The Saga of the Greenlanders

Original Texts, Translations, and Word Lists

Translated by
Matthew Leigh Embleton

Copyright ©2025 Matthew Leigh Embleton. All rights reserved.

The Saga of the Greenlanders

The Saga of the Greenlanders (*Old Norse*) 4
The Saga of the Greenlanders (*Old Icelandic*) 41
Word List *(Norse to English)* 77
Word List *(English to Norse)* 108

Cover: Old Norse text over an outline of Iceland. Author's design.

The original Old Icelandic and Old Norse texts are in the public domain.
These translations ©2021 Matthew Leigh Embleton
©2025 Matthew Leigh Embleton (This Edition)

Acknowledgments

I have long been fascinated by languages and history, and I am very grateful to the special people in my life who have supported and encouraged me in my work. Thank you for believing in me. You know who you are.

Introduction

The Saga of the Greenlanders (Grœnlendinga Saga) is one of the two Icelandic Sagas which make up the Vínland Sagas (Vínlandingasögur), along with The Saga of Erik the Red (Eiríks Saga Rauða), which tell the story of the Norse discovery of North America. The rich tradition of Icelandic literature survived by oral tradition over several centuries before being written down in the 13th Century.

Old Norse is a North Germanic language spoken by inhabitants of Scandinavia from about the 7th to the 15th centuries. Old Icelandic is a variety of Old West Norse that emerged during the Norse settlement of Iceland in the second half of the 9th century.

The meaning of the word 'saga' (plural: 'sǫgur' or 'sögur') translates as 'that which is said', or more widely: a 'saying', 'statement', 'story', 'tale', or 'narrative'.

This book contains:
- The Saga of the Greenlanders (Grœnlendinga Saga) (Old Norse Version)
- The Saga of the Greenlanders (Grœnlendinga Saga) (Old Icelandic Version)

The texts are presented in their original Norse, with a literal word-for-word line-by-line translation, and a Modern English translation, all side-by-side. In this way, it is possible to see and feel how the Norse language worked and how it has evolved. Also included is a word list with 1,935 Norse words translated in to English, and 1,142 English words translated into Norse.

This book is designed to be of use and interest to anyone with a passion for the Old Norse or Old Icelandic language, Norse history, or languages and history in general.

The Saga of the Greenlanders (*Old Norse*)

Old Norse	Literal	English
1	*1*	*1*
Þorvaldr hét maðr, sonr Ásvalds Úlfssonar, Öxna-Þórissonar.	Thorvald was-called a-man son-of Asvald's Ulfson, Oxna-Thorison.	There was a man named Thorvald, son of Asvald, son of Ulf, son of Oxna-Thorri.
Þorvaldr ok Eiríkr inn rauði, sonr hans, fóru af Jaðri til Íslands fyrir víga sakir.	Thorvald and Erik the Red, son his, travelled from Jaeren to Iceland because-of-a killing conviction.	Thorvald and Erik the Red, his son, travelled from Jaeran to Iceland because of a conviction for a killing.
Þá var víða byggt Ísland.	Then was widely settled Iceland.	Then Iceland was widely settled.
Þeir bjuggu fyrst at Dröngum á Hornströndum.	They lived first at Drangar on Hornstrandir.	They lived first at Drangar in Hornstrandir.
Þar andaðist Þorvaldr.	There died Thorvald.	There Thorvald died.
Eiríkr fekk þá Þjóðhildar, dóttur Jörundar Úlfssonar ok Þorbjargar Knarrarbringu, er þá átti Þorbjörn inn haukdælski.	Erik married then Thjodhild, daughter-of Jorund Ulfson and Thorbjorg Knarrarbringu, who then married Thorbjorn of Haukadal.	Erik then married Thjodhild, daughter of Jorund, son of Ulf, and Thorbjorg Knarrabringu, who then married Thorbjorn of Haukadal.
Réðst Eiríkr þá norðan ok bjó á Eiríksstöðum hjá Vatnshorni.	Went Erik then northwards and lived at Eriksstadir near Vatnshorn.	Erik then went northwards and lived at Eriksstadir near Vantshorn.
Sonr Eiríks ok Þjóðhildar hét Leifr.	Son Erik's and Thjodhild's was-called Leif.	Erik and Thjodhild's son was named Leif.
Enn eftir víg Eyjólfs saurs ok Hólmgöngu-Hrafns var Eiríkr gerr brott ór Haukadal.	But after killing-of Eyolf's the-Foul and Raven-the-Dueller was Erik made away from Haukadal.	But after the killing of Eyolf the Foul and Raven the Dueller, Erik was made to leave Haukadal.
Fór hann vestr til Breiðafjarðar ok bjó í Öxney á Eiríksstöðum.	Travelled he west to Breidafjord and lived at Oxney at Eriksstadir.	He then travelled west to Breidafjord and lived at Oxney in Eriksstadir.
Hann léði Þorgesti á breiðabólstað setstokka ok náði eigi, er hann kallaði til.	He lent Thorgest to upholstery seat-posts and got-not, when he called for them.	He lent Thorgest some upholstery seat posts, and when he asked for them back, he did not get them.

The Saga of the Greenlanders (Old Norse)

Old Norse	Literal	English
Þaðan af gerðust deilur ok bardagar með þeim Þorgesti, sem segir í sögu Eiríks.	From-there of made disputes and battle between them Thorgest, as said in saga Erik's.	From then on there were disputes and battles between him and Thorgest, as told in Erik's Saga.
Styrr Þorgrímsson veitti Eiríki at málum ok Eyjólfr ór Svíney, ok synir Þorbrands ór Álftafirði ok Þorbjörn Vífilsson.	Styrr Thorgrimson supported Erik in case and Eyolf of Sviney, and sons Thorbrand of Alftafjord and Thorbjorn Vifilson.	Styrr Thorgrimson supported Erik in the matter, and Eyolf of Sviney, and Thorbrand's sons of Alftafjord, and Thorbjorn Vifilson.
En Þorgestlingum veittu synir Þórðar gellis ok Þorgeirr ór Hítardal.	But Thorgest's-sons supported sons Thord Howler and Thorgeir of Hitardal.	But Thorgest's sons were supported by Thord Howler, and Thorgeir of Hitardal.
Eiríkr varð sekr á Þórsnessþingi.	Erik was outlawed at-the Thorsnes-assembly.	Erik was outlawed at the Thorsness assembly.
Bjó Eiríkr þá skip sitt til hafs í Eiríksvági.	Prepared Erik then ship his to sea in Eriksvog.	He then prepared his ship to go to sea at Eriksvog.
En er hann var búinn, fylgðu þeir Styrr honum út um eyjar.	And when he was ready, followed they Styrr him out about the-island.	And when he was ready, Styrr followed them about the island.
Eiríkr sagði þeim, at hann ætlaði at leita lands þess, er Gunnbjörn, sonr Úlfs kráku, sá, er hann rak vestr um haf, þá er hann fann Gunnbjarnarsker.	Erik told them, that he intended to search land this, which Gunnbjorn, son-of Ulf Crow, saw, when he-was driven west at sea, when was he found Gunnbjarnarsker.	Erik told them that he intended to search for a land, which Gunnbjorn, son of Ulf Crow, saw when he was driven west at sea, when he found Gunnbjorn's Skerries.
Kveðst hann aftr mundu leita til vina sinna, ef hann fyndi landit.	Said he return would seek to friends his, if he found land.	He said he would return to seek his friends if he found land.
Eiríkr sigldi undan Snæfellsjökli.	Erik sailed from Snaefellsjokli.	Erik sailed from Snaefellsjokli.
Hann fann landit, ok kom útan at því, þar sem hann kallaði Miðjökul.	He found land, and came out of for, there which he call Midjokul.	He found land, and came out therefore, there he called Modjokul.
Sá heitir nú Bláserkr.	This is-called now Blaserkur.	This is now named Blaserkur.
Hann fór þá þaðan suðr með landinu at leita, ef þaðan væri byggjanda landit.	He went then from-there south along land to seek, if there was habitable land.	He travelled south from there along land to see if there was habitable land.

The Saga of the Greenlanders (Old Norse)

Old Norse	Literal	English
Hann var inn fyrsta vetr í Eiríksey, nær miðri inni eystri byggð.	He was the first winter in Eriksey, near-the middle of-the eastern settlement.	The first winter he was at Eriksey, near the middle of the Eastern Settlement.
Um várit eftir fór hann til Eiríksfjarðar ok tók sér þar bústað.	About spring after returned he to Eriksfjord and took he there abode.	After about spring he travelled to Eriksfjord and took he there a dwelling.
Hann fór þat sumar í ina vestri óbyggð ok gaf víða örnefni.	He returned that summer to the western settlement and gave many place-names.	He travelled that summer to the Western Settlement and gave many places names.
Hann var annan vetr í Hólmum við Hvarfsgnípu, en it þriðja sumarit fór allt norðr til Snæfells ok inn í Hrafnsfjörð.	He was second winter at Holm in Hvarfsgnipu, but the third summer went all north to Snaefell and then into Hrafnsfjord.	The second winter he was at Holm in Hvarfsgnipu, but the third summer travelled all the way north to Snaefell and then to Hrafnsfjord.
Þá kvaðst hann kominn fyrir botn Eiríksfjarðar.	Then said he coming for-the bottom-of Eriksfjord.	Then he said he came to the bottom of Eriksfjord.
Hvarf hann þá aftr ok var inn þriðja vetr í Eiríksey fyrir mynni Eiríksfjarðar.	Disappeared he then returned and was the third winter in Eriksey at the-inlet Eriksfjord.	After that he then disappeared and was for the third winter in Eriksey before the inlet Eriksfjord.
Eftir um sumarit fór hann til Íslands ok kom skipi sínu í Breiðafjörð.	After about summer went he to Iceland and came ship his into Breidafjord.	After about summer he travelled to Iceland and his ship came to Breidafjord.
Hann kallaði land þat, er hann hafði fundit, Grænland, því at hann kvað þat mundu fýsa menn þangat, ef landit héti vel.	He called land that, which he had found, Greenland, because as he said they would be-attracted people there, if the-land named well.	He called the land which he had found Greenland, because as he said, it would attract people there if it was named well.
Eiríkr var á Íslandi um vetrinn, en um sumarit eftir fór hann at byggja landit.	Erik was in Iceland about winter, but about summer after went he to colonise land.	Erik was in Iceland over winter, but after around summer he travelled to settle the land.
Hann bjó í Brattahlíð í Eiríksfirði.	He dwelt at Brattahlid in Eriksfjord.	He lived at Brattahlid in Eriksfjord.
Svá segja fróðir menn, at á því sama sumri, er Eiríkr rauði fór at byggja Grænland, þá fór hálfr þriði tögr skipa ór Breiðafirði ok Borgarfirði, enn fjórtán kómust út þangat.	So say wise people, that at since same summer, that Erik the-Red went to colonise Greenland, then travelled half-of thirty-and twenty ships from Breidafjord and Borgafjord, but fourteen arrived out there.	So wise men say that after that same summer, Erik the Red travelled to settle Greenland, then half of thirty and twenty ships travelled from Breidafjord and Borgafjord, but fourteen arrived there.

The Saga of the Greenlanders (Old Norse)

Old Norse	Literal	English
Sum rak aftr, en sum týndust.	Some driven back, but some lost.	Some were driven back, but some were lost.
Þat var fimmtán vetrum fyrr en kristni var lögtekin á Íslandi.	This was fifteen winters before that Christianity was law-taken in Iceland.	This was fifteen winters before Christianity became law in Iceland.
Á því sama sumri fór útan Friðrekr biskup ok Þorvaldr Koðránsson.	Then since same summer travelled out Fridrek bishop and Thorvald Kodranson.	After that same summer travelled out Bishop Fridrek and Thorvald Kodranson.
Þessir menn námu land á Grænlandi, er þá fóru út með Eiríki: Herjólfr Herjólfsfjörð, hann bjó á Herjólfsnesi, Ketill Ketilsfjörð, Hrafn Hrafnsfjörð, Sölvi Sölvadal, Helgi Þorbrandsson Álftafjörð, Þorbjörn glóra Siglufjörð, Einarr Einarsfjörð, Hafgrímr Hafgrímsfjörð ok Vatnahverfi, Arnlaugr Arnlaugsfjörð.	These men took land on Greenland, when then travelled out with Erik: Herjolf Herjolfsfjord, he lived at Herjólfsnes, Ketil Ketilsfjord, Hrafn Hrafnsfjord, Sölvi Solvadal, Helgi Thorbrandson Alftafjord, Thorbjorn the-Sensible Siglefjord, Einar Einarsfjord, Hafgrim Hafgrimsfjord and Vatnahverfi, Arnlaug Arnlaugsfjord.	These men took land in Greenland, when they travelled out with Erik: Herjolf took Herjolfsfjord, he lived on Herjolfsnes, Ketil took Ketilsfjord, Hrafn took Hrafnsfjord, Solvi took Solvadal, Helgi Thorbrandson took Alftafjord, Hafgrim took Hafgrimsfjord and Vatnahverfi, and Arnlaug took Arnlaugsfjord.
En sumir fóru til Vestribyggðar.	But some went to Western-Settlement.	But some travelled to the Western Settlement.
2	2	2
Herjólfr var Bárðarson Herjólfssonar.	Herjolf was Bard's-son Herjolf's-son	Herjolf was Bard's son, the son of Herjolf.
Hann var frændi Ingólfs landnámamanns.	He was kinsman Ingolf's land-taking-man.	He was kinsman to Ingolf the land taking man.
Þeim Herjólfi gaf Ingólfr land á milli Vágs ok Reykjaness.	To Herjolf gave Ingolf land in between Vog and Reykjanes.	Ingolf gave to them land between Vogs and Reykjanes.
Herjólfr bjó fyrst á Drepstokki.	Herjolf lived first at Drepstokk.	Herjolf lived first at Drepstokk.
Þorgerðr hét kona hans, en Bjarni sonr þeira ok var inn efniligsti maðr.	Thorgerd was-called wife his, and Bjarni son theirs and was a promising man.	His wife was named Thorgerd and their son Bjarni was a promising man.
Hann fýstist útan þegar á unga aldri.	He desired travel already from young age.	He desired to travel out at a young age.

The Saga of the Greenlanders (Old Norse)

Old Norse	Literal	English
Varð honum gott bæði til fjár ok mannvirðingar, ok var sinn vetr hvárt, útan lands eða með feðr sínum.	Was he good both to wealth and man-worthiness-(respect) and was he winter either, out-of lands or with father his.	He was good in both wealth and worthiness, and in winter he was either travelling or with his father.
Brátt átti Bjarni skip í förum.	Soon had Bjarni ship to travel.	Soon Bjarni had a ship to travel.
Ok inn síðasta vetr, er hann var í Nóregi, þá brá Herjólfr til Grænlandsferðar með Eiríki ok brá búi sínu.	And the last winter, that he was in Norway, then prepared Herjolf to Greenland-voyage with Erik and prepared farm his.	And the last winter that he was in Norway, then Herjolf prepared for the voyage to Greenland with Erik and prepared his farm.
Með Herjólfi var á skipi suðreyskr maðr, kristinn, sá er orti Hafgerðingadrápu.	With Herjolf was in ship south-islander man, Christian, that who wrote sea-poem.	With Herjolf in his ship was a man from the southern islands, a Christian who wrote a sea poem.
Þar er þetta stef í:	There which this stave in:	There is this stave:
Mínar biðk at munka reyni meinalausan farar beina. Heiðis haldi hárar foldar hallar dróttinn yfir mér stalli.	My bid I that monks tester harmlessly travel assist, heath hold high folds hall master over my altar.	I ask you, monks' tester to assist my travel harmless, holding the heath's high folds hall master over my altar.
Herjólfr bjó á Herjólfsnesi.	Herjolf lived at Herjólfsnes.	Herjolf lived at Herjolfsness.
Hann var inn göfgasti maðr.	He was a respectable man.	He was a respectable man.
Eiríkr rauði bjó í Brattahlíð.	Erik the Red lived-at Brattahlid.	Erik the Red settled at Brattahlid.
Hann var þar með mestri virðingu, ok lutu allir til hans.	He was there with most worthiness, and lent all to him.	He was there given the most respect by all.
Þessi váru börn Eiríks: Leifr, Þorvaldr ok Þorsteinn, en Freydís hét dóttir hans.	These were children Erik's: Leif, Thorvald and Thorstein, but Freydis was-named daughter his.	Erik's children were: Leif, Thorvald, and Thorstein, and his daughter was named Freydis.
Hon var gift þeim manni, er Þorvarðr hét, ok bjuggu þau í Görðum, þar sem nú er biskupsstóll.	She was married to a-man who Thorvald was-named and lived they in Gardar, there where now is bishop's-seat.	She was married to a man named Thorvard, and they lived at Gardar, where the bishop's seat now is.
Hon var svarri mikill, enn Þorvarðr var lítilmenni.	She was haughty very, but Thorvald was little-man.	She was haughty, but Thorvard was not much of a man.

The Saga of the Greenlanders (Old Norse)

Old Norse	Literal	English
Var hon mjök gefin til fjár.	Was she much married to wealth.	She married him very much for this wealth.
Heiðit var fólk á Grænlandi í þann tíma.	Heathen were people in Greenland at this time.	Heathen were the people in Greenland at this time.
Þat sama sumar kom Bjarni skipi sínu á Eyrar, er faðir hans hafði brot siglt um várit.	That same summer came Bjarni ship his to Eyrar where father his had away sailed about spring.	That same summer came Bjarni's ship to Eyrar, where his father had sailed from in the spring.
Þau tíðendi þóttu Bjarna mikil ok vildi eigi bera af skipi sínu.	These tidings thought Bjarni great and willed not unload from ship his.	This news greatly affected Bjarni and he did not want to unload his ship.
Þá spurðu hásetar hans, hvat er hann bærist fyrir, en hann svarar, at hann ætlaði at halda siðvenju sinni ok þiggja at föður sínum vetrvist, "ok vil ek halda skipinu til Grænlands, ef þér vilið mér fylgð veita".	Then asked crew he what was he bearing for but he answered that he intended that to hold custom his and receive by father his winter "and will I hold ship to Greenland if you will me follow lead".	His crew asked him what he wanted to do but he answered that he wanted to keep his custom of spending the winter with his father "and I want to sail to Greenland if you will follow me".
Allir kváðust hans ráðum fylgja vilja.	All said his counsel follow would.	All of them said they would follow his counsel.
Þá mælti Bjarni: "Óvitrlig mun þykkja vár ferð, þar sem engi vár hefir komit í Grænlandshaf".	Then said Bjarni: "Unwisely will seem our voyage there since none been have come to Greenland-sea".	Then Bjarni said: "Our voyage will look unwise, since none of us have sailed the Greenland sea".
Enn þó halda þeir nú í haf, þegar þeir váru búnir, ok sigldu þrjá daga, þar til er landit var vatnat, en þá tók af byrina ok lagði á norrænur ok þokur, ok vissu þeir eigi, hvert at þeir fóru, ok skipti þat mörgum dægrum.	But though held they now to sea when they were ready and sailed three days there until was land was water-taken but then took of fair-wind and lay on north-wind and fog and knew they not where that they travelled and time that many days.	But they set sail once they were ready and sailed for three days, until the land disappeared below the horizon, but then the fair wind dropped, and they were met with winds from the north and fog, and they did not know where they were travelling for many days.

The Saga of the Greenlanders (Old Norse)

Old Norse	Literal	English
Eftir þat sá þeir sól ok máttu þá deila ættir, vinda nú segl ok sigla þetta dægr, áðr þeir sá land, ok ræddu um með sér, hvat landi þetta mun vera, en Bjarni kveðst hyggja, at þat mundi eigi Grænland.	After that saw they the-sun and could then share direction, wind now sails and sailed this day before they saw land and discussed among with them what land that could be but Bjarni said thought it that could not-be Greenland.	After that they saw the sun and took their bearings, they hoisted their sails and sailed for the rest of the day before they saw land, and they discussed among themselves what land it could be, but Bjarni said that it could not be Greenland.
Þeir spyrja, hvárt hann vill sigla at þessu landi eðr eigi.	They asked whether he wished sail to this land or not.	They asked whether he wished to sail close to the land or not.
Hann svarar: "Þat er mitt ráð at sigla í nánd við landit".	"It is my advice to sail to close with land".	"I advise that we sail close to the land".
Ok svá gera þeir ok sá þat brátt, at landit var ófjöllótt ok skógi vaxit, ok smár hæðir á landinu, ok létu landit á bakborða ok létu skaut horfa á land.	And so did they and saw that soon that land was without-mountains and forests grown and small heights on land and left land on port-side and let stern turn on land.	And so they did, and saw that the land was not mountainous, but did have small hills and was covered with forests, so keeping land on their port side, they turned their sail-end landwards and angled away from the shore.
Síðan sigla þeir tvau dægr, áðr þeir sá land annat.	Afterwards sailed they two days before they saw land another.	Then they sailed for two days before they saw any more land.
Þeir spyrja, hvárt Bjarni ætlaði þat enn Grænland.	They asked if Bjarni supposed this was Greenland.	They asked Bjarni if he thought this land was Greenland.
Hann kvaðst eigi heldr ætla þette Grænland en it fyrra, "því at jöklar eru mjök miklir sagðir á Grænlandi".	He said not rather supposed this Greenland as the first "because the glaciers are very large said in Greenland"	He said that he did not think this was Greenland as the first "because there are said to be very large glaciers in Greenland".
Þeir nálguðust brátt þetta land ok sá þat vera slétt land ok viði vaxit.	They approached soon this land and saw it was flat land and woods growing.	They soon approached this land and saw that it was flat and wooded.
Þá tók af byr fyrir þeim.	Then took of fair-wind before them.	Then the wind died.
Þá ræddu hásetar þat, at þeim þótti þat ráð at taka þat land, en Bjarni vill þat eigi.	Then advised crew that to them thought that advised to take that land but Bjarni willed that not.	Then the crew advised that they put ashore, but Bjarni did not want to.

The Saga of the Greenlanders (Old Norse)

Old Norse	Literal	English
Þeir þóttust bæði þurfa við ok vatn.	They thought both needed wood and water.	They said that they needed wood and water.
At engu eruð þér því óbirgir, segir Bjarni, en þó fekk hann af því nökkut ámæli af hásetum sínum.	"In nothing are you for without-supplies" said Bjarni but though got he of for some reproach from crew his.	"There are no supplies you are lacking" said Bjarni, but he was criticised by his crew for this.
Hann bað þá vinda segl, ok svá var gert, ok settu framstafn frá landi ok sigla í haf útsynnings byr þrjú dægr ok sá þá landit it þriðja.	He bid them wind sails and so was done and set prow from land and sailing to sea south-west-wind three days and saw then land third.	He told them to hoist the sail and they did so, setting the bow away from land and sailing seawards, for three days they sailed with wind from the south west and then saw a third land.
En þat land var hátt ok fjöllótt ok jökull á.	And this land was high and mountainous and glaciers on.	And this land was high and mountainous and was capped by glaciers.
Þeir spyrja þá, ef Bjarni vildi at landi láta þar, en hann kvaðst eigi þat vilja, "því at mér lízt þetta land ógagnvænligt".	They asked then if Bjarni willed to land put there but he said not that willed "for to me appears this land uninviting".	They asked if Bjarni wished to make land here, but he said that he did not "for this land appears uninviting".
Nú lögðu þeir eigi segl sitt, halda með landinu fram ok sá, at þat var eyland, settu enn stafn við því landi ok heldu í haf inn sama byr.	Now lay they not sails these, held along land from and saw it that was island, turned yet stern with for land and held to sea the same fair-wind.	Now they did not lower the sail, but followed along the shore until they saw that it was an island, they turned the stern landwards and sailed out to sea with the same breeze.
En veðr óx í hönd, ok bað Bjarni þá svipta ok eigi sigla meira en bæði dygði vel skipi þeira ok reiða, sigldu nú fjögr dægr.	But weather grew at hand and bid Bjarni then shorten and not sail greater than both enough well ships theirs and decided, sailed now four days.	But the wind grew and Bjarni told them to lower the sail and not sail faster than the ship could manage, they sailed for four days.
Þá sá þeir land it fjórða. *Þá spurðu þeir Bjarna, hvárt hann ætlaði þetta vera Grænland, eða eigi.*	Then saw they land the fourth. Then asked they Bjarni whether he supposed this was Greenland or not.	Then they saw a fourth land. They asked Bjarni if he thought this was Greenland or not.
Bjarni svarar: "Þetta er líkast því, er mér er sagt frá Grænlandi, ok hér munum vér at landi halda".	Bjarni answered: "This is like therefore which to-me was said from Greenland and here should we by land hold".	Bjarni answered: "This land appears to me as was described about Greenland, and we'll head for the shore here".

The Saga of the Greenlanders (Old Norse)

Old Norse	Literal	English
Svá gera þeir ok taka land undir einhverju nesi at kveldi dags, ok var þar bátr á nesinu.	So did they and took land under some headland at evening day, and was there boat by headland.	So they did and took land under some headland in the evening of the day, and there was a boat by the headland.
En þar bjó Herjólfr, faðir Bjarna, á því nesi, ok af því hefir nesit nafn tekit ok er síðan kallat Herjólfsnes.	But there lived Herjolf, father Bjarni's, on that headland, and of because has headland name taken and was since called Herjólfsnes.	And there lived Herjolf, Bjarni's father, on that headland, and because of this the headland was taken and was since called Herjolfsnes.
Fór Bjarni nú til föður síns ok hættir nú siglingum ok er með föður sínum, meðan Herjólfr lifði, ok síðan bjó hann þar eftir föður sinn.	Went Bjarni now to father his and gave-up now sailing and was with father his, while Herjolf lived, and afterwards dwelt he there after father his.	Bjarni went now to his father and gave up his sailing, and afterwards settled he there after his father had died.
3	3	3
Þat er nú þessu næst, at Bjarni Herjólfsson kom útan af Grænlandi á fund Eiríks jarls, ok tók jarl við honum vel.	It is now this next that Bjarni Son-of-Herjolf came out of Greenland to meet Erik earl and took earl with him well.	It now happened that Bjarni Herjolfson came to Greenland to meet earl Erik, and the earl received him well.
Sagði Bjarni frá ferðum sínum, er hann hafði lönd sét, ok þótti mönnum hann verit hafa óforvitinn, er hann hafði ekki at segja af þeim löndum, ok fekk han af því nökkut ámæli.	Said Bjarni from voyages his that he had land seen and thought men he had-been having no-curiosity when he had nothing to say of these lands and got he of therefore some reproach.	Bjarni told of his voyages and that he had seen land, and people thought he had lacked curiosity when he had nothing much to say about these lands, and he received criticism for this.
Bjarni gerðist hirðmaðr jarls ok fór út til Grænlands um sumarit eftir. Var nú mikil umræða um landaleitan.	Bjarni became court-man earl's and travelled out to Greenland about summer after. Was now much talk about land-exploring.	Bjarni became one of the earl's followers and travelled out to Greenland the next summer. There was now much talk of exploring these lands.
Leifr, sonr Eiríks rauða ór Brattahlíð, fór á fund Bjarna Herjólfssonar ok keypti skip at honum ok réð til háseta, svá at þeir váru hálfr fjórði tögr manna saman.	Leif son Erik's the-Red from Brattahlid travelled to meet Bjarni Herjolfsson and bought ship of his and appointed to men so that there were half fourth twenty men together.	Leif, Erik the Red's son from Brattahlid, travelled to meet Bjarni Herjolfsson and bought his ship and hired a crew of thirty five men altogether.
Leifr bað föður sinn, Eirík, at hann mundi enn fyrir vera förinni.	Leif bid father his Erik that he would still for be voyage.	Leif asked his father Erik to lead the expedition.
Eiríkr talðist heldr undan, kveðst þá vera hniginn í aldr ok kveðst minna mega við vási öllu en var.	Erik told rather away, saying then being declining in age and said less able with cold-and-wet all but was.	Erik was reluctant, saying that he was getting old and less able to cope with the cold weather as he once was.

The Saga of the Greenlanders (Old Norse)

Old Norse	Literal	English
Leifr kveðr hann enn mundu mestri heill stýra af þeim frændum.	Leif said he still would most luck steer of them kinsmen.	Leif said that he still had the most luck of all his kinsmen.
Ok þetta lét Eiríkr eftir Leifi ok riðr heiman, þá er þeir eru at því búnir, ok var þá skammt at fara til skipsins.	And this allowed Erik after Leif and rode home then as they were to for prepared and was then short to go to ship.	Erik gave in to Leif, and they rode from home as they were ready and had a short distance to go to the ship.
Drepr hestrinn fæti, sá er Eiríkr reið, ok fell hann af baki, ok lestist fótr hans.	Failed horse's feet, that was Erik riding, and fell he from back and injured foot his.	The horse that Erik was riding stumbled, and Erik fell injuring his foot.
Þá mælti Eiríkr: "Ekki mun mér ætlat at finna lönd fleiri enn þetta, er nú byggjum vér.	Then said Erik "Not should to-me intend to find land more but this that now inhabit we.	Then Erik said "I am not intended to find any other land than the one where we now live.
Munum vér nú ekki lengr fara allir samt".	Should we now nothing longer go all together".	This will be the end of our travelling together".
Fór Eiríkr heim í Brattahlíð, en Leifr réðst til skips, ok félagar hans með honum, hálfr fjórði tögr manna.	Travelled Erik home to Brattahlid but Leif rode to ship and companions his with him, half fourth twenty men.	Erik travelled home to Brattahlid but Leif rode to the ship with his companions, thirty five men.
Þar var Suðrmaðr einn í ferð, er Tyrkir hét.	There was southern-man one on voyage was Tyrkir named.	There was a southern man on the voyage who was named Tyrkir.
Nú bjuggu þeir skip sitt ok sigldu í haf, þá er þeir váru búnir, ok fundu þá þat land fyrst, er þeir Bjarni fundu síðast.	Now prepared they ship theirs and sailed to sea then when they were ready and found then that land first which there Bjarni found last.	Now they prepared their ship and sailed to sea, then they were ready and found first land that Bjarni had found last.
Þar sigla þeir at landi, ok köstuðu akkerum ok skkutu báti ok fóru á land ok sá þar eigi gras.	There sailed they to land and cast anchor and launched boats and travelled to land and saw there not grass.	They sailed to the land, cast anchor, put out a boat and rowed ashore, and saw there was no grass.
Jöklar miklir váru allt it efra, en sem ein hella væri allt til jöklanna frá sjónum, ok sýndist þeim þat land vera gæðalaust.	Glaciers great were all the over but which a stone-slab was all to mountains from the-sea and seemed to-them that land was without-quality.	Large glaciers covered the highlands, but the land was like a stone slab from the mountains to the sea, and it seemed to them that this land was of little use.
Þá mælti Leifr: "Eigi er oss nú þat orðit um þetta land sem Bjarna, at vér hafim eigi komit á landit.	Then said Leif: "Not are we now that word about this land as Bjarni that we have not come on land.	Then Leif said: "Now we cannot have word about this land like Bjarni that we did not come on land.
Nú mun ek gefa nafn landinu, ok kalla Helluland".	Now will I give name land and call Helluland".	Now I will give the land a name and call it Helluland".
Síðan fóru þeir til skips.	Since travelled they to ship.	Afterwards they returned to the ship.

The Saga of the Greenlanders (Old Norse)

Old Norse	Literal	English
Eftir þetta sigla þeir í haf ok fundu land annat, sigla enn at landi ok kasta akkerum, skjóta síðan báti ok ganga á landit.	After that sailed they to sea and found land another, sailed yet to land and cast anchor, launched then boats and went to land.	After that they sailed to sea and found another land, sailed close to the land and cast anchor, put out a boat and went to shore.
Þat land var slétt ok skógi vaxit, ok sandar hvítir víða, þar sem þeir fóru, ok ósæbratt.	That land was flat and forest grown and sands white widely there as they travelled and unbroken-sea.	This land was flat and forested, with many white beaches, wide as they travelled and unbroken by the sea.
Þá mælti Leifr: "Af kostum skal þessu landi nafn gefa ok kalla Markland", fóru síðan ofan aftr til skips sem fljótast.	Then said Leif: "Of benefit shall this land name give and call Markland". Travelled since on back to ship as immediately.	Then Leif said: "This land shall be named by its benefit, and will be called Markland". Afterwards they travelled back to the ship immediately.
Nú sigla þeir þaðan í haf landnyrðingsveðr ok váru úti tvau dægr, áðr þeir sá land, ok sigldu at landi ok kómu at ey einni, er lá norðr af landinu, ok gengu þar upp ok sást um í góðu veðri ok fundu þat, at dögg var á grasinu, ok varð þeim þat fyrir, at þeir tóku höndum sínum í döggina ok brugðu í munn sér ok þóttust ekki jafnsætt kennt hafa sem þat var.	Now sailed they from-there to sea North-East-Wind and were out two days before they saw land and sailed to land and came to island one which lay north from land and went there up and looked about in good weather and found that to dew was on grass and were they that at-hand that they took hands theirs to dew and brought to mouths theirs and thought not as-sweet known have as that was.	Now they sailed from there to the sea with a north east wind, and sailed for two days before they saw land, they sailed towards it and came to an island that lay to the north of the land, they went up to the shore and looked about, in fine weather they found dew on the grass, that they took in their hands, and brought to their mouths, and they thought nothing was as sweet as that was.
Síðan fóru þeir til skip síns ok sigldu í sund þat, er lá milli eyjarinnar ok ness þess, er norðr gekk af landinu, stefndu í vestrætt fyrir nesit.	Since travelled they to ship theirs and sailed to strait that which lay between island and headland this was north going of land, steered at westwards before headland.	Afterwards they travelled to their ship and sailed to the strait that lay between the island and the headland that stretched out north from the land, they steered westwards around the headland.
Þar var grunnsævi mikit at fjöru sjávar, ok stóð þá uppi skip þeira, ok var þá langt til sjávar at sjá frá skipinu.	There were shallows much at tide sea and stood then up ship theirs and was then long to sea to see from ship.	There were many shallows at low tide and their ship was stranded, and then the sea was a long way out as seen by those on the ship.
En þeim var svá mikil forvitni á at fara til landsins, at þeir nenntu eigi þess at bíða, at sjór felli undir skip þeira, ok runnu til lands, þar er á ein fell ór vatni einu.	But they were so much curiosity of to travel to land, that they bothered not this to wait, by sea rising under ship theirs, and ran to land, there was on one lake from river one.	Their curiosity to travel to land was so great, that they did not bother to wait for the sea to rise under their ship, and ran aground where there was a river from a lake.

The Saga of the Greenlanders (Old Norse)

Old Norse	Literal	English
En þegar sjór fell undir skip þeira, þá tóku þeir bátinn ok reru til skipsins ok fluttu þat upp í ána, síðan í vatnit, ok köstuðu þar akkerum ok báru af skipi húðföt sín ok gerðu þar búðir, tóku þat ráð síðan at búast þar um þann vetr ok gerðu þar hús mikil.	But then sea fell under ship theirs, then took they boat and rowed to ship and floated that up into river, then into lake, and cast there anchor and brought off ship skin-cots theirs and made there booths, took they counsel then to stay there about then winter and make there houses large.	But when the sea flowed under their ship, they took the boat and rowed it to the ship, and floated up into the river, then into the lake, and cast anchor there, and brought off the ship their sleeping-sacks and built booths, they then decided to stay there for the winter and make large houses there.
Hvárki skorti þar lax í ánni né í vatninu ok stærra lax en þeir hefði fyrr sét.	Neither shortage there salmon in river nor in lake and larger salmon than they have before seen.	There was no shortage of salmon there, neither in the river nor in the lake, and larger salmon than they had seen before.
Þar var svá góðr landskostr, at því er þeim sýndist, at þar mundi engi fénaðr fóðr þurfa á vetrum.	There was so good land-benefits, in therefore as they seemed, that there would not cattle fodder need in winter.	The land was so good, that it seemed to them that cattle would not need fodder in winter.
Þar kómu engi frost á vetrum, ok lítt rénuðu þar grös.	There came no frost in winter, and little receded there grass.	There was no frost in winter, and the grass only receded a little.
Meira var þar jafndægri en á Grænlandi eða Íslandi.	More was there equal-day than on Greenland or Iceland.	The days and nights were more equal in length than in Greenland or Iceland.
Sól hafði þar eyktar stað ok dagmála stað um skammdegi.	Sun had there three-hours stood and morning stood during short-time-of-day.	The sun stood by mid morning and stood during mid afternoon, during winter and the shortest time of day.
En er þeir höfðu lokit húsgerð sinni, þá mælti Leifr við föruneyti sitt: "Nú vil ek skipta láta liði váru í tvá staði, ok vil ek kanna láta landit, ok skal helmingr liðs vera við skála heima, enn annarr helmingr skal kanna landit ok fara eigi lengra en þeir komi heim at kveldi, ok skilist eigi".	And when they had ended house-building theirs then talked Leif with companions his: "Now will I divide let company ours into two parts and will I explore let land and shall half company be with cabin home but another half shall explore land and go not further than they come home by evening and separate not".	And when they had finished their house building, Leif said to his companions: "Now I wish to have our company divided into two groups and explore the land, I wish that half the company shall be home at the cabin, and the other half shall explore the land and go no further than they can come home by evening, and no one separate".
Nú gerðu þeir svá um stund. Leifr gerði ýmisst, at hann fór með þeim eða var heima at skála.	Now did they so about awhile. Leif did either, that he travelled with them or was home at cabin.	Now they did this for a while. Leif either travelled with them or he was home at the cabin.

The Saga of the Greenlanders (Old Norse)

Old Norse	Literal	English
Leifr var mikill maðr ok sterkr, manna sköruligastr at sjá, vitr maðr ok góðr hófsmaðr um alla hluti.	Leif was great man and strong, man striking to see, wise man and good moderate-man about all things.	Leif was a great and strong man, striking in appearance, and a wise man who was moderate about all things.
4	4	4
Á einhverju kveldi bar þat til tíðenda, at manns var vant af liði þeira, ok var þat Tyrkir Suðrmaðr.	On some evening bore that to news, that man was missing of team theirs, and was that Tyrkir southern-man.	One evening came the news that a man was missing from their team, and that was Tyrkir the southerner.
Leifr kunni því stórilla, því at Tyrkir hafði lengi verit með þeim feðgum, ok elskat mjök Leif í barnæsku.	Leif knew therefore greatly, because for Tyrkir had long been with them father-and-son, and loved much Leif in childhood.	Leif was affected by this, because Tyrkir had spent many years with him and his father, and he had treated Leif very affectionately as a child.
Taldi Leifr nú mjök á hendr förunautum sínum ok bjóst til ferðar at leita hans ok tólf menn með honum.	Told Leif now much to hand people his and prepared to go to seek him and twelve men with him.	Leif told off his people and prepared to seek him with twelve men.
En er þeir váru skammt komnir frá skála, þá gekk Tyrkir í mót þeim, ok var honum vel fagnat.	But when they were short came from cabin, then going Tyrkir in meeting them, and was he well welcomed.	But when they were a short way away from the cabin, Tyrkir came towards them, and he was gladly welcomed.
Leifr fann þat brátt, at fóstra hans var skapgott.	Leif found that soon, that foster-father his was well-tempered.	Leif soon found that his foster-father was in a good mood.
Hann var brattleitr ok lauseygr, smáskitlegr í andliti, lítill vexti ok vesallegr, en íþróttamaðr á alls konar hagleik.	He was steep-looking and loose-eyed, dirty in face, little grown and poor-wretch, but excellent in all kinds-of pursuits.	He had a protruding forehead and darting eyes, with dark wrinkles in his face, he was short and frail looking, but excellent in many pursuits.
Þá mælti Leifr til hans: "Hví varstu svá seinn, fóstri minn, ok fráskili föruneytinu?"	Then said Leif to him: "Why were so late, foster mine, and separated companions?"	Then Leif said to him: "Why were you so late, foster-father, and how were you separated from your companions?".
Hann talaði þá fyrst lengi á þýzku ok skaut marga vega augunum ok gretti sik.	He talked then first long in German and shot many ways eyes and frowned himself.	He talked at length first in German with his eyes darting in many directions and frowning.
En þeir skilðu eigi, hvat er hann sagði.	But they knew not, what was he said.	The others did not know what he was saying.
Hann mælti þá á norrænu, er stund leið: "Ek var genginn eigi miklu lengra en þit.	He said then in Norse, a while way: "I was going not much longer than you.	After a while, he spoke in Norse: "I had only gone a little farther than you.
Kann ek nökkur nýnæmi at segja.	Know I something new to say.	I know some news to tell you:

The Saga of the Greenlanders (Old Norse)

Old Norse	Literal	English
Ek fann vínvið ok vínber".	I found vines and grapes".	I found grapevines and grapes".
Mun þat satt, fóstri minn? kvað Leifr.	"Would that true, foster mine?" said Leif.	"Is this true, foster-father?" said Leif.
At vísu er þat satt, kvað hann, "því at ek var þar fæddr, er hvárki skorti vínvið né vínber".	"To know is that true", said he, "because that I was there fathered, where neither shortage vines nor grapes".	"I know this is true", said he, "because where I was brought up, there was no shortage of grapevines and grapes".
Nú sváfu þeir af þá nótt, en um morguninn mælti Leifr við háseta sína: "Nú skal hafa tvennar sýslur fram, ok skal sinn dag hvárt, lesa vínber eða höggva við ok fella mörkina, svá at þat verði farmr til skips míns". Ok þetta var ráðs tekit.	Now slept they of then night, but about morning said Leif to crew his: "Now shall have two pursuits from, and shall the day either, gather grapes or fell with and fell trees, so by that be cargo to ship mine". And that was counsel taken.	They went to sleep that night, and around morning Leif said to his crew: "Now we shall have two pursuits each day, either picking grapes or cutting vines, or felling trees to make cargo for my ship". And that advice was taken.
Svá er sagt, at eftirbátr þeira var fylldr af vínberjum. *Nú var höggvinn farmr á skipit.*	So is said, that boat theirs was filled of grapes. Now was cut-down cargo for ship.	So it was said that their boat was filled with grapes. Now they cut down wood as cargo for the ship.
Ok er várar, þá bjuggust þeir ok sigldu burt, ok gaf Leifr nafn landinu eftir landkostum ok kallaði Vínland, sigla nú síðan í haf, ok gaf þeim vel byri, þar til er þeir sá Grænland ok fjöll undir jöklum.	And when spring, then prepared they and sailed away, and gave Leif named land after land-benefits and called Vinland, sailed now since into sea, and gave them well fair-wind, there until was they saw Greenland and mountains below glaciers.	And when spring came, they made ready and sailed away, and Leif named the land after its features and called it Vinland, they now sailed to sea, and they were given fair wind until they saw Greenland and the mountains under glaciers.
Þá tók einn maðr til máls ok mælti við Leif: "Hví stýrir þú svá undir veðr skipinu?" *Leifr svarar: "Ek hygg at stjórn minni, en þó enn at fleira,* *eðr hvat sjáið þér til tíðenda?".* *Þeir kváðust ekki sjá, þat er tíðindum sætti.*	Then took one man to speak and said to Leif: "Why steer you so up-to wind the-ship? Leif answered: "I think to steering less, but though still to more, or what see you to news?". They said not see, that which news agreed.	Then one man said to Leif: "Why do you steer the ship so close to the wind?" Leif answered: "I am aware of my course, but there is more to it than that, do you see anything of note?". They said that they did not see anything of note.
Ek veit eigi, segir Leifr, "hvárt ek sé skip eðr sker".	"I know not", said Leif, "Whether I see ship or skerry".	"I don't know", said Leif, "whether I see a ship or a rock".

17

The Saga of the Greenlanders (Old Norse)

Old Norse	Literal	English
Nú sjá þeir ok kváðu sker vera.	Now looked they and said skerry was.	Now they looked and said that it was a rock.
Hann sá því framar en þeir, at hann sá menn í skerinu.	He saw that from but they, that he saw men on the-skerry.	He saw so much better than them, that he could see men on the rock.
Nú vil ek, at vér beitim undir veðrit, segir Leifr, "svá at vér náim til þeira, ef menn eru þurftugir at ná várum fundi, ok er nauðsyn á at duga þeim. En með því at þeir sé eigi friðmenn, þá eigum vér allan kost undir oss, en þeir ekki undir sér".	"Now will I, that we apply up-to wind", said Leif, "So that we near to them, if men are in-need by near we meet, and is necessity to that help them. But as-well for by they so not peaceful-men, then own we all advantage behind us, but they not behind them".	"Now I wish to steer us close to the wind", said Leif, "so that we are near to them, if these men are in need of help, we must help them. But equally if they are hostile, then we have all the advantages, and they have none".
Nú sækja þeir undir skerit ok lægðu segl sitt, ok köstuðu akkeri ok skutu litlum báti öðrum, er þeir höfðu haft með sér.	Now sought they under the-skerry and lowered sails theirs, and cast anchor and launched little boat other, that they had had with them.	Now they searched about the rock, lowered their sails, cast anchor, and launched the second of their small boats that they had with them.
Þá spurði Tyrkir, hverr þar réði fyrir liði.	Then asked Tyrkir, who there leader present team.	Then Tyrkir asked who there was the leader of their company.
Sá kveðst Þórir heita, ok vera norrænn maðr at kyni.	So said Thorir called, and was north man by kin.	The man who replied said his name was Thorir, and that he was of Norwegian origin.
"Eða hvert er þitt nafn?"	"But what is your name?"	"But what is your name?"
Leifr segir til sín.	Leif said to them.	Leif told them.
Ertu sonr Eiríks rauða ór Brattahlíð? segir hann.	"Are-you son-of Erik's the-Red out-of Brattahlid?" said he.	"Are you the son of Erik the Red from Brattahlid?" he said.
Leifr kvað svá vera.	Leif said so was.	Leif said it was so.
"Nú vil ek", segir Leifr, "bjóða yðr öllum á mitt skip, ok fémunum þeim, er skipit má við taka".	"Now will I", said Leif, "Invite you all on my ship, and goods those, which ship may with take".	"Now I wish", said Leif, "to invite you all on to my ship and any goods, which the ship may carry".
Þeir þágu þann kost ok sigldu síðan til Eiríksfjarðar með þeim farmi, þar til er þeir kómu til Brattahlíðar, báru farminn af skipi.	They accepted that choice and sailed afterwards to Eriksfjord with them cargo, there to then they came to Brattahlid, brought cargo off ship.	They accepted his offer and then they sailed to Eriksfjord with their cargo, until they reached Brattahlid, where they brought the cargo off the ship.

The Saga of the Greenlanders (Old Norse)

Old Norse	Literal	English
Síðan bauð Leifr Þóri til vistar með sér ok Guðríði, konu hans, ok þremr mönnum öðrum, en fekk vistir öðrum hásetum, bæði Þóris ok sínum félögum.	Afterwards invited Leif Thorir to stay with him and Guthrid, wife his, and three men other, but got provisions other seamen, as-well Thorir and his companions.	Afterwards Leif invited Thorir to stay with him, along with Thorir's wife Gudrid, and three other men, and found provisions for the other seamen, both Thorir's and his companions.
Leifr tók fimmtán menn ór skerinu.	Leif took fifteen men from the-skerry.	Leif rescued fifteen men from the rock.
Hann var síðan kallaðr Leifr inn heppni.	He was afterwards called Leif the lucky.	After this he was called Leif the Lucky.
Leifi varð nú bæði gott til fjár ok mannvirðingar.	Leif was now both benefited to wealth and worthiness.	Leif now became very wealthy and gained much respect.
Þann vetr kom sótt mikil í lið Þóris, ok andist hann Þórir ok mikill hluti liðs hans.	That winter came sickness great among team Thorir, and died he Thorir and much part-of men his.	That winter there came a great sickness among Thorir's companions, and Thorir died along with many of his company.
Þann vetr andaðist ok Eiríkr rauði.	That winter died also Erik the-Red.	That winter Erik the Red also died.
Nú var umræða mikil um Vínlandsför Leifs, ok þótti Þorvaldi bróður hans, of óvíða kannat hafa verit landit.	Now was talk much about Vinland-voyage Leif's, and thought Thorvald brother his, about little-wide explored had been land.	There was great discussion of Leif's Vinland-voyage, and his brother Thorvald thought that the land had been little explored.
Þá mælti Leifr við Þorvald: "Þú skalt fara með skip mitt, bróðir, ef þú vill, til Vínlands, ok vil ek þó, at skipit fari áðr eftir viði þeim, er Þórir átti á skerinu".	Then said Leif to Thorvald: "You shall go with ship mine, brother, if you will, to Vinland, and will I though, that ship go return after timber that, was Thorir had on the-skerry".	Leif then said to Thorvald: "You go to Vinland, brother, if you wish, but I wish for that ship to return after the timber, that Thorir had on that rock".
Ok svá var gert.	And so was done.	And so it was done.
5	5	5
Nú bjóst Þorvaldr til þeirar ferðar með þrjá tigu manna með umráði Leifs, bróður síns.	Now prepared Thorvald to their voyage with three ten men with counsel Leif, brother his.	Now Thorvald prepared their voyage with advice from his brother Leif, with thirty companions.
Síðan bjuggu þeir skip sitt ok heldu í haf, ok er engi frásögn um ferð þeira, fyrr en þeir koma til Vínlands, til Leifsbúða, ok bjuggu þar um skip sitt ok sátu um kyrrt þann vetr ok veiddu fiska til matar sér.	After prepared they ship theirs and held to sea, and is nothing said about voyage theirs, before but they came to Vinland, to Leif's-camp, and settled there about ship theirs and sat about still they winter and caught fish for food theirs.	They made their ship ready and put to sea, and nothing is said about their voyage before they came to Vinland, to Leif's camp, and they settled their ship, and stayed in place that winter and caught fish for their food.

The Saga of the Greenlanders (Old Norse)

Old Norse	Literal	English
En um várit mælti Þorvaldr, at þeir skyldu búa skip sitt ok skyldi eftirbátr skipsins ok nökkurir menn með fara fyrir vestan landit ok kanna þar um sumarit.	But about spring said Thorvald, that they should prepare ship theirs and should boat ship's and some men with travel for western land and explore there about summer.	Then about spring Thorvald said that they should prepare their ship, and with the ship's boat some men should travel west of the land and explore there during the summer.
Þeim sýndist landit fagrt ok skógótt ok skammt milli skóga ok sjávar ok hvítir sandar.	They seemed land beautiful and wooded and short between woods and sea and white sands.	To them the land seemed beautiful and well forested, and a short distance between the woods and the sea were white sands.
Þar var eyjótt mjök ok grunnsævi mikit.	There were islands much and shallows much.	There were many islands and large stretches of shallow sea.
Þeir fundu hvergi manna vistir né dýra.	They found neither men food nor animals.	The found neither sign of men nor animals.
En í eyju einni vestarliga fundu þeir kornhjálm af tré.	But on island one westward found they corn-shed of wood.	But on one of the westward islands they found a wooden corn shed.
Eigi fundu þeir fleiri mannaverk ok fóru aftr ok kómu til Leifsbúða at hausti.	Not found they more men's-work and went back and came to Leif's-camp in autumn.	They did not find any more work by human hands and came back to Leif's camp in the autumn.
En at sumri öðru fór Þorvaldr fyrir austan með kaupskipit ok it nyrðra fyrir landit.	But at summer the-next went Thorvald for eastward with ship and the north for land.	The next summer Thorvald journeyed eastwards with the ship and north around the land.
Þá gerði at þeim veðr hvasst fyrir andnesi einu, ok rak þá þar upp, ok brutu kjölinn undan skipinu ok höfðu þar langa dvöl ok bættu skip sitt.	Then was to them weather stormy before headland one, and driven then there up, and broke keel under ship and had there long dwelled and repaired ship theirs.	Then they encountered stormy weather around one of the headlands, and they were driven ashore, and their keel brooke under their ship, and they stayed there a long time repairing their ship.
Þá mælti Þorvaldr við förunauta sína: "Nú vil ek, at vér reisim hér upp kjölinn á nesinu ok kallim Kjalarnes". *Ok svá gerðu þeir.*	Then said Thorvald to companions his: "Now will I, that we raise here up keel on headland and call Kjalarnes". And so did they.	Then Thorvald said to his companions: "Now I wish that we raise the keel up on the headland and call it Kjalarnes". And so they did.
Síðan sigla þeir þaðan í braut ok austr fyrir landit ok inn í fjarðarkjafta þá, er þar váru næstir, ok at höfða þeim, er þar gekk fram.	Afterwards sailed they there to away and eastern for land and then into fjord-mouth then, which there was nearest, and to headland they, which there going from.	Afterwards they sailed away to the east of the land and then into the mouth of the next fjords, and then to a cape stretching out from there to the sea.
Hann var allr skógi vaxinn.	It was all wood grown.	It was covered with forest.

The Saga of the Greenlanders (Old Norse)

Old Norse	Literal	English
Þá leggja þeir fram skip sitt í lægi ok skjóta bryggjum á land, ok gengr Þorvaldr þar á land upp með alla förunauta sína.	There let they from ship theirs to lay and launched bridge to land, and went Thorvald there to land up with all companions his.	There they lay their ship and set out gangways to the land, and Thorvald and his companions went to shore.
Hann mælti þá: "Hér er fagrt, ok hér vilda ek bæ minn reisa",	He said then: "Here is beautiful, and here will I settlement mine raise",	Then he said: "It is beautiful here, and I wish to build a farm here",
ganga síðan til skips ok sjá á sandinum inn frá höfðanum þrjár hæðir, ok fóru til þangat ok sjá þar húðkeipa þrjá ok þrjá menn undir hverjum.	Went then to ship and saw on sands in from headland three heights, and went to there and saw there hide-boats three and three men under each.	Afterwards as they went back to the ship, they saw three hillocks on the beach inland from the cape, and saw three canoes with three men under each of them.
Þá skiptu þeir liði sínu ok höfðu hendr á þeim öllum, nema einn komst á burt með keip sinn.	Then divided they people theirs and had caught to they all, taken one came to away with canoe his.	They divided their forces and caught all of them, except one who escaped with his canoe.
Þeir drepa hina átta ok ganga síðan aftr á höfðann ok sjást þar um ok sjá inn í fjörðinn hæðir nökkurar, ok ætluðu þeir þat vera byggðir.	They killed the eight and went since back to headland and looked there about and saw that in fjord heights some, and supposed they that were dwellings.	They killed the other eight and afterwards went back to the cape, and they looked and saw that in some of the fjord heights, what they assumed to be settlements.
Eftir þat sló á þá höfga svá miklum, at þeir máttu eigi vöku halda, ok sofna þeir allir.	After that struck on then heaviness so much, that they may not awake keep, and slept they all.	After that they became so heavy with weariness, that they could not stay awake, and the all fell asleep.
Þá kom kall yfir þá, svá at þeir vöknuðu allir.	Then came shout over then, so that they awoke all.	Then a voice called to them, and they all awoke.
Svá segir kallit: "Vaki þú, Þorvaldr, ok allt föruneyti þitt, ef þú vill líf þitt hafa, ok far þú á skip þitt ok allir menn þínir, ok farit frá landi sem skjótast".	So said call: "Wake you, Thorvald, and all companions yours, if you will lives yours have, and go you to ship yours and all men yours, and travel from land which quickly".	The voice called: "Wake up, Thorvald, and all your companions, if you wish to save your lives, get to your ship and all your men, and leave this land as quickly as you can".
Þá fór innan eftir firðinum ótal húðkeipa, ok lögðu at þeim.	Then went within behind fjord countless hide-boats, and lay at them.	Then from within the fjord came countless canoes heading towards them.
Þorvaldr mælti þá: "Vér skulum færa út á borð vígfleka ok verjast sem bezt, en vega lítt í mót".	Thorvald said then: "We should bring out to board battle and defend as best, but fight little to against".	Then Thorvald said: "We should bring out breastworks along the sides of the ship and defend as best we can, but fight back as little as we can".

The Saga of the Greenlanders (Old Norse)

Old Norse	Literal	English
Svá gera þeir, en Skrælingar skutu á þá um stund, en flýja síðan burt sem ákafast, hverr sem mátti.	So did they, but Skraelings shot towards then about awhile, but fled afterwards away as fast, each as may.	So they did, but the Skraelings shot at them for a while, they fled as rapidly as they could.
Þá spurði Þorvaldr menn sína, ef þeir væri nökkut sárir.	Then asked Thorvald men his, if they had any wounds.	Then Thorvald asked his men if any of them had been wounded.
Þeir kváðust eigi sárir vera.	They said not wounded were.	They said that they were not wounded.
"Ek hefi fengit sár undir hendi", segir hann, "ok fló ör milli skipborðsins ok skjaldarins undir hönd mér, ok er hér örin, en mun mik þetta til bana leiða.	"I have caught wound under arm", said he, "And flew arrow between ship's-berth and shield under arm to-me, and is here arrow, then should me this to death lead.	"I have been wounded under my arm", he said, "and an arrow flew between the ship's berth and the shield into my armpit, and this shall lead to my death.
Nú ræð ek, at þér búið ferð yðra sem fljótast aftr á leið, en þér skuluð færa mik á höfða þann, er mér þótti byggiligast vera.	Now advise I, to you prepare travel depart as quickly return to journey, but you should bring me to headland that, which me thinks dwelling shall-be.	Now I advise you to prepare for your return journey as quickly as possible, but take me to that cape that I thought would make a good farm.
Má þat vera, at mér hafi satt á munn komit, at ek muni þar búa á um stund.	May that be, by me have true to mouth come, that I should there dwell on for awhile.	Maybe the words I spoke shall prove true, that I shall dwell there for awhile.
Þar skuluð þér mik grafa ok setja krossa at höfði mér ok at fótum, ok kallið þat Krossanes jafnan síðan".	There should you me engrave and set cross at head mine and at feet, and call that Krossanes ever after".	There you should bury me and put a cross at my head and feet, and call that Krossanes ever after".
Grænland var þá kristnat, en þó andaðist Eiríkr rauði fyrir kristni.	Greenland was then Christian, but though died Erik the-Red before Christianity.	Greenland was then Christian, but Erik died before the conversion to Christianity.
Nú andaðist Þorvaldr, en þeir gerðu allt eftir því, sem hann hafði mælt, ok fóru síðan ok hittu þar förunauta sína, ok sögðu hvárir öðrum slík tíðendi sem vissu ok bjuggu þar þann vetr ok fengu sér vínber ok vínvið til skipsins.	Now died Thorvald, but they did all after according, which he had said, and went since and met their companions theirs, and said each other such tidings which knew and dwelt there that winter and gathered they grapes and vines to ship.	Now Thorvald died, and they did everything as he had said, and afterwards they went to meet their companions, and each group told its news to the others, and they stayed there that winter and gathered grapes and vines in their ship.
Nú búast þeir þaðan um várit eftir til Grænlands ok kómu skipi sínu í Eiríksfjörð ok kunnu Leifi at segja mikil tíðendi.	Now prepared they there about spring after to Greenland and came ship theirs in Eriksfjord and known Leif that said much tidings.	Now they prepared their ship about spring to return to Greenland, and their ship came in to Eriksfjord and had much news to tell Leif.

6   6   6

The Saga of the Greenlanders (Old Norse)

Old Norse	Literal	English
Þat hafði gerzt til tíðenda meðan á Grænlandi, at Þorsteinn í Eiríksfirði hafði kvángazt ok fengit Guðríðar Þorbjarnardóttur, er átt hafði Þórir Austmaðr, er fyrr var frá sagt.	It had made to news meanwhile to Greenland, that Thorstein in Eriksfjord had married and married Guthrid Thorbjarnardottur, who had married Thorir Easterner, as before was from said.	Among the news meanwhile in Greenland was that Thorstein in Eriksfjord had married Gudrid Thorbjornadottir, who had previously been married to Thorir the Easterner who was spoken of earlier.
Nú fýstist Þorsteinn Eiríksson at fara til Vínlands eftir líki Þorvalds, bróður síns, ok bjó skip it sama, ok valði hann lið at afli ok vexti ok hafði með sér hálfan þriðja tög manna ok Guðríði, konu sína, ok sigla í haf, þegar þau eru búin, ok ór landsýn.	Now desired Thorstein Eriksson to travel to Vinland after body Thorvald's, brother his, and prepared ship the same, and chose he team in strength and well-built and had with him half third twenty men and Guthrid, wife his, and sailed to sea, then they were ready, and out-of land-sight.	Now Thorstein Eriksson wished to travel to Vinland and retrieve the body of his brother Thorvald, and made the same ship ready, and he chose his company for their strength and size, and had with him twenty five men and his wife Gudrid, and when they were ready the sailed to sea, and out of sight of land.
Þau velkði úti allt sumarit, ok vissu eigi, hvar þau fóru.	They drove about all summer, and knew not, where they went.	They were driven about all summer, and they did not know where they went.
Ok er vika var af vetri, þá tóku þeir land í Lýsufirði á Grænlandi í inni vestri byggð.	And when week was of winter, then took they land in Lysufjord in Greenland in the western settlement.	And when the first week of winter had passed, they made land in Lysufjord, in the Western Settlement of Greenland.
Þorsteinn leitaði þeim um vistir ok fekk vistir öllum hásetum sínum. *En hann var vistlauss ok kona hans.* *Nú váru þau eftir at skipi tvau nökkurar nætr.* *Þá var enn ung kristni á Grænlandi.*	Thorstein sought them about shelter and got lodging all crew his. But he was without-lodging and wife his. Now were they remained in ship two some nights. Then was yet young Christianity in Greenland.	Thorstein found them shelter and got lodgings for all of his crew. But he and his wife were without lodgings. Now they remained on the ship for several nights. Then Christianity was still young in Greenland.
Þat var einn dag, at menn kómu at tjaldi þeira snemma. *Sá spurði, er fyrir þeim var, hvat manna væri í tjaldinu.*	It was one day, that people came by tent theirs early. So asked, who present they were, what men were in tent.	One day some men came early to their tent. The asked what men were in the tent.
Þorsteinn svarar: "Tveir menn", segir hann, "eða hverr spyrr at?"	Thorstein answered: "Two people", said he, "But who asks to?"	Thorstein answered: "Two people", he said, "but who is asking?".

The Saga of the Greenlanders (Old Norse)

Old Norse	Literal	English
"Þorsteinn heiti ek, ok em ek kallaðr Þorsteinn svartr. En þat er erendi mitt hingat, at ek vil bjóða ykkr báðum hjónunum til vistar til mín".	"Thorstein called I, and am I called Thorstein the-Black. But that is errand mine here, that I will bid you both couple to lodging to mine".	"I am called Thorstein, Thorstein the Black. My reason for coming here is to invite you both to stay with me".
Þorsteinn kveðst vilja hafa umræði konu sinnar, en hon bað hann ráða, ok nú játar hann þessu.	Thorstein said will have discussion wife his, but she bid he decide, and now accepted he this.	Thorstein said he wished to discuss this with his wife, but she asked him to decide, and he now accepted.
"Þá mun ek koma eftir ykkur á morgin með eyki, því at skortir ekki til at veita ykkr vist, en fásinni er mikit með mér at vera, því at tvau erum vit þar hjón, því at ek em einþykkr mjök".	"Then should I come back to-you in morning with animals, for by shortage not to by supply you provisions, but remote is very with me by being, for that two we-are with there couple, because that I am solitary much".	"Then I shall come back to you in the morning with oxen, I have no shortage of supplies for you, but it is remote being here with me, because there are only two of us, my wife and I, and I am very much a solitary man.
Annan sið hefi ek ok en þér hafið, ok ætla ek þann þó betra, er þér hafið.	Another tradition have I and than you have, and suppose I that yet better, is you have".	Also I have another faith than you, but I suspect yours is the better of the two".
Nú kom hann eftir þeim um morgininn með eyki, ok fóru þau með Þorsteini svarta til vistar, ok veitti hann þeim vel.	Now came he after them about morning with animals, and went they with Thorstein the-Black to lodge, and supported he them well.	Now he came back to them around morning with oxen, and they went to stay with Thorstein the Black, and he provided for them generously.
Guðríðr var skörulig kona at sjá ok vitr kona ok kunni vel at vera með ókunnum mönnum.	Guthrid was strong woman to see and wise woman and knew well at being with unknown people.	Gudrid was a strong woman, of striking appearance, and a wise woman who knew how to behave among strangers.
Þat var snemma vetrar, at sótt kom í lið Þorsteins Eiríkssonar, ok önduðust þar margir förunautar hans.	That was early winter, that sickness came to companions Thorstein's Eriksson, and died there many companions his.	It was early that winter that sickness came to Thorstein Eriksson's companions, and many of them died there.
Þorsteinn bað gera kistur at líkum þeira, er önduðust, ok færa til skips ok búa þar um, "því at ek vil láta flytja til Eiríksfjarðar at sumri öll líkin".	Thorstein asked made coffins for bodies theirs, who died, and brought to ship and laid there about, "For that I will lay carry to Eriksfjord in summer all bodies".	Thorstein asked that coffins be made for their bodies who had died, and brought back to the ship and laid there, "For I will carry all of them to Eriksfjord in the summer".

The Saga of the Greenlanders (Old Norse)

Old Norse	Literal	English
Nú er þess skammt at bíða, at sótt kemr í hýbýli Þorsteins, ok tók kona hans sótt fyrst, er hét Grímhildr.	Now was this short to wait, that sickness came into dwelling Thorstein's, and took wife his sickness first, who called Grimhild.	It was not long until the sickness came to Thorstein the Black's house, and his wife Grimhild was the first to fall ill.
Hon var ákafliga mikil ok sterk sem karlar, en þó kom sóttin henni undir.	She was very large and strong as men, but yet came sickness her under.	She was a very large woman, strong as a man, yet she bowed to the sickness.
Ok brátt eftir þat tók sóttina Þorsteinn Eiríksson, ok lágu þau bæði senn, ok andaðist Grímhildr, kona Þorsteins svarta.	And soon after that took sickness Thorstein Eriksson, and lay they both same, and died Grimhild, wife Thorstein the-Black's.	And soon after that Thorstein Eriksson was stricken, and both of them laid there, and Grimhild, the wife of Thorstein the Black died.
En er hon var dauð, þá gekk Þorsteinn fram ór stofunni eftir fjöl at leggja á líkit.	But when she was dead, then went Thorstein from out room after plank to lay on body.	And when she had died, Thorstein the Black went from the main room to look for a plank to lay her body on.
Guðríðr mælti þá: "Vertu litla hríð á brott, Þorsteinn minn", segir hon.	Guthrid said then: "Be little time to away, Thorstein mine", said she.	Gudrid then spoke: "Don't be away long, dear Thorstein" she said.
Hann kvað svá vera skyldu.	He said so be should.	He said so it would be.
Þá mælti Þorsteinn Eiríksson: "Með undarligum hætti er nú um húsfreyju vára, því at nú örglast hon upp við ölnboga ok þokar fótum sínum frá stokki ok þreifar til skúa sinna".	Then said Thorstein Eriksson: "With strange way is now about housewife going, for that now rises she up with elbows and stretches feet hers from bed and feels for shoes hers".	Then Thorstein Eriksson said: "Strange are the actions of the mistress of the house now, she's struggling to raise herself up on her elbows, and stretches her feet from the bed and feels for her shoes".
Ok í því kom Þorsteinn bóndi inn, ok lagðist Grímhildr niðr í því, ok brakaði þá í hverju tré í stofunni.	And in for came Thorstein farmer the, and lay Grimhild down in for, and creaked then in each beam in room.	And in came Thorstein the farmer, and Grimhild fell back down, and every beam in the room creaked.
Nú gerir Þorsteinn kistu at líki Grímhildr ok færði í brott ok bjó um.	Now made Thorstein coffin for body Grimhild's and took it out and dwelling about.	Thorstein then made a coffin for Grimhild's body and took it away from the house.
Hann var bæði mikill maðr ok sterkr, ok þurfti hann þess alls, áðr hann kom henni burt af bænum.	He was both large man and strong, and needed he this all, before he came her away out-of dwelling.	He was a large and strong man, and he needed all his strenngth to carry her out of the house.
Nú elnaði sóttin Þorsteini Eiríkssyni, ok andaðist hann.	Now attacked sickness Thorstein Eriksson, and died he.	Now the sickness attacked Thorstein Eriksson, and he died.
Guðríðr, kona hans, kunni því lítt.	Guthrid, wife his, knew therefore little.	Gudrid, his wife, was overtaken with grief and knew little else.

The Saga of the Greenlanders (Old Norse)

Old Norse	Literal	English
Þá váru þau öll í stofunni.	Then were they all in room.	All of them were in the main room.
Guðríðr hafði setit á stóli frammi fyrir bekknum, er hann hafði legit, Þorsteinn, bóndi hennar.	Guthrid had sat on stool from before bench, which he had laid, Thorstein, husband hers.	Gudrid sat on a stool in front of the bench where her husband Thorstein had lain.
Þá tók Þorsteinn bóndi Guðríði af stólinum í fang sér ok settist í annan bekkinn með hana gegnt líki Þorsteins ok talði um fyrir henni marga vega ok huggaði hana ok hét henni því, at hann mundi fara með henni til Eiríksfjarðar með líki Þorsteins, bónda hennar, ok förunauta hans.	Then took Thorstein the-farmer Guthrid from stool into grasp his and sat on another bench with he opposite body Thorstein's and talked about before her many ways and comforted he and called her therefore, that he would go with her to Eriksfjord with body Thorstein's, husband hers, and companions his.	Thorstein the farmer then took Gudrid from the stool into his arms and sat with her on the bench across from her husband Thorstein's corpse and said many comforting things, consoling her and promising her that he would take her to Eriksfjord with her husband Thorstein's body, and those of his companions.
Ok svá skal ek taka hingat hjón fleiri, segir hann, "þér til hugganar ok skemmtanar".	"And so shall I take there couple more", said he, "You to comfort and entertain".	"And we'll invite other people to stay here", he said, "to provide you with solace and companionship".
Hon þakkaði honum.	She thanked him.	She thanked him.
Þorsteinn Eiríksson settist þá upp ok mælti: "Hvar er Guðríðr?"	Thorstein Eriksson sat then up and said: "Where is Guthrid?"	Thorstein Eriksson then sat up and said: "Where is Gudrid?"
Þrjá tíma mælti hann þetta, en hon þagði.	Three times said he this, but she silent.	Three times he said this, but she remained silent.
Þá mælti hon við Þorstein bónda: "Hvárt skal ek svör veita hans máli eða eigi?"	Then said she to Thorstein the-farmer: "However shall I answer know his speech or not?"	Then she said to Thorstein the farmer: "Shall I answer him or not?",
Hann bað hana eigi svara.	He bid she not answer.	He told her not to answer.
Þá gekk Þorsteinn bóndi yfir gólfit ok settist á stólinn, en Guðríðr sat í knjám honum.	Then went Thorstein the-farmer over floor and sat on stool, but Guthrid sat on knees his.	Thorstein the farmer then crossed the floor and sat on the stool, and Gudrid on his knee.
Ok þá mælti Þorsteinn bóndi: "Hvat viltu, nafni?" segir hann.	And then said Thorstein the-farmer "What will-you, namesake?" said he.	Then Thorstein the farmer spoke: "What is it that you want, namesake?", he said.

The Saga of the Greenlanders (Old Norse)

Old Norse	Literal	English
Hann svarar, er stund leið: "Mér er annt til þess, at segja Guðríði forlög sín, til þess at hon kunni þá betr andláti mínu, því at ek em kominn til góðra hvíldastaða.	He answered, at time way: "I who wish to this, to say Guthrid fortune hers, to this by she could then better death mine, for that I am come to good resting-place.	He answered after a short while: "I want to tell Gudrid her fate, to make it easier for her to deal with my death, for I have gone to a good resting place.
En þat er þér at segja, Guðríðr, at þú munt gift vera íslenzkum manni, ok munu langar vera samfarir ykkrar, ok margt manna mun frá ykkr koma, þroskasamt, bjart ok ágætt, sætt ok ilmat vel.	But this is you to say, Guthrid, that you shall married be Icelander man, and shall long be together you, and many people shall from you come, promising, bright and fine, settled and favoured well.	I say this to you, Gudrid, that you shall marry an Icelander, and you will long be together, and you shall have many descendants, promisinig, bright, and fine, sweet and well favoured.
Munuð þit fara af Grænlandi til Nóregs ok þaðan til Íslands ok gera bú á Íslandi.	Shall you travel from Greenland to Norway and from-there to Iceland and make settlement on Iceland.	You will travel from Greenland to Norway, and from there to Iceland, and settle on Iceland.
Þar munuð þit lengi búa, ok muntu honum lengr lifa.	There shall you long live, and shall him longer live.	There you will live a long time, longer than your husband.
Þú munt útan fara ok ganga suðr ok koma út aftr til Íslands til bús þíns, ok þá mun þar kirkja reist vera, ok muntu þar vera ok taka nunnuvígslu, ok þar muntu andast".	You shall out travel and go south and come from return to Iceland to home yours, and then shall there church raised be, and shall there be and take nun's-vows, and there shall die".	You will travel and go south, and return to Iceland to your farm, and there a church will be raised, and there you will take a nun's vows, and there you will die".
Ok þá hnígr Þorsteinn aftr, ok var búit um lík hans ok fært til skips.	And then fell Thorstein back, and was prepared about body his and taken to ship.	And then Thorstein Eriksson fell back, and his corpse was prepared and taken to the ship.
Þorsteinn bóndi efndi vel við Guðríði allt þat, er hann hafði heitit.	Thorstein the-farmer kept well with Guthrid all that, which he had promised.	Thorstein the farmer kept all his promises to Gudrid.
Hann seldi um várit jörð sína ok kvikfé ok fór til skips með Guðríði með allt sitt, bjó skipit ok fekk menn til ok fór síðan til Eiríksfjarðar.	He sold about spring land his and livestock and went to ship with Guthrid with all his, prepared ship and got men to and went then to Eriksfjord.	In the spring he sold his land and livestock, and went to the ship with all his posessions, prepared the ship, hired a crew, and sailed to Eriksfjord.
Váru nú líkin jörðuð at kirkju.	Were now bodies buried by church.	The bodies were now buried by a church.
Guðríðr fór til Leifs í Brattahlíð, en Þorsteinn svarti gerði bú í Eiríksfirði ok bjó þar, meðan hann lifði, ok þótti vera inn vaskasti maðr.	Guthrid travelled to Leif in Brattahlid, but Thorstein the-Black made dwelling at Eriksfjord and dwelt there, meantime he lived, and thought was he capable man.	Gudrid travlelled to Leif in Brattahlid, and Thorstein the Black built a farm in Eriksfjord and settled there as long as he lived, and he was thought of as a most capable man.

The Saga of the Greenlanders (Old Norse)

Old Norse	Literal	English
Þat sama sumar kom skip af Nóregi til Grænlands.	That same summer came ship from Norway to Greenland.	That same summer a ship came from Norway and arrived in Greenland.
Sá maðr hét Þorfinnr karlsefni, er því skipi stýrði.	The man called Thorfin Karlsefni, who for ship steered.	The captain of the ship was named Thorfin Karlsefni.
Hann var sonr Þórðar hesthöfða Snorrasonar, Þórðarsonar frá Höfða.	He was son-of Thord Horse-Head Snorrason, Thordarson from Hofdi.	He was the son of Thord Horse-Head, the son of Snorri Thordarson of Hofdi.
Þorfinnr karlsefni var stórauðigr at fé, ok var um vetrinn í Brattahlíð með Leifi Eiríkssyni. Brátt felldi hann hug til Guðríðar ok bað hennar, en hon veik til Leifs svörum fyrir sik.	Thorfin Karlsefni was wealthy in cattle, and was about winter in Brattahlid with Leif Eriksson. Soon fell he thoughts to Guthrid and asked her, but she referred to Leif's answer to him.	Thorfin Karlsefni was wealth in cattle, and he spent the winter in Brattahlid with Leif Eriksson. He was soon attracted to Gudrid and asked her to marry him, but she referred him to Leif for his answer.
Síðan var hon honum föstnuð ok gert brúðlaup þeira á þeim vetri.	Afterwards was she to-him betrothed and was wedding theirs in that winter.	Afterwards she was engaged to him and their wedding was that winter.
In sama var umræða á Vínlandsför sem fyrr, ok fýstu menn Karlsefni mjök þeirar ferðar, bæði Guðríðr ok aðrir menn. Nú var ráðin ferð hans, ok réð hann sér skipverja sex tigu karla ok konur fimm.	The same was discussed to Vinland-voyage as before, and urged people Karlsefni much there to-journey, both Guthrid and other people. Now was agreed travel his, and hired he the crew six ten men and women five.	The discussion of a voyage to Vinland continued as before, and people urged Karlsefni to make the journey, both Gudrid and others. Now he was decided to travel, he hired a crew of sixty men and five women.
Þann máldaga gerðu þeir Karlsefni ok hásetar hans, at jöfnum höndum skyldi þeir hafa allt þat, er þeir fengi til gæða. Þeir höfðu með sér allskonar fénað, því at þeir ætluðu at byggja landit, ef þeir mætti þat.	Then agreed was they Karlsefni and crew his, that even handed should they have all that, which they get to quality. They have with them all-kinds livestock, for that they intended to settle land, if they may that.	Then Karlsefni and his crew agreed that all goods they obtained would be divided equally among them. They had with them all kinds of livestock, for they intended to settle the land if they could.
Karlsefni bað Leif húsa á Vínlandi, en hann kveðst ljá mundu húsin, en gefa eigi.	Karlsefni asked Leif houses in Vinland, but he said loan would houses, but give not.	Karlsefni asked Leif for his houses in Vinland, and Leif said he would lend them, but not give them to him.
Síðan heldu þeir í haf skipinu ok kómu til Leifsbúða með heilu ok höldnu ok báru þar upp húðföt sín.	Then held they to sea ship and came to Leif's-camp with whole and safe and carried there up skin-cots theirs.	Then they put the ship to sea and all arrived at Leif's camp safely and unloaded their sleeping-sacks.

The Saga of the Greenlanders (Old Norse)

Old Norse	Literal	English
Þeim bar brátt í hendr mikil föng ok góð, því at reyðr var þar upp rekin, bæði mikil ok góð, fóru til síðan ok skáru hvalinn, skorti þá eigi mat.	They bore soon to hand much provisions and good, for a rorqual was there up driven, both large and good, went to then and cut whale, shortage then not food.	They soon had plenty of good provisions, since a large and fine rorqual was driven up to shore, they had no shortage of food.
Skorti þá eigi mat.	Shortage then not food.	They had no shortage of food.
Fénaðr gekk þar á land upp, en þat var brátt, at graðfé varð úrigt ok gerði mikit um sik.	Cattle went there to land up, but that was soon, the cattle were irritable and made greatly about themselves.	The livestock went inland, but the males were soon irritable and hard to handle.
Þeir höfðu haft með sér griðung einn.	They had had with them bull one.	They had with them a bull.
Karlsefni lét fella viðu ok telgja til skips síns ok lagði viðinn á bjarg eitt til þurrkunar.	Karlsefni let fell wood and hewn to ships theirs and lay trees on rock along to dry.	Karlsefni had trees felled and hewn for their ships, and lay the timber on a rock to dry.
Þeir höfðu öll gæði af landkostum, þeim er þar váru, bæði af vínberjum ok alls konar veiðum ok gæðum.	They had all quality of land-benefits, they which there were, both of grapes and all kinds fish and quality.	They had all kinds of benefit from the land, which included grapes, all kinds of fish and game, and other quality things.
Eftir þann vetr inn fyrsta kom sumar.	After that winter the first came summer.	After the first winter passed and summer came,
Þá urðu þeir varir við Skrælinga, ok fór þar ór skógi fram mikill flokkr manna.	Then became they aware with Skraelings, and went there out woods from large group men.	They became aware of the Skraelings, a large group of men came out of the woods.
Þar var nær nautfé þeira, en graðungr tók at belja ok gjalla ákafliga hátt.	There was near cattle there, but bull took to bellowing and snorting very loudly.	There cattle were near, and the bull took to bellowing and snorting very loudly.
En þat hræddust Skrælingar ok lögðu undan með byrðar sínar, en þat var grávara ok safali ok alls konar skinnavara, ok snúa til bæjar Karlsefnis ok vildu þar inn í húsin, en Karlsefni lét verja dyrrnar.	But that frightened Skraelings and laid away with burdens theirs, but they were grey-skins and sables and all kinds furs, and turned towards farm Karlsefni's and willed there the into house, but Karlsefni laid protection door.	Then this frightened the Skraelings and they ran away with their burdens, which included grey skins, sables, and all kinds of fur, they turned towards Karlsefni's farm and wanted to get into the house, but Karlsefni had protected the door.
Hvárigir skilðu annars mál.	Neither knew others' language.	Neither knew the others' language.
Þá tóku Skrælingar ofan bagga sína ok leystu ok buðu þeim ok vildu vápn helzt fyrir, en Karlsefni bannaði þeim at selja vápnin.	Then took Skraelings off bags theirs and loosened and offered they and willed weapons preferably for, but Karlsefni banned they to sell weapons.	Then the Skraelings took off their bags and opened them, offering their goods, preferably in exchange for weapons, but Karlsefni forbade them to trade weapons.

The Saga of the Greenlanders (Old Norse)

Old Norse	Literal	English
Ok nú leitar hann ráðs með þeim hætti, at hann bað konur bera út búnyt at þeim, ok þegar er þeir sá búnyt, þá vildu þeir kaupa þat, en ekki annat.	And now sought he solution with them to-stop, that he asked women bring out milk-products by them, and then when they saw milk-products, then willed they buy that, and nothing else.	And now he sought a solution to this, he asked the women to bring out milk-products, and when they saw these milk-products, they wanted to buy that and nothing else.
Nú var sú kaupför Skrælinga, at þeir báru sinn varning í brott í mögum sínum, en Karlsefni ok förunautar hans höfðu eftir bagga þeira ok skinnvöru.	Now were their trading-with Skraelings, by them bearing their goods in away in stomachs theirs, but Karlsefni and companions his had after bags theirs and skin-wares.	The trading with the Skraelings resulted in them carrying away their purchases in their stomachs, leaving their packs and skins with Karlsefni.
Fóru þeir við svá búit í burt.	Went they with so settlement to away.	When this was done, they went away.
Nú er frá því at segja, at Karlsefni lætr gera skíðgarð rammligan um bæ sinn, ok bjuggust þar um.	Now was from therefore to say, that Karlsefni laid made fence strong about farm theirs, and prepared there about.	Now from this is to be told, that Karlsefni had a strong fence made around their farm to be prepared.
Í þann tíma fæddi Guðríðr sveinbarn, kona Karlsefnis, ok hét sá sveinn Snorri.	In that time bore Guthrid baby-boy, wife Karlsefni's, and called the boy Snorri.	At this time Karlsefni's wife Gudrid gave birth to a baby boy who was named Snorri.
Á öndverðum öðrum vetri þá kómu Skrælingar til móts við þá ok váru miklu fleiri en fyrr ok höfðu slíkan varnað sem fyrr.	The beginning next winter then came Skraelings to meet with then and were much more than before and had such wares as before.	At the beginning of the next winter the Skraelings came to meet with them in much greater numbers than before.
Þá mælti Karlsefni við konur: "Nú skuluð þér bera út slíkan mat sem fyrr var rífastr, en ekki annat".	Then said Karlsefni to women: "Now should you bring out such food as before was demanded, but nothing else".	Karlsefni then spoke to the women: "Now you should bring out whatever food was most in demand, and nothing else".
Ok er þeir sá þat, þá köstuðu þeir böggunum sínum inn yfir skíðgarðinn.	And when they saw that, they threw they bags theirs the over fence.	And when the natives saw this, they cast their bags over the fence.
En Guðríðr sat í durum inni með vöggu Snorra, sonar síns.	But Guthrid sat in doorway in with cradle Snorri, son hers.	But Gudrid sat in the doorway with the cradle of her son Snorri.
Þá bar skugga í dyrrin, ok gekk þar inn kona í svörtum námkyrtli, heldr lág, ok hafði dregil um höfuð ok ljósjörp á hár, fölleit ok mjök eygð, svá at eigi hafði jafnmikil augu sét í einum mannshausi.	Then carried shadow in doorway, and going there the woman in dark gown, held tightly, and had shawl about head and bright-chestnut of hair, pale and much eyed, so that not had equal eyes seen in any people's-heads.	Then a shadow fell across the doorway, and there came a woman in a dark gown, held tightly, and had a shawl around her head of bright chestnut hair, pale and large eyes, such that no one had seen eyes like them in anyone's head.

The Saga of the Greenlanders (Old Norse)

Old Norse	Literal	English
Hon gekk þar at, er Guðríðr sat, ok mælti: "Hvat heitir þú?" segir hon.	She went there by, was Guthrid sat, and spoke: "What called-are you?" said she.	She came to where Gudrud sat, and spoke: "What is your name?", she said.
"Ek heiti Guðríðr, eða hvert er þitt heiti?".	"I am-called Guthrid, but what is your name?".	"I am called Gudrid, but what is your name?".
"Ek heiti Guðríðr", segir hon.	"I am-called Guthrid", said she.	"I am called Gudrid", she said.
Þá rétti Guðríðr húsfreyja hönd sína til hennar, at hún sæti hjá henni, en þat bar allt saman, at þá heyrði Guðríðr brest mikinn, ok var þá konan horfin, ok í því var ok veginn einn Skrælingr af einum húskarli Karlsefnis, því at hann hafði viljat taka vápn þeira, ok fóru nú brott sem tíðast, en klæði þeira lágu þar eftir ok varningr.	Then extended Guthrid housewife hand hers to her, that she sit by her, but that bore all together, that then heard Guthrid crash great, and was then woman disappeared, and in therefore was also slain one Skraeling from one houseman Karlsefnis, because that he had willed take weapon theirs, and went now away that swiftly, but clothing theirs laid there left and goods.	Then Gudrid the housewife extended her hand to her, to sit by her, but then there was a great crash, and the woman disappeared, at that moment one of the natives had been killed by one of Karlsefni's men, because he had tried to take their weapons, and they went away swiftly, but their clothing lay there behind with other goods.
Engi maðr hafði konu þessa sét útan Guðríðr ein.	No man had woman this seen of Guthrid alone.	No one had seen the woman except for Gudrid.
Nú munum vér þurfa til ráða at taka, segir Karlsefni, "því at ek hygg, at þeir muni vitja vár it þriðja sinn með ófriði ok fjölmenni. *Nú skulum vér taka þat ráð, at tíu menn fari fram á nes þetta ok sýni sik þar, en annat lið várt skal fara í skóg ok höggva þar rjóðr fyrir nautfé váru, þá er liðit kemr fram ór skóginum.*	"Now should we need to plan to take", said Karlsefni, "Because that I think, that they shall visit will the third they with warlike and many. Now should we take that plan, that ten men go from to headland this and show themselves there, while second team ours shall go into forest and strike there clearing for cattle ours, then as team come from out forest.	"Now we need to make a plan", said Karlsefni, "because I think that they will visit us a third time with hostility and in many numbers. Now shall we follow this plan, that ten men will go out on this headland and show themselves there, while our second team will go into the forest and strike there a clearing for the cattle, then as a team come from out of the forest.
Vér skulum ok taka gríðung várn ok láta hann fara fyrir oss".	We shall also take bull ours and let him go ahead-of us".	We shall also take our bull and let him go before us".
En þar var svá háttat, er fundr þeira var ætlaðr, at vatn var öðrum megin, en skógr á annan veg. *Nú váru þessi ráð höfð, er Karlsefni lagði til.*	But there was so the-way where battle theirs was intended, by water was the-other side, but forest on-the other way. Now was this plan taken, as Karlsefni had to.	There where their battle was intended, there was water on one side, and a forest on the other. Now the followed the plan that Karlsefni had made.

The Saga of the Greenlanders (Old Norse)

Old Norse	Literal	English
Nú kómu Skrælingar í þann stað, er Karlsefni hafði ætlat til bardaga. Nú var þar bardagi, ok fell fjölði af liði Skrælinga.	Now came Skraelings to the place, where Karlsefni had intended to battle. Now was there battle, and fell many of people Skraelings.	Now the Skraelings came to the place where Karlsefni had intended to battle. Now was there a battle, and many of the Skraeling people fell.
Einn maðr var mikill ok vænn í liði Skrælinga, ok þótti Karlsefni, sem hann mundi vera höfðingi þeira.	One man was tall and handsome in group Skraelings, and thought Karlsefni, that he would be leader theirs.	One of them men in their group was tall and handsome, and Karlsefni thought that he was probably their leader.
Nú hafði einn þeira Skrælinga tekit upp öxi eina ok leit á um stund ok reiddi at félaga sínum ok hjó til hans.	Now had one of-them Skraelings taken up axe one and looked to about awhile and aimed at companion his and struck to him.	Now one of the Skraelings took up an axe and looked around awhile and aimed at one of his companions and struck him.
Sá fell þegar dauðr.	So fell then dead.	So he then fell dead.
Þá tók sá inn mikli maðr við öxinni ok leit á um stund ok varp henni síðan á sjóinn, sem lengst mátti hann.	Then took so the tall man to axe and looked to about awhile and threw he then to sea, as long as-may he.	Then the tall man took the axe and looked around for awhile, and then he thew it into the sea as far as he could.
En síðan flýja þeir á skóginn, svá hverr sem fara mátti, ok lýkr þar nú þeira viðskiptum.	But afterwards fled they to woods, so each as went may, and ended there now their dealings.	After that they fled into the woods as fast as they could, and they had no more dealings with them.
Váru þeir Karlsefni þar þann vetr allan.	Were they Karlsefni there that winter all.	Karlsefni and his companions were there all winter.
En at vári þá lýsir Karlsefni, at hann vill eigi þar vera lengr ok vill fara til Grænlands.	But at spring then declared Karlsefni, that he willed not there be longer and will travel to Greenland.	But in the spring, Karlsefni declared that he did not wish to be there any longer and wished to travel to Greenland.
Nú búa þeir ferð sína ok höfðu þaðan mörg gæði í vínviði ok berjum ok skinnvöru.	Now prepared they journey theirs and had there many quality in vines and berries and skin-wares.	Now they prepared for their journey and they had much good quality vines, berries, and skins.
Nú sigla þeir í haf ok kómu til Eiríksfjarðar skipi sínu heilu ok váru þar um vetrinn.	Now sailed they to sea and came to Eriksfjord ship theirs whole and were there about winter.	Now they sailed to sea and their ship came safely to Eriksfjord and they stayed there over the winter.
8	8	8
Nú tekst umræða at nýju um Vínlandsferð, því at sú ferð þykkir bæði góð til fjár ok virðingar.	Now took discussion that again about Vinland-voyage, since by that trip seemed both good to wealth and worthiness.	Now the discussion was taken to again about a Vinland voyage, since the trip seemed to bring both wealth and respect.

The Saga of the Greenlanders (Old Norse)

Old Norse	Literal	English
Þat sama sumar kom skip af Nóregi til Grænlands, er Karlsefni kom af Vínlandi.	That same summer came ship of Norway to Greenland, when Karlsefni came of Vinland.	That same summer a ship came from Norway when Karlsefni came back from Vinland.
Því skipi stýrðu bræðr tveir, Helgi ok Finnbogi, ok váru þann vetr á Grænlandi.	For ship steered brothers two, Helgi and Finnbogi, and were they wintered in Greenland.	The captains were two brothers, Helgi and Finnbogi, and they spent the winter in Greenland.
Þeir bræðr váru íslenzkir at kyni ok ór Austfjörðum.	Those brothers were Icelanders by kin and from Austfjord.	The brothers were Icelanders, from the East Fjords.
Þar er nú til at taka, at Freydís Eiríksdóttir gerði ferð sína heiman ór Görðum ok fór til fundar við þá bræðr, Helga ok Finnboga, ok beiddi þá, at þeir færi til Vínlands með farkost sinn ok hafa helming gæða allra við hana, þeira er þar fengist.	There is now to that take, that Freydis Eriksdottir made journey hers home from Gardar and went to meet with then brothers, Helgi and Finnbogi, and propose then, that they journey to Vinland with vessel theirs and have half quality everyone's with her, their which there caught.	Now we turn to Freydis Eriksdottir, who journeyed from here home at Gardar and then travelled to meet with the brothers, Helgi and Finnbogi, to invite them to travel to Vinland with their vessel and have a half share of any profits from it.
Nú játtu þeir því.	Now agreed they accordingly.	They agreed to this.
Þaðan fór hon á fund Leifs, bróður síns, ok bað, at hann gæfi henni hús þau, er hann hafði gera látit á Vínlandi.	There travelled she to meet Leif, brother hers, and asked, to him give her houses those, which he had made laid in Vinland.	There she travelled to meet Leif, her brother, to ask him to give her those houses which he had made in Vinland.
En hann svarar inu sama, kveðst ljá mundu hús, en gefa eigi.	But he answered the same, said loan would houses, but give not.	But he answered the same as before, he said that he would loan the houses, but not give them to her.
Sá var máldagi með þeim bræðrum ok Freydísi, at hvárir skyldu hafa þrjá tigu vígra manna á skipi ok konur um fram.	So were matters with they brothers and Freydis, that each should have three ten fighting men on ship and women about from.	So were matters between the brothers and Freydis, that each should have thirty fighting men on their ships and women in addition.
En Freydís brá af því þegar ok hafði fimm mönnum fleira ok leyndi þeim, ok urðu þeir bræðr eigi fyrri við þá varir en þeir kómu til Vínlands.	But Freydis drew off for already and had five men more and concealed them, and became they brothers not before to then foreseen but they came to Vinland.	But Freydis broke the agreement straight away and had five extra men, concealing them so that the brothers would not be aware of this until they came to Vinland.
Nú létu þau í haf ok höfðu til þess mælt áðr, at þau myndi samflota hafa, ef svá vildi verða, ok þess var lítill munr.	Now laid they to sea and had to this said before, that they should together have, if so will be, and this was little difference.	Now they put to sea and had said before that they should be together if they could, which they almost did.

The Saga of the Greenlanders (Old Norse)

Old Norse	Literal	English
En þó kómu þeir bræðr nökkuru fyrri ok höfðu upp borit föng sín til húsa Leifs.	But though came they brothers sometime before and had up carried possessions theirs to houses Leif's.	Though the brothers arrived sometime before and carried their possessions to Leif's houses.
En er Freydís kom at landi, þá ryðja þeir skip sitt ok bera upp til húss föng sín.	But when Freydis came to land, then cleared they ship theirs and carried up to houses possessions theirs.	Then when Freydis came to land, they cleared their ship and carried their possessions up to their houses.
Þá mælti Freydís: "Hví báruð þér inn hér föng yður?"	Then spoke Freydis: "Why carried you in here possessions yours?"	Then Freydis spoke: "Why have you carried your posessions in here?".
"Því, at vér hugðum", segja þeir, "at haldast mundi öll ákveðin orð með oss".	"Because that we thought", said they, "That hold would all agreed word with us".	"Because we thought", they said, "that you would keep your agreement with us".
Mér léði Leifr húsanna, segir hon, "en eigi yðr".	"To-me lent Leif houses", said she, "But not you".	"Leif lent the houses to me", she said, "not you".
Þá mælti Helgi: "Þrjóta mun okkr bræðr illsku við þik",	Then said Helgi: "Scarcely would-be we brothers ill-will with you",	Then Helgi said: "We brothers would scarcely be a match for your ill-will".
báru nú út föng ok gerðu sér skála ok settu þann skála firr sjónum á vatnsströndu ok bjuggu vel um.	Carried now out possessions and made they cabin and placed they cabin further-from the-sea towards a-lake and settled well about.	They removed their posessions and they made a longhouse further from the sea towards a lake, and settled in well.
En Freydís lét fella viðu til skips síns.	Then Freydis had wood felled for ship hers.	Then Freydis had wood cut to make a load for her ship.
Nú tók at vetra, ok töluðu þeir bræðr, at takast myndi upp leikar ok væri höfð skemmtan.	Now took in winter, and talked they brothers, that take should up games and would have amusement.	Now winter took, and the brothers talked of taking up games that would bring entertainment.
Svá var gert um stund, þar til er menn bárust verra í milli.	So was done about awhile, there until were men brought worse in between.	And so they did for a while, until disagreements arose between them.
Ok þá gerðist sundrþykki með þeim, ok tókust af leikar, ok engar gerðust kvámur milli skálanna, *ok fór svá fram lengi vetrar.*	And then made disagreement with them, and took of games, and none did come between cabins and went so from long winter.	And then was a rift between them, and the activities ceased, and none came or went between their cabins, and so it went all winter long.

The Saga of the Greenlanders (Old Norse)

Old Norse	Literal	English
Þat var einn morgin snemma, at Freydís stóð upp ór rúmi sínu ok klæddist ok fór eigi í skóklæðin, en veðri var svá farit, at dögg var fallin mikil.	It was one morning early, that Freydis stood up out-of room theirs and dressed and went not in shoes, but weather was such going, that dew was fallen much.	It was early one morning, that Freydis got up and dressed, but did not wear any shoes, but the weather had left much dew fallen on the ground.
Hon tók kápu bónda síns ok fór í, en síðan gekk hon til skála þeira bræðra ok til dura.	She took cape husband hers and went into, but then went she to cabin theirs brothers and to door.	She took her husband's cape and went out, and then she went to the door of the brothers' cabin.
En maðr einn hafði út gengit litlu áðr ok lokit hurð aftr á miðjan klofa.	But man one had out gone little before and left door back to middle gap.	One of the men had gone out shortly before and left the door half open.
Hon lauk upp hurðinni ok stóð í gáttum stund þá ok þagði.	She closed up door and stood in doorway awhile then and silent.	She closed the door and stood silently in the doorway awhile.
En Finnbogi lá innstr í skálanum ok vakði.	But Finnbogi lay inside in cabin and awoke.	Finnbogi lay inside the cabin and awoke.
Hann mælti: "Hvat villtu hingat, Freydís?"	He said: "What will-you here, Freydis?".	He said: "What do you want here Freydis?".
Hon svarar: "Ek vil, at þú standir upp ok gangir út með mér, ok vil ek tala við þik".	She answered: "I will, that you stand up and go out with me, and will I speak with you".	She answered: "I want you to get up and come outside, and I want to speak with you".
Svá gerir hann.	So did he.	So he did.
Þau ganga at tré, er lá undir skálavegginum, ok settust þar niðr.	They went to tree, that lay near cabins, and sat there down.	They went to a tree that lay near the cabins, and there sat down.
Hversu líkar þér? segir hon.	"How like you?" said she.	"How do you like it here?" she said.
Hann svarar: "Góðr þykkir mér landkostr, en illr þykkir mér þústr sá, er vár á milli er, því ek kalla ekki hafa til orðit".	He answered: "Good think me land-benefits, but ill think me discord so, that sprung to between as, for I call not have to word".	He answered: "I think the land here has much benefit, but I don't like the ill feeling that has arisen between us, as I have no words for it".
Þá segir þú sem er, segir hon,	"Then say you as is", said she,	"What you say is true", she said,
"ok svá þykkir mér. En þat er erendi mitt á þinn fund, at ek vilda kaupa skipum við ykkr bræðr, því at þit hafið meira skip en ek, ok vilda ek í brott heðan".	"And so think I. But that which business mine to you find, that I will purchase ship with you brothers, because that you have more ship than I, and will I to away hence".	"And I agree. But my purpose in meeting with you, is that I wish to buy yours and your brother's ship, because you have more ship than I, and I wish to leave soon".

The Saga of the Greenlanders (Old Norse)

Old Norse	Literal	English
Þat mun ek láta gangast, segir hann, "ef þér líkar þá vel".	"That should I let go", said he, "If you like then well".	"That I could agree to", he said, "If that pleases you".
Nú skilja þau við þat, gengr hon heim, en Finnbogi til hvílu sinnar.	Now separated they with that, went she home, and Finnbogi to bed his.	Now with that they separated, and she went home, and Finnbogi to his bed.
Hon stígr upp í rúmit köldum fótum, ok vaknar hann Þorvarðr við ok spyrr, hví at hon væri svá köld ok vát.	She climbed up into room cold feet, and awoke he Thorvald to and asked, why that she was so cold and wet.	She climbed up into the room with cold feet, and Thorvard woke and asked why she was so cold and wet.
Hon svarar með miklum þjósti: "Ek var gengin", segir hon, "til þeira bræðra at fala skip af þeim, ok vilda ek kaupa meira skip. *En þeir urðu við þat svá illa, at þeir börðu mik ok léku sárliga, en þú, vesall maðr, munt hvárki vilja reka minnar skammar né þinnar, ok mun ek þat nú finna, at ek em í brottu af Grænlandi, ok mun ek gera skilnað við þik, útan þú hefnir þessa".*	She answered with much vehemence: "I was gone", said she, "To the brothers to bargain ship of them, and wished I purchase bigger ship. But they became with that so bad, that they beat me and played woundingly, but you, miserable man, would neither will expel my shame nor yours, and should I that now find, that I am in gone from Greenland, and should I make separate with you, outside-of you avenge this".	She answered vehemently: "I was gone", she said, "to the brothers to purchase their ship from them, and wished I to buy a bigger ship. With that they became so angry, that they beat me, and struck me woundingly, but you, miserable man, will neither expel my shame or yours, and if that's the case, then I will leave Greenland, and divorce you, unless you avenge this".
Ok nú stóðst hann eigi átölur hennar ok bað menn upp standa sem skjótast ok taka vápn sín,	And now stood he not reproaches hers and ordered men up stand while quickly and take weapons theirs,	And now, unable to withstand her reproaches, he ordered that the men get up quickly and get their weapons,
Ok svá gera þeir ok fara þegar til skála þeira bræðra ok gengu inn at þeim soföndum ok tóku þá ok færðu í bönd ok leiddu svá út hvern, sem bundinn var.	And so did they and went straightaway to cabin they brothers and went in by them sleeping and took then and went in binding and lead so out each, who bound was.	And so they did, travelling straightaway to the brothers' cabin, and went in while they were sleeping, took them, bound them, and led them outside as they were bound.
En Freydís lét drepa hvern, sem út kom.	Then Freydis had killled each, who out came.	Then Freydis had each one killed as they came out.
Nú váru þar allir karlar drepnir, en konur váru eftir, ok vildi engi þær drepa.	Now were there all men killed, but women were left, and willed none they kill.	Now all the men were killed, there remained the women, but no one wanted to kill them.
Þá mælti Freydís: "Fái mér öxi í hönd".	Then said Freydis: "Give me axe into hand".	Then Freydis said: "Give me the axe in my hand".
Svá var gert.	So was done.	So was it done.

The Saga of the Greenlanders (Old Norse)

Old Norse	Literal	English
Síðan vegr hon at konum þeim fimm, er þar váru, ok gekk af þeim dauðum.	Then slayed she that women they five, who there were, and went of them dead.	Then she slayed the five women who were there, and all of them were dead.
Nú fóru þau til skála síns eftir þat it illa verk, ok fannst þat eitt á, at Freydís þóttist allvel hafa um ráðit, ok mælti við félaga sína: "Ef oss verðr auðit at koma til Grænlands", segir hon, "þá skal ek þann mann ráða af lífi, er segir frá þessum atburðum.	Now went they to cabin theirs after that the evil work, and found that one all, that Freydis thought all-well have about resolved, and said to companions hers: "If we worth fated to come to Greenland", said she, "Then shall I then men rule of life, who says from these events.	Now they went back to their cabin after that evil work, and they all found that Freydis thought all was well done, and she spoke to her companions: "If we are fated to return to Greenland", she said, "Then I shall have killed any man who says anything about these events.
Nú skulum vér þat segja, at þau búi hér eftir, þá er vér fórum í brott".	Now should we this say, that they remained here behind, when were we travelling to away".	Now shall we say of this that they remained here, when we travelled away".
Nú bjuggu þeir skipit snemma um várit, þat er þeir bræðr höfðu átt, með þeim öllum gæðum, er þau máttu til fá ok skipit bar, sigla síðan í haf ok urðu vel reiðfara ok kómu í Eiríksfjörð skipi sínu snemma sumars.	Now readied they ship early about spring, that was the brothers had had, with them all quality, that they may to get and ship carry, sailed after to sea and became well voyage and came to Eriksfjord ship theirs early summer.	Early in the spring they prepared the ship which the brothers had owned, with all the goods that the ship could carry, then afterwards sailed to sea and they had a good voyage and their ship came into Eriksfjord early in the summer.
Nú var þar Karlsefni fyrir ok hafði albúit skip sitt til hafs ok beið byrjar, ok er þat mál manna, at eigi mundi auðgara skip gengit hafa af Grænlandi en þat, er hann stýrði.	Now was there Karlsefni already and had prepared ship his to sea and waited begin, and is that said men, that not would richer ship go sea off Greenland but that, which he steered.	Karlsefni was there already, and had his ship all prepared for sea, waiting for a favourable wind, and it was said that none would go to sea with a richer ship from Greenland than that which he captained.

9

Old Norse	Literal	English
Freydís fór nú til bús síns, því at þat hafði staðit meðan óskatt.	Freydis travelled now to dwelling hers, for as that had stood meantime uninjured.	Freydis travelled now to her farm, which withstood her absence without injury.
Hon fekk mikinn feng fjár öllu föruneyti sínu, því at hon vildi leyna láta ódáðum sínum.	She gave great gifts wealth all companions hers, for that she would conceal let dishonour hers.	She gave great gifts of wealth to all her companions, so that she could conceal her dishonour.
Sitr hon nú í búi sínu.	Sat she now in house hers.	She remained at her farm.

The Saga of the Greenlanders (Old Norse)

Old Norse	Literal	English
Eigi urðu allir svá haldinorðir, at þegði yfir ódáðum þeira eða illsku, at eigi kæmi upp um síðir.	Not became all so held-words, by silence over dishonour theirs or evil, that not came up about eventually.	Not all words were held in silence over their dishonour or evil, that didn't come up eventually.
Nú kom þetta upp um síðir fyrir Leif, bróður hennar, ok þótti honum þessi saga allill.	Now came this up about eventually before Leif, brother hers, and thought he this story evil.	Now this came up before Leif, her brother, and he thought this story was most evil.
Þá tók Leifr þrjá menn af liði þeira Freydísar ok píndi þá til sagna um þenna atburð allan jafnsaman, ok var með einu móti sögn þeira.	Then took Leif three men of band theirs Freydis and tortured then to say about these events all equally, and was with one towards story theirs.	Then Leif took three men from Freydis's company and tortured them to talk about those events, they were all equal and as one in their telling.
Eigi nenni ek, segir Leifr, "at gera þat við Freydísi, systur mína, sem hon væri verð, en spá mun ek þeim þess, at þeira afkvæmi muni lítt at þrifum verða".	"Not bother I", said Leif, "To do that to Freydis, sister mine, which she would deserve, but prophecy should I that these, by their offspring should little by thriving be".	"I am not the one", said Leif, "to do to Freydis, my sister, that which she deserves, but I should prophecise this, that their offspring shall little thriving become".
Nú leið þat svá fram, at engum þótti um þau vert þaðan í frá nema ills.	Now laid that so from, that none thought about them worthy there in from taking ill.	Now as it happened, none thought anything of them except evil.
Nú er at segja frá því, er Karlsefni býr skip sitt ok sigldi í haf. *Honum fórst vel ok kom til Nóregs með heilu ok höldnu ok sat þar um vetrinn ok seldi varning sinn ok hafði þar gott yfirlæti ok þau bæði hjón af inum göfgustum mönnum í Nóregi,* *en um várit eftir bjó hann skip sitt til Íslands.*	Now is to say from therefore, when Karlsefni prepared ship his and sailed to sea. He travelled well and came to Norway with whole and safe and sat there about winter and sold wares his and had there benefit respectable and they both couple of the respectable people in Norway, but about spring after prepared he ship his to Iceland.	Now to turn to Karlsefni, he prepared his ship and sailed to sea. He travelled well and came to Norway safe an well, and remained there over the winter and sold his goods, and both him and his wife were treated well by the noble people in Norway, and after about spring, he prepared his ship for Iceland.
Ok er hann var albúinn ok skip hans lá til byrjar fyrir bryggjunum, þá kom þar at honum Suðrmaðr einn, ættaðr af Brimum ór Saxlandi. *Hann falar at Karlsefni húsasnotru hans.*	And when he was ready and ship his lay to fair-wind for bridge, then came there to him southern-man one, descended from Bremen of Saxony. He bargained-for that Karlsefni carved decoration his.	And when he was ready and his ship waited for a fair wind on the gangways, then came a southern man, descended from Bremen of Saxony. He asked Karlsefni to sell him the carved decoration on the prow.
Ek vil eigi selja", sagði hann.	"I will not sell", said he.	"I don't care to sell it", he said.

The Saga of the Greenlanders (Old Norse)

Old Norse	Literal	English
Ek mun gefa þér við hálfa mörk gulls, segir Suðrmaðr.	"I would give you to half mark gold", said southern-man.	"I'll give you half a mark of gold for it", said the southern man.
Karlsefni þótti vel við boðit, ok keyptu síðan.	Karlsefni thought well with offer, and sold afterwards.	Karlsefni thought this was a good offer, and then sold it.
Fór Suðrmaðr í burt með húsasnotruna, en Karlsefni vissi eigi, hvat tré var.	Went southern-man to away with carved-decoration, but Karlsefni knew not, what wood was.	The southern man went away with his carved decoration, but Karlsefni did not know what wood it was made of.
En þat var mösurr, kominn af Vínlandi.	But that was burl-wood, coming from Vinland.	But it was made of burl wood, which came from Vinland.
Nú siglir Karlsefni í haf ok kom skipi sínu fyrir norðan land í Skagafjörð, ok var þar upp sett skip hans um vetrinn.	Now sailed Karlsefni to sea and came ship his for north land to Skagafjord, and was there up set ship his about winter.	Now Karlsefni sailed to sea and his ship came to the north of the land to Skagafjord, and he set up his ship there for the winter.
En um várit keypti hann Glaumbæjarland ok gerði bú á ok bjó þar, meðan hann lifði, ok var it mesta göfugmenni, ok er margt manna frá honum komit ok Guðríði, konu hans, ok góðr ættbogi.	Then about spring bought he Glaumbær and made dwelling on and lived there, long-as he lived, and was the most greatest, and which many people from him came and Guthrid, wife his, and good descendents.	Then in the spring he purchased land at Glaumbaer and made a farm there, as long as he lived, and was the the most respected, and many pepople are came from him and his wife Gudrid, with good descendents.
Ok er Karlsefni var andaðr, tók Guðríðr við búsvarðveizlu ok Snorri, sonr hennar, er fæddr var á Vínlandi.	And when Karlsefni was dead, took Guthrid to farming and Snorri, son hers, who born was in Vinland.	And when Karlsefni died, Gudrid took over the farm with her son Snorri, who had been born in Vinland.
Ok er Snorri var kvángaðr, þá fór Guðríðr útan ok gekk suðr ok kom út aftr til bús Snorra, sonar síns, ok hafði hann þá látit gera kirkju í Glaunbæ.	And when Snorri was married, then went Guthrid out and went south and came out returning to house Snorri, son hers, and had he then caused made church in Glaumbær.	And when Snorri was married, Gudrid travelled abroad, and went south, returning to her son Snorri's farm, and he had built a church in Glaumbaer.
Síðan varð Guðríðr nunna ok einsetukona ok var þar, meðan hon lifði.	Afterwards was Guthrid a-nun and recluse and was there, long-as she lived.	Later Gudrid became a nun and an anchoress and remained there as long as she lived.
Snorri átti son þann, er Þorgeirr hét.	Snorri had son that, was Thorgeir named.	Snorri has a son who was named Thorgeir.
Hann var faðir Yngvildar, móður Brands biskups.	He was father-of Yngvild, mother Brand Bishop's	He was the father of Yngvild, who was mother to Bishop Brand.

The Saga of the Greenlanders (Old Norse)

Old Norse	Literal	English
Dóttir Snorra Karlsefnissonar hét Hallfríðr.	Daughter Snorri Karlsefnison's was-called Hallfrid.	Snorri Karlsefnison's daughter was called Hallfrid.
Hon var kona Runólfs, föður Þorláks biskups.	She was wife Runolf's, father Thorlak Bishop's	She was the wife of Runolf, father of Bishop Thorlak.
Björn hét sonr Karlsefnis ok Guðríðar.	Bjorn was-called son-of Karlsefni's and Guthrid's.	Karlsefni and Gudrid had a son called Bjorn.
Hann var faðir Þórunnar, móður Bjarnar biskups.	He was father-of Thorun, mother Bjarn Bishop's	He was the father of Thorun, mother to Bishop Bjorn.
Fjölði manna er frá Karlsefni kominn, ok er hann kynsæll maðr orðinn.	Many people were from Karlsefni come, and was he kin-blessed man become.	Many people are descended from Karlesfni, and his was a prosperous clan.
Ok hefir Karlsefni gerst sagt allra manna atburði um farar þessar allar, er nú er nökkut orði á komit.	And has Karlsefni made said every people's events about voyages these all, which now is somewhat recited to came.	It was Karlsefni who told of people's events about these voyages, some of which came to words.

The Saga of the Greenlanders (*Old Icelandic*)

Old Icelandic	Literal	English
1	1	1
Þorvaldur hét maður, sonur Ásvalds Úlfssonar, Öxna-Þórissonar.	Thorvald was-named a-man, son-of Asvald's Son-of-Ulfson, Son-of-Oxna-Thorri.	There was a man named Thorvald, son of Asvald, son of Ulf, son of Oxna-Thorri.
Þorvaldur og Eiríkur hinn rauði, sonur hans, fóru af Jaðri til Íslands fyrir víga sakir.	Thorvald and Erik the Red, son his, travelled from Jaeren to Iceland because-of-a killing conviction.	Thorvald and Erik the Red, his son, travelled from Jaeran to Iceland because of a conviction for a killing.
Þá var víða byggt Ísland.	Then was widely settled Iceland.	Then Iceland was widely settled.
Þeir bjuggu fyrst að Dröngum á Hornströndum.	They lived first at Drangar on Hornstrandir.	They lived first at Drangar in Hornstrandir.
Þar andaðist Þorvaldur.	There died Thorvald.	There Thorvald died.
Eiríkur fekk þá Þjóðhildar, dóttur Jörundar Úlfssonar og Þorbjargar knarrarbringu, er þá átti Þorbjörn hinn haukdælski.	Erik married then Thjodhild, daughter-of Jorund Son-of-Ulf and Thorbjorg Knarrarbringu, who then married Thorbjorn of Haukadal.	Erik then married Thjodhild, daughter of Jorund, son of Ulf, and Thorbjorg Knarrabringu, who then married Thorbjorn of Haukadal.
Réðst Eiríkur þá norðan og bjó á Eiríksstöðum hjá Vatnshorni.	Went Erik then northwards and lived at Eriksstadir near Vatnshorn.	Erik then went northwards and lived at Eriksstadir near Vantshorn.
Sonur Eiríks og Þjóðhildar hét Leifur.	Son-of Erik's and Thjodhild's was-named Leif.	Erik and Thjodhild's son was named Leif.
Enn eftir víg Eyjólfs saurs og Hólmgöngu-Hrafns var Eiríkur gerður brott úr Haukadal.	But after killing-of Eyolf's the-Foul and Raven-the-dueller was Erik made away from Haukadal.	But after the killing of Eyolf the Foul and Raven the Dueller, Erik was made to leave Haukadal.
Fór hann vestur til Breiðafjarðar og bjó í Öxney á Eiríksstöðum.	Travelled he west to Breidafjord and lived at Oxney on Eriksstadir.	He then travelled west to Breidafjord and lived at Oxney in Eriksstadir.
Hann léði Þorgesti á Breiðabólstað setstokka og náði eigi, er hann kallaði til.	He lent Thorgest to Upholstery seat-posts and got not, when he called to.	He lent Thorgest some upholstery seat posts, and when he asked for them back, he did not get them.
Þaðan af gerðust deilur og bardagar með þeim Þorgesti, sem segir í sögu Eiríks.	From-there from made disputes and battle between them Thorgest, as said in saga Erik's.	From then on there were disputes and battles between him and Thorgest, as told in Erik's Saga.
Styrr Þorgrímsson veitti Eiríki að málum og Eyjólfur úr Svíney, og synir Þorbrands úr Álftafirði og Þorbjörn Vífilsson.	Styrr Thorgrimson supported Erik in the-matter and Eyjolf of Sviney, and sons Thorbrand's of Alftafjord and Thorbjorn Vifilson.	Styrr Thorgrimson supported Erik in the matter, and Eyolf of Sviney, and Thorbrand's sons of Alftafjord, and Thorbjorn Vifilson.

The Saga of the Greenlanders (Old Icelandic)

Old Icelandic	Literal	English
En Þorgestlingum veittu synir Þórðar Gellis ok Þorgeir úr Hítardal.	But Thorgest's-sons supported sons Thord Howler and Thorgeir of Hitardal.	But Thorgest's sons were supported by Thord Howler, and Thorgeir of Hitardal.
Eiríkur varð sekur á Þórsnessþingi.	Erik was outlawed at-the Thorsness-assembly.	Erik was outlawed at the Thorsness assembly.
Bjó Eiríkur þá skip sitt til hafs í Eiríksvogi.	Prepared Erik then ship his to sea at Eriksvog.	He then prepared his ship to go to sea at Eriksvog.
En er hann var búinn, fylgdu þeir Styrr honum út um eyjar.	And when he was ready, followed they Styrr him out about the-island.	And when he was ready, Styrr followed them about the island.
Eiríkur sagði þeim, að hann ætlaði at leita lands þess, er Gunnbjörn, sonur Úlfs kráku, sá, er hann rak vestur um haf, þá er hann fann Gunnbjarnarsker.	Erik told them, that he intended to search land this, which Gunnbjorn, son-of Ulf Crow, saw, when he driven west at sea, when was he found Gunnbjarnarsker.	Erik told them that he intended to search for a land, which Gunnbjorn, son of Ulf Crow, saw when he was driven west at sea, when he found Gunnbjorn's Skerries.
Kveðst hann aftur mundu leita til vina sinna, ef hann fyndi landið.	Said he return would seek to friends his, if he found land.	He said he would return to seek his friends if he found land.
Eiríkur sigldi undan Snæfellsjökli.	Erik sailed from Snaefellsjokli.	Erik sailed from Snaefellsjokli.
Hann fann landið, og kom utan að því, þar sem hann kallaði Miðjökul.	He found land, and came out of for, there which he called Midjokul.	He found land, and came out therefore, there he called Modjokul.
Sá heitir nú Bláserkur.	This is-named now Blaserkur.	This is now named Blaserkur.
Hann fór þá þaðan suður með landinu at leita, ef þaðan væri byggjandi landið.	He travelled then from-there south along land to seek, if there was habitable land.	He travelled south from there along land to see if there was habitable land.
Hann var hinn fyrsta vetur í Eiríksey, nær miðri hinni eystri byggð.	He was the first winter in Eriksey, near-the middle of-the Eastern Settlement.	The first winter he was at Eriksey, near the middle of the Eastern Settlement.
Um vorið eftir fór hann til Eiríksfjarðar og tók sér þar bústað.	About spring after travelled he to Eriksfjord and took he there abode.	After about spring he travelled to Eriksfjord and took he there a dwelling.
Hann fór það sumar í hina vestri óbyggð og gaf víða örnefni.	He travelled that summer to the western settlement and gave many place-names.	He travelled that summer to the Western Settlement and gave many places names.
Hann var annan vetur í Hólmum við Hvarfsgnípu, en hið þriðja sumar fór allt norður til Snæfells og inn í Hrafnsfjörð.	He was second winter at Holm in Hvarfsgnipu, but the third summer travelled all North to Snaefell and then to Hrafnsfjord.	The second winter he was at Holm in Hvarfsgnipu, but the third summer travelled all the way north to Snaefell and then to Hrafnsfjord.
Þá kvaðst hann kominn fyrir botn Eiríksfjarðar.	Then said he coming for-the bottom-of Eriksfjord.	Then he said he came to the bottom of Eriksfjord.

The Saga of the Greenlanders (Old Icelandic)

Old Icelandic	Literal	English
Hvarf hann þá aftur og var hinn þriðja vetur í Eiríksey fyrir mynni Eiríksfjarðar.	Disappeared he then after and was the third winter in Eriksey before the-inlet Eriksfjord.	After that he then disappeared and was for the third winter in Eriksey before the inlet Eriksfjord.
Eftir um sumarið fór hann til Íslands og kom skipi sínu í Breiðafjörð.	After about summer travelled he to Iceland and came ship his to Breidafjord.	After about summer he travelled to Iceland and his ship came to Breidajord.
Hann kallaði land það, er hann hafði fundið, Grænland, því að hann kvað það mundu fýsa menn þangað, ef landið héti vel.	He called land that, which he had found, Greenland, because as he said it would attract men there, if the-land was-named well.	He called the land which he had found Greenland, because as he said, it would attract people there if it was named well.
Eiríkur var á Íslandi um veturinn, en um sumarið eftir fór hann að byggja landið.	Erik was in Iceland about winter, but about summer after travelled he to settle land.	Erik was in Iceland over winter, but after around summer he travelled to settle the land.
Hann bjó í Brattahlíð í Eiríksfirði.	He dwelt at Brattahlid in Eriksfjord.	He lived at Brattahlid in Eriksfjord.
Svo segja fróðir menn, að á því sama sumri, er Eiríkur rauði fór að byggja Grænland, þá fór hálfur þriði tugur skipa úr Breiðafirði og Borgarfirði, en fjórtán komust út þangað.	So say wise men, that at since same summer, that Erik the-Red travelled to settle Greenland, then travelled half-of thirty twenty ships from Breidafjord and Borgafjord, but fourteen arrived out there.	So wise men say that after that same summer, Erik the Red travelled to settle Greenland, then half of thirty and twenty ships travelled from Breidafjord and Borgafjord, but fourteen arrived there.
Sum rak aftur, en sum týndust.	Some driven back, but some lost.	Some were driven back, but some were lost.
Það var fimmtán vetrum fyrr en kristni var lögtekin á Íslandi.	This was fifteen winters before that christianity was law-taken on Iceland.	This was fifteen winters before Christianity became law in Iceland.
Á því sama sumri fór utan Friðrekur biskup og Þorvaldur Koðránsson.	Then since same summer travelled out Fridrek bishop and Thorvald Kodranson.	After that same summer travelled out Bishop Fridrek and Thorvald Kodranson.
Þessir menn námu land á Grænlandi, er þá fóru út með Eiríki: Herjólfur Herjólfsfjörð, - hann bjó á Herjólfsnesi, - Ketill Ketilsfjörð, Hrafn Hrafnsfjörð, Sölvi Sölvadal, Helgi Þorbrandsson Álftafjörð, Hafgrímur Hafgrímsfjörð og Vatnahverfi, Arnlaugur Arnlaugsfjörð.	These men took land in Greenland, when then travelled out with Erik: Herjolf Herjolfsfjord, - he lived on Herjólfsnes, - Ketil Ketilsfjord, Hrafn Hrafnsfjord, Sölvi Solvadal, Helgi Thorbrandson Alftafjord, Hafgrim Hafgrimsfjord and Vatnahverfi, Arnlaug Arnlaugsfjord.	These men took land in Greenland, when they travelled out with Erik: Herjolf took Herjolfsfjord, he lived on Herjolfsnes, Ketil took Ketilsfjord, Hrafn took Hrafnsfjord, Solvi took Solvadal, Helgi Thorbrandson took Alftafjord, Hafgrim took Hafgrimsfjord and Vatnahverfi, and Arnlaug took Arnlaugsfjord.
En sumir fóru til Vestribyggðar.	But some travelled to Western-settlement.	But some travelled to the Western Settlement.

2 2 2

The Saga of the Greenlanders (Old Icelandic)

Old Icelandic	Literal	English
Herjúlfur var Bárðarson Herjúlfssonar.	Herjolf was Bard's-son Son-of-Herjolf.	Herjolf was Bard's son, the son of Herjolf.
Hann var frændi Ingólfs landnámamanns.	He was kinsman Ingolf's land-taking-man.	He was kinsman to Ingolf the land taking man.
Þeim Herjúlfi gaf Ingólfur land á milli Vogs og Reykjaness.	To-them Herjolf gave Ingolf land on between Vogs and Reykjanes.	Ingolf gave to them land between Vogs and Reykjanes.
Herjúlfur bjó fyrst á Drepstokki.	Herjolf lived first on Drepstokk.	Herjolf lived first at Drepstokk.
Þorgerður hét kona hans en Bjarni son þeirra og var hinn efnilegsti maður.	Thorgerd was-named wife his but Bjarni son theirs and was a promising man.	His wife was named Thorgerd and their son Bjarni was a promising man.
Hann fýstist utan þegar á unga aldri.	He desired out-travel already at young age.	He desired to travel out at a young age.
Varð honum gott bæði til fjár og mannvirðingar og var sinn vetur hvort, utan lands eða með föður sínum.	Was he good both to wealth and man-worthiness and was he winter either, out-of lands or with father his.	He was good in both wealth and worthiness, and in winter he was either travelling or with his father.
Brátt átti Bjarni skip í förum.	Soon had Bjarni ship to travel.	Soon Bjarni had a ship to travel.
Og hinn síðasta vetur er hann var í Noregi þá brá Herjúlfur til Grænlandsferðar með Eiríki og brá búi sínu.	And the last winter that he was in Norway then prepared Herjolf to Greenland-voyage with Erik and prepared farm his.	And the last winter that he was in Norway, then Herjolf prepared for the voyage to Greenland with Erik and prepared his farm.
Með Herjúlfi var á skipi suðureyskur maður, kristinn, sá er orti Hafgerðingadrápu.	With Herjolf was in ship south-islander man, christian, that who wrote Sea-poem.	With Herjolf in his ship was a man from the southern islands, a Christian who wrote a sea poem.
Þar er þetta stef í:	There which this stave is:	There is this stave:
Mínar bið eg að munka reyni meinalausan farar beina, heiðis haldi hárrar foldar hallar drottinn yfir mér stalli.	My bid I that monks tester harmlessly travel assist, heath hold high folds hall master over my altar.	I ask you, monks' tester to assist my travel harmless, holding the heath's high folds hall master over my altar.
Herjúlfur bjó á Herjúlfsnesi.	Herjolf lived on Herjolfsness.	Herjolf lived at Herjolfsness.
Hann var hinn göfgasti maður.	He was a respectable man.	He was a respectable man.
Eiríkur rauði bjó í Brattahlíð.	Erik the-Red settled at Brattahlid.	Erik the Red settled at Brattahlid.
Hann var þar með mestri virðingu og lutu allir til hans.	He was there with most worthiness and lent all to his.	He was there given the most respect by all.
Þessi voru börn Eiríks: Leifur, Þorvaldur og Þorsteinn en Freydís hét dóttir hans.	These were children Erik's: Leif, Thorvald also, and Thorstein but Freydis was-named daughter his.	Erik's children were: Leif, Thorvald, and Thorstein, and his daughter was named Freydis.

The Saga of the Greenlanders (Old Icelandic)

Old Icelandic	Literal	English
Hún var gift þeim manni er er Þorvarður hét og bjuggu þau í Görðum þar sem nú er biskupsstóll.	She was married they a-man who was Thorvard was-named and lived they at Gardar there as now who bishop's-seat.	She was married to a man named Thorvard, and they lived at Gardar, where the bishop's seat now is.
Hún var svarri mikill en Þorvarður var lítilmenni.	She was haughty very but Thorvard was little-man.	She was haughty, but Thorvard was not much of a man.
Var hún mjög gefin til fjár.	Was she much married to wealth.	She married him very much for this wealth.
Heiðið var fólk á Grænlandi í þann tíma.	Heathen were folk in Greenland at this time.	Heathen were the people in Greenland at this time.
Það sama sumar kom Bjarni skipi sínu á Eyrar er faðir hans hafði brott siglt um vorið.	That same summer came Bjarni ship his to Eyrar where father his had away sailed about spring.	That same summer came Bjarni's ship to Eyrar, where his father had sailed from in the spring.
Þau tíðindi þóttu Bjarna mikil og vildi eigi bera af skipi sínu.	These tidings thought Bjarni great and willed not unload from ship his.	This news greatly affected Bjarni and he did not want to unload his ship.
Þá spurðu hásetar hans hvað er hann bærist fyrir en hann svaraði að hann ætlaði að að halda siðvenju sinni og þiggja að föður sínum veturvist "og vil eg halda skipinu til Grænlands ef þér viljið mér fylgd veita".	Then asked crew he what was he bearing for but he answered that he intended that to hold custom his and receive by father his winter "and will I hold ship to Greenland if you will me follow lead".	His crew asked him what he wanted to do but he answered that he wanted to keep his custom of spending the winter with his father "and I want sail to Greenland if you will follow me".
Allir kváðust hans ráðum fylgja vilja.	All said his counsel follow would.	All of them said the would follow his counsel.
Þá mælti Bjarni: "Óviturleg mun þykja vor ferð þar sem engi vor hefir komið í Grænlandshaf".	Then said Bjarni: "Unwisely will seem our voyage there since none been have come to Greenland-sea".	Then Bjarni said: "Our voyage will look unwise, since none of us have sailed the Greenland sea".
En þó halda þeir nú í haf þegar þeir voru búnir og sigldu þrjá daga þar til er landið var vatnað en þá tók af byrina og lagði á norrænur og þokur og vissu þeir eigi hvert að þeir fóru og skipti það mörgum dægrum.	But though held they now to sea when they were ready and sailed three days there until was land was water-taken but then took of fair-wind and lay on north-wind and fog and knew they not where that they travelled and time that many days.	But they set sail once they were ready and sailed for three days, until the land disappeared below the horizon, but then the fair wind dropped, and they were met with winds from the north and fog, and they did not know where they were travelling for many days.

The Saga of the Greenlanders (Old Icelandic)

Old Icelandic	Literal	English
Eftir það sáu þeir sól og máttu þá deila áttir, vinda nú segl og sigla þetta dægur áður þeir sáu land og ræddu um með sér hvað landi þetta mun vera en Bjarni kveðst hyggja að það mundi eigi Grænland.	After that saw they the-sun and could then share direction, wind now sails and sailed this day before they saw land and discussed among with them what land that could be but Bjarni said thought it that could not-be Greenland.	After that they saw the sun and took their bearings, they hoisted their sails and sailed for the rest of the day before they saw land, and they discussed among themselves what land it could be, but Bjarni said that it could not be Greenland.
Þeir spyrja hvort hann vill sigla að þessu landi eða eigi.	They asked whether he wished sail to this land or not.	They asked whether he wished to sail close to the land or not.
"Það er mitt ráð að sigla í nánd við landið".	"It is my advice to sail to close with land".	"I advise that we sail close to the land".
Og svo gera þeir og sáu það brátt að landið var ófjöllótt og skógi vaxið og smár hæðir á landinu og létu landið á bakborða og létu skaut horfa á land.	And so did they and saw that soon that land was without-mountains and forests grown and small heights on land and left land on port-side and let stern turn on land.	And so they did, and saw that the land was not mountainous, but did have small hills and was covered with forests, so keeping land on their port side, they turned their sail-end landwards and angled away from the shore.
Síðan sigla þeir tvö dægur áður þeir sáu land annað.	Afterwards sailed they two days before they saw land another.	Then they sailed for two days before they saw any more land.
Þeir spyrja hvort Bjarni ætlaði það enn Grænland.	They asked if Bjarni supposed this was Greenland.	They asked Bjarni if he thought this land was Greenland.
Hann kvaðst eigi heldur ætla þetta Grænland en hið fyrra "því að jöklar eru mjög miklir sagðir á Grænlandi"	He said not rather supposed this Greenland as the first "because the glaciers are very large said in Greenland"	He said that he did not think this was Greenland as the first "because there are said to be very large glaciers in Greenland".
Þeir nálguðust brátt þetta land og sáu það vera slétt land og viði vaxið. *Þá tók af byr fyrir þeim.*	They approached soon this land and saw it was flat land and woods growing. Then took of fair-wind before them.	They soon approached this land and saw that it was flat and wooded. Then the wind died.
Þá ræddu hásetar það að þeim þótti það ráð að taka það land en Bjarni vill það eigi. *Þeir þóttust bæði þurfa við og vatn.*	Then advised crew that to them thought that advised to take that land but Bjarni willed that not. They thought both needed wood and water.	Then the crew advised that they put ashore, but Bjarni did not want to. They said that they needed wood and water.

The Saga of the Greenlanders (Old Icelandic)

Old Icelandic	Literal	English
"Að öngu eruð þér því óbirgir" segir Bjarni en þó fékk hann af því nokkuð ámæli af hásetum sínum.	"In nothing are you for without-supplies" said Bjarni but though got he of for some reproach from crew his.	"There are no supplies you are lacking" said Bjarni, but he was criticised by his crew for this.
Hann bað þá vinda segl og svo var gert og settu framstafn frá landi og sigla í haf útsynningsbyr þrjú dægur og sáu þá landið þriðja.	He bid them wind sails and so was done and set prow from land and sailing to sea south-west-wind three days and saw then land third.	He told them to hoist the sail and they did so, setting the bow away from land and sailing seawards, for three days they sailed with wind from the south west and then saw a third land.
En það land var hátt og fjöllótt og jökull á.	And this land was high and mountainous and glaciers on.	And this land was high and mountainous and was capped by glaciers.
Þeir spyrja þá ef Bjarni vildi að landi láta þar en hann kvaðst eigi það vilja "því að mér líst þetta land ógagnvænlegt".	They asked then if Bjarni willed to land put there but he said not that willed "for to me appears this land uninviting".	They asked if Bjarni wished to make land here, but he said that he did not "for this land appears uninviting".
Nú lögðu þeir eigi segl sitt, halda með landinu fram og sáu að það var eyland, settu enn stafn við því landi og héldu í haf hinn sama byr.	Now lay they not sails these, held along land from and saw it that was island, turned yet stern with for land and held to sea the same fair-wind.	Now they did not lower the sail, but followed along the shore until they saw that it was an island, they turned the stern landwards and sailed out to sea with the same breeze.
En veður óx í hönd og bað Bjarni þá svipta og eigi sigla meira en bæði dygði vel skipi þeirra og reiða, sigldu nú fjögur dægur.	But weather grew at hand and bid Bjarni then shorten and not sail greater than both enough well ships theirs and decided, sailed now four days.	But the wind grew and Bjarni told them to lower the sail and not sail faster than the ship could manage, they sailed for four days.
Þá sáu þeir land hið fjórða. Þá spurðu þeir Bjarna hvort hann ætlaði þetta vera Grænland eða eigi.	Then saw they land the fourth. Then asked they Bjarni whether he supposed this was Greenland or not.	Then they saw a fourth land. They asked Bjarni if he thought this was Greenland or not.
Bjarni svarar: "Þetta er líkast því er mér er sagt frá Grænlandi og hér munum vér að landi halda".	Bjarni answered: "This is like therefore which to-me was said from Greenland and here should we by land hold".	Bjarni answered: "This land appears to me as was was described about Greenland, and we'll head for the shore here".

3

3

3

| *Það er nú þessu næst að Bjarni Herjúlfsson kom utan af Grænlandi á fund Eiríks jarls og tók jarl við honum vel.* | It is now this next that Bjarni Son-of-Herjolf came out of Greenland to meet Erik earl and took earl with him well. | It now happened that Bjarni Herjolfson came to Greenland to meet earl Erik, and the earl received him well. |

The Saga of the Greenlanders (Old Icelandic)

Old Icelandic	Literal	English
Sagði Bjarni frá ferðum sínum er hann hafði lönd séð og þótti mönnum hann verið hafa óforvitinn er hann hafði ekki að segja af þeim löndum og fékk hann af því nokkuð ámæli.	Said Bjarni from voyages his that he had land seen and thought men he had-been having no-curiosity when he had nothing to say of these lands and got he of therefore some reproach.	Bjarni told of his voyages and that he had seen land, and people thought he had lacked curiosity when he had nothing much to say about these lands, and he received criticism for this.
Bjarni gerðist hirðmaður jarls og fór út til Grænlands um sumarið eftir. Var nú mikil umræða um landaleitan.	Bjarni became court-man earl's and travelled out to Greenland about summer after. Was now much talk about land-exploring.	Bjarni became one of the earl's followers and travelled out to Greenland the next summer. There was now much talk of exploring these lands.
Leifur son Eiríks rauða úr Brattahlíð fór á fund Bjarna Herjúlfssonar og keypti skip að honum og réð til háseta svo að þeir voru hálfur fjórði tugur manna saman. Leifur bað föður sinn Eirík að hann mundi enn fyrir vera förinni.	Leif son Erik's the-Red from Brattahlid travelled to meet Bjarni Herjolfsson and bought ship of his and appointed to men so that there were half fourth twenty men together. Leif bid father his Erik that he would still for be voyage.	Leif, Erik the Red's son from Brattahlid, travelled to meet Bjarni Herjolfsson and bought his ship and hired a crew of thirty five men altogether. Leif asked his father Erik to lead the expedition.
Eiríkur taldist heldur undan, kveðst þá vera hniginn í aldur og kveðst minna mega við vosi öllu en var. Leifur kveður hann enn mundu mestri heill stýra af þeim frændum. Og þetta lét Eiríkur eftir Leifi og ríður heiman þá er þeir eru að því búnir og var þá skammt að fara til skipsins. Drepur hesturinn fæti, sá er Eiríkur reið, og féll hann af baki og lestist fótur hans.	Erik told rather away, saying then being declining in age and said less able with cold-and-wet all but was. Leif said he still would most luck steer of them kinsmen. And this allowed Erik after Leif and rode home then as they were to for prepared and was then short to go to ship. Failed horse's feet, that was Erik riding, and fell he from back and injured foot his.	Erik was reluctant, saying that he was getting old and less able to cope with the cold weather as he once was. Leif said that he still had the most luck of all his kinsmen. Erik gave in to Leif, and they rode from home as they were ready and had a short distance to go to the ship. The horse that Erik was riding stumbled, and Erik fell injuring his foot.
Þá mælti Eiríkur "Ekki mun mér ætlað að finna lönd fleiri en þetta er nú byggjum vér. Munum vér nú ekki lengur fara allir samt".	Then said Erik "Not should to-me intend to find land more but this that now inhabit we. Should we now nothing longer go all together".	Then Erik said "I am not intended to find any other land than the one where we now live. This will be the end of our travelling together".
Fór Eiríkur heim í Brattahlíð en Leifur réðst til skips og félagar hans með honum, hálfur fjóði tugur manna.	Travelled Erik home to Brattahlid but Leif rode to ship and companions his with him, half fourth twenty men.	Erik travelled home to Brattahlid but Leif rode to the ship with his companions, thirty five men.

The Saga of the Greenlanders (Old Icelandic)

Old Icelandic	Literal	English
Þar var suðurmaður einn í ferð er Tyrkir hét.	There was southern-man one on voyage was Tyrkir named.	There was a southern man on the voyage who was named Tyrkir.
Nú bjuggu þeir skip sitt og sigldu í haf þá er þeir voru búnir og fundu þá það land fyrst er þeir Bjarni fundu síðast.	Now prepared they ship theirs and sailed to sea then when they were ready and found then that land first which there Bjarni found last.	Now they prepared their ship and sailed to sea, then they were ready and found first land that Bjarni had found last.
Þar sigla þeir að landi og köstuðu akkerum og skutu báti og fóru á land og sáu þar eigi gras.	There sailed they to land and cast anchor and launched boats and travelled to land and saw there not grass.	They sailed to the land, cast anchor, put out a boat and rowed ashore, and saw there was no grass.
Jöklar miklir voru allt hið efra en sem ein hella væri allt til jöklanna frá sjónum og sýndist þeim það land vera gæðalaust.	Glaciers great were all the over but which a stone-slab was all to mountains from the-sea and seemed to-them that land was without-quality.	Large glaciers covered the highlands, but the land was like a stone slab from the mountains to the sea, and it seemed to them that this land was of little use.
Þá mælti Leifur: "Eigi er oss nú það orðið um þetta land sem Bjarna að vér höfum eigi komið á landið.	Then said Leif: "Not are we now that word about this land as Bjarna that we have not come on land.	Then Leif said: "Now we cannot have word about this land like Bjarni that we did not come on land.
Nú mun eg gefa nafn landinu og kalla Helluland".	Now will I give name land and call Helluland".	Now I will give the land a name and call it Helluland".
Síðan fóru þeir til skips.	Since travelled they to ship.	Afterwards they returned to the ship.
Eftir þetta sigla þeir í haf og fundu land annað, sigla enn að landi og kasta akkerum, skjóta síðan báti og ganga á landið.	After that sailed they to sea and found land another, sailed yet to land and cast anchor, launched then boats and went to land.	After that they sailed to sea and found another land, sailed close to the land and cast anchor, put out a boat and went to shore.
Það land var slétt og skógi vaxið og sandar hvítir víða þar sem þeir fóru og ósæbratt.	That land was flat and forest grown and sands white widely there as they travelled and unbroken-sea.	This land was flat and forested, with many white beaches, wide as they travelled and unbroken by the sea.
Þá mælti Leifur: "Af kostum skal þessu landi nafn gefa og kalla Markland".	Then said Leif: "Of benefit shall this land name give and call Markland".	Then Leif said: "This land shall be named by its benefit, and will be called Markland".
Fóru síðan ofan aftur til skips sem fljótast.	Travelled since on back to ship as immediately.	Afterwards they travelled back to the ship immediately.

The Saga of the Greenlanders (Old Icelandic)

Old Icelandic	Literal	English
Nú sigla þeir þaðan í haf landnyrðingsveður og voru úti tvö dægur áður þeir sáu land og sigldu að landi og komu að ey einni er lá norður af landinu og gengu þar upp og sáust um í góðu veðri og fundu það að dögg var á grasinu og varð þeim það fyrir að þeir tóku höndum sínum í döggina og brugðu í munn sér og þóttust ekki jafnsætt kennt hafa sem það var.	Now sailed they from-there to sea North-East-Wind and were out two days before they saw land and sailed to land and came to island one which lay north from land and went there up and looked about in good weather and found that to dew was on grass and were they that at-hand that they took hands theirs to dew and brought to mouths theirs and thought not as-sweet known have as that was.	Now they sailed from there to the sea with a north east wind, and sailed for two days before they saw land, they sailed towards it and came to an island that lay to the north of the land, they went up to the shore and looked about, in fine weather they found dew on the grass, that they took in their hands, and brought to their mouths, and they thought nothing was as sweet as that was.
Síðan fóru þeir til skips síns og sigldu í sund það er lá milli eyjarinnar og ness þess er norður gekk af landinu, stefndu í vesturátt fyrir nesið.	Since travelled they to ship theirs and sailed to strait that which lay between island and headland this was north going of land, steered at westwards before headland.	Afterwards they travelled to their ship and sailed to the strait that lay between the island and the headland that stretched out north from the land, they steered westwards around the headland.
Þar var grunnsævi mikið að fjöru sjóvar og stóð þá uppi skip þeirra og var þá langt til sjóvar að sjá frá skipinu.	There were shallows much at tide sea and stood then up ship theirs and was then long to sea to see from ship.	There were many shallows at low tide and their ship was stranded, and then the sea was a long way out as seen by those on the ship.
En þeim var svo mikil forvitni á að fara til landsins að þeir nenntu eigi þess að bíða að sjór félli undir skip þeirra og runnu til lands þar er á ein féll úr vatni einu. En þegar sjór féll undir skip þeirra þá tóku þeir bátinn og réru til skipsins og fluttu það upp í ána, síðan í vatnið og köstuðu þar akkerum og báru af skipi húðföt sín og gerðu þar búðir, tóku það ráð síðan að búast þar um þann vetur og gerðu þar hús mikil.	But they were so much curiosity of to travel to land, that they bothered not this to wait, by sea rising under ship theirs, and ran to land, there was on one lake from river one. But then sea fell under ship theirs, then took they boat and rowed to ship and floated that up into river, then into lake, and cast there anchor and brought off ship skin-cots theirs and made there booths, took they counsel then to stay there about then winter and make there houses large.	Their curiosity to travel to land was so great, that they did not bother to wait for the sea to rise under their ship, and ran aground where there was a river from a lake. But when the sea flowed under their ship, they took the boat and rowed it to the ship, and floated up into the river, then into the lake, and cast anchor there, and brought off the ship their sleeping-sacks and built booths, they then decided to stay there for the winter and make large houses there.
Hvorki skorti þar lax í ánni né í vatninu og stærra lax en þeir hefðu fyrr séð.	Neither shortage there salmon in river nor in lake and larger salmon than they have before seen.	There was no shortage of salmon there, neither in the river nor in the lake, and larger salmon than they had seen before.

The Saga of the Greenlanders (Old Icelandic)

Old Icelandic	Literal	English
Þar var svo góður landskostur, að því er þeim sýndist, að þar mundi engi fénaður fóður þurfa á vetrum.	There was so good land-benefits, in therefore as they seemed, that there would not cattle fodder need in winter.	The land was so good, that it seemed to them that cattle would not need fodder in winter.
Þar komu engi frost á vetrum og lítt rénuðu þar grös.	There came no frost in winter, and little receded there grass.	There was no frost in winter, and the grass only receded a little.
Meira var þar jafndægri en á Grænlandi eða Íslandi.	More was there equal-day than on Greenland or Iceland.	The days and nights were more equal in length than in Greenland or Iceland.
Sól hafði þar eyktarstað og dagmálastað um skammdegi.	Sun had there three-hours stood and morning stood during short-time-of-day.	The sun stood by mid morning and stood during mid afternoon, during winter and the shortest time of day.
En er þeir höfðu lokið húsgerð sinni þá mælti Leifur við föruneyti sitt: "Nú vil eg skipta láta liði voru í tvo staði og vil eg kanna láta landið og skal helmingur liðs vera við skála heima en annar helmingur skal kanna landið og fara eigi lengra en þeir komi heim að kveldi og skiljist eigi".	And when they had ended house-building theirs then talked Leif with companions his: "Now will I divide let company ours into two parts and will I explore let land and shall half company be with cabin home but another half shall explore land and go not further than they come home by evening and separate not".	And when they had finished their house building, Leif said to his companions: "Now I wish to have our company divided into two groups and explore the land, I wish that half the company shall be home at the cabin, and the other half shall explore the land and go no further than they can come home by evening, and no one separate".
Nú gerðu þeir svo um stund.	Now did they so about awhile.	Now they did this for a while.
Leifur gerði ýmist, að hann fór með þeim eða var heima að skála.	Leif did either, that he travelled with them or was home at cabin.	Leif either travelled with them or he was home at the cabin.
Leifur var mikill maður og sterkur, manna skörulegastur að sjá, vitur maður og góður hófsmaður um alla hluti.	Leif was great man and strong, man striking to see, wise man and good moderate-man about all things.	Leif was a great and strong man, striking in appearance, and a wise man who was moderate about all things.
4	4	4
Á einhverju kveldi bar það til tíðinda að manns var vant af liði þeirra og var það Tyrkir suðurmaður.	At one-such evening bore that to news that man was missing from company theirs and was that Tyrkir southern-man.	One evening came the news that a man was missing from their team, and that was Tyrkir the southerner.
Leifur kunni því stórilla því að Tyrkir hafði lengi verið með þeim feðgum og elskað mjög Leif í barnæsku.	Leif knew therefore greatly because that Tyrkir had long been with them father-and-son and loved much Leif in childhood.	Leif was affected by this, because Tyrkir had spent many years with him and his father, and he had treated Leif very affectionately as a child.

The Saga of the Greenlanders (Old Icelandic)

Old Icelandic	Literal	English
Taldi Leifur nú mjög á hendur förunautum sínum og bjóst til ferðar að leita hans og tólf menn með honum.	Told Leif now much on hand travelling-men his and prepared to go to seek him and twelve men with him.	Leif told off his people and prepared to seek him with twelve men.
En er þeir voru skammt komnir frá skála þá gekk Tyrkir í mót þeim og var honum vel fagnað.	But when they were short came from cabin, then going Tyrkir in meeting them, and was he well welcomed.	But when they were a short way away from the cabin, Tyrkir came towards them, and he was gladly welcomed.
Leifur fann það brátt að fóstra hans var skapgott.	Leif found that soon, that foster-father his was well-tempered.	Leif soon found that his foster-father was in a good mood.
Hann var brattleitur og lauseygur, smáskitlegur í andliti, lítill vexti og vesallegur en íþróttamaður á alls konar hagleik.	He was steep-looking and loose-eyed, dirty in face, little grown and poor-wretch, but excellent in all kinds-of pursuits.	He had a protruding forehead and darting eyes, with dark wrinkles in his face, he was short and frail looking, but excellent in many pursuits.
Þá mælti Leifur til hans: "Hví varstu svo seinn fóstri minn og fráskili föruneytinu?"	Then said Leif to him: "Why were so late, foster mine, and separated companions?"	Then Leif said to him: "Why were you so late, foster-father, and how were you separated from your companions?".
Hann talaði þá fyrst lengi á þýsku og skaut marga vega augunum og gretti sig. *En þeir skildu eigi hvað er hann sagði.*	He talked then first long in German and shot many ways eyes and frowned himself. But they knew not, what was he said.	He talked at length first in German with his eyes darting in many directions and frowning. The others did not know what he was saying.
Hann mælti þá á norrænu er stund leið: "Eg var genginn eigi miklu lengra en þið. *Kann eg nokkur nýnæmi að að segja.* *Eg fann vínvið og vínber".*	He said then in Norse, a while way: "I was going not much longer than you. Know I something new to say. I found vines and grapes".	After a while, he spoke in Norse: "I had only gone a little farther than you. I know some news to tell you: I found grapevines and grapes".
"Mun það satt fóstri minn?" kvað Leifur.	"Would that true, foster mine?" said Leif.	"Is this true, foster-father?" said Lef.
Að vísu er það satt, kvað hann, "því að eg var þar fæddur er hvorki skorti vínvið né vínber".	"To know is that true", said he, "because that I was there fathered, where neither shortage vines nor grapes".	"I know this is true", said he, "because where I was brought up, there was no shortage of grapevines and grapes".

The Saga of the Greenlanders (Old Icelandic)

Old Icelandic	Literal	English
Nú sváfu þeir af þá nótt en um morguninn mælti Leifur við háseta sína: "Nú skal hafa tvennar sýslur fram og skal sinn dag hvort, lesa vínber eða höggva vínvið og fella mörkina svo að það verði farmur til skips míns".	Now slept they of then night, but about morning said Leif to crew his: "Now shall have two pursuits from, and shall the day either, gather grapes or fell with and fell trees, so by that be cargo to ship mine".	They went to sleep that night, and around morning Leif said to his crew: "No we shall have two pursuits each day, either picking grapes or cutting vines, or felling trees to make cargo for my ship".
Og þetta var ráðs tekið.	And that was counsel taken.	And that advice was taken.
Svo er sagt að eftirbátur þeirra var fylltur af vínberjum.	So is said, that boat theirs was filled of grapes.	So it was said that their boat was filled with grapes.
Nú var hogginn farmur á skipið.	Now was cut-down cargo for ship.	Now they cut down wood as cargo for the ship.
Og er vorar þá bjuggust þeir og sigldu burt og gaf Leifur nafn landinu eftir landkostum og kallaði Vínland, sigla nú síðan í haf og gaf þeim vel byri þar til er þeir sáu Grænland og fjöll undir jöklum.	And when spring, then prepared they and sailed away, and gave Leif named land after land-benefits and called Vinland, sailed now since into sea, and gave them well fair-wind, there until was they saw Greenland and mountains below glaciers.	And when spring came, they made ready and sailed away, and Leif named the lanf after its features and called it Vinland, they now sailed to sea, and they were given fair wind until they saw Greenland and the mountains under glaciers.
Þá tók einn maður til máls og mælti við Leif: "Hví stýrir þú svo mjög undir veður skipinu?"	Then took one man to speak and said to Leif: "Why steer you so up-to wind the-ship?	Then one man said to Leif: "Why do you steer the ship so close to the wind?"
Leifur svaraði: "Eg hygg að stjórn minni en þó enn að fleira. Eða hvað sjáið þér til tíðinda?"	Leif answered: "I think to steering less, but though still to more, or what see you to news?".	Leif answered: "I am aware of my course, but there is more to it than that, do you see anything of note?".
Þeir kváðust ekki sjá það er tíðindum sætti.	They said not see, that which news agreed.	They said that they did not see anything of note.
Eg veit eigi, segir Leifur, "hvort eg sé skip eða sker".	"I know not", said Leif, "Whether I see ship or skerry".	"I don't know", said Leif, "whether I see a ship or a rock".
Nú sjá þeir og kváðu sker vera.	Now looked they and said skerry was.	Now they looked and said that it was a rock.
Hann sá því framar en þeir að hann sá menn í skerinu.	He saw that from but they, that he saw men on the-skerry.	He saw so much better than them, that he could see men on the rock.

The Saga of the Greenlanders (Old Icelandic)

Old Icelandic	Literal	English
Nú vil eg að vér beitum undir veðrið, segir Leifur, "svo að vér náum til þeirra ef menn eru þurftugir að ná vorum fundi og er nauðsyn á að duga þeim.	"Now will I, that we apply up-to wind", said Leif, "So that we near to them, if men are in-need by near we meet, and is necessity to that help them.	"Now I wish to steer us close to the wind", said Leif, "so that we are near to them, if these men are in need of help, we must help them.
En með því að þeir séu eigi friðmenn þá eigum vér allan kost undir oss en þeir ekki undir sér".	But as-well for by they so not peaceful-men, then own we all advantage behind us, but they not behind them".	But equally if they are hostile, then we have all the advantages, and they have none".
Nú sækja þeir undir skerið og lægðu segl sitt, köstuðu akkeri og skutu litlum báti öðrum er þeir höfðu haft með sér.	Now sought they under the-skerry and lowered sails theirs, and cast anchor and launched little boat other, that they had had with them.	Now they searched about the rock, lowered their sails, cast anchor, and launched the second of their small boats that they had with them.
Þá spurði Leifur hver þar réði fyrir liði.	Then asked Leif who there leader for company.	Then Leif asked who there was the leader of their company.
Sá kveðst Þórir heita og vera norænn maður að kyni,	So said Thorir called, and was north man by kin.	The man who replied said his name was Thorir, and that he was of Norwegian origin.
"eða hvert er þitt nafn?"	"But what is your name?"	"But what is your name?"
Leifur segir til sín.	Leif said to them.	Leif told them.
"Ertu son Eiríks rauða úr Brattahlíð?" segir hann.	"Are-you son-of Erik's the-Red out-of Brattahlid?" said he.	"Are you the son of Erik the Red from Brattahlid?" he said.
Leifur kvað svo vera:	Leif said so was.	Leif said it was so.
"Nú vil eg", segir Leifur, "bjóða yður öllum á mitt skip og fémunum þeim er skipið má við taka".	"Now will I", said Leif, "Invite you all on my ship, and goods those, which ship may with take".	"Now I wish", said Leif, "to invite you all on to my ship and any goods, which the ship may carry".
Þeir þágu þann kost og sigldu síðan til Eiríksfjarðar með þeim farmi þar til er þeir komu til Brattahlíðar, báru farminn af skipi.	They accepted that choice and sailed afterwards to Eriksfjord with them cargo, there to then they came to Brattahlid, brought cargo off ship.	They accepted his offer and then they sailed to Eriksfjord with their cargo, until they reached Brattahlid, where they brought the cargo off the ship.
Síðan bauð Leifur Þóri til vistar með sér og Guðríði konu hans og þrem mönnum öðrum en fékk vistir öðrum hásetum, bæði Þóris og sínum félögum.	Afterwards invited Leif Thori to stay with him and Guthrid, wife his, and three men other, but got provisions other seamen, as-well Thori and his companions.	Afterwards Leif invited Thorir to stay with him, along with Thorir's wife Gudrid, and three other men, and found provisions for the other seamen, both Thorir's and his companions.
Leifur tók fimmtán menn úr skerinu.	Leif took fifteen men from the-skerry.	Leif rescued fifteen men from the rock.

The Saga of the Greenlanders (Old Icelandic)

Old Icelandic	Literal	English
Hann var síðan kallaður Leifur hinn heppni.	He was afterwards called Leif the lucky.	After this he was called Leif the Lucky.
Leifi varð nú bæði gott til fjár og mannvirðingar.	Leif was now both benefited to wealth and worthiness.	Leif now became very wealthy and gained much respect.
Þann vetur kom sótt mikil í lið Þóris og andaðist hann Þórir og mikill hluti liðs hans.	That winter came sickness great among team Thorir, and died he Thorir and much part-of men his.	That winter there came a great sickness among Thorir's companions, and Thorir died along with many of his company.
Þann vetur andaðist og Eiríkur rauði.	That winter died also Erik the-Red.	That winter Erik the Red also died.
Nú var umræða mikil um Vínlandsför Leifs og þótti Þorvaldi bróður hans of óvíða kannað hafa verið landið.	Now was talk much about Vinland-voyage Leif's, and thought Thorvald brother his, about little-wide explored had been land.	There was great discussion of Leif's Vinland-voyage, and his brother Thorvald thought that the land had been little explored.
Þá mælti Leifur við Þorvald: "Þú skalt fara með skip mitt bróðir ef þú vilt til Vínlands og vil eg þó að skipið fari áður eftir viði þeim er Þórir átti í skerinu".	Then said Leif to Thorvald: "You shall go with ship mine, brother, if you will, to Vinland, and will I though, that ship go return after timber that, was Thorir had on the-skerry".	Leif then said to Thorvald: "You go to Vinland, brother, if you wish, but I wish for that ship to return after the timber, that Thorir had on that rock".
Og svo var gert.	And so was done.	And so it was done.
5	5	5
Nú bjóst Þorvaldur til þeirrar ferðar með þrjá tigi manna með umráði Leifs bróður síns.	Now prepared Thorvald to their voyage with three ten men with counsel Leif, brother his.	Now Thorvald prepared their voyage with advice from his brother Leif, with thirty companions.
Síðan bjuggu þeir skip sitt og héldu í haf og er engi frásögn um ferð þeirra fyrr en þeir koma til Vínlands til Leifsbúða og bjuggu þar um skip sitt og sátu um kyrrt þann vetur og veiddu fiska til matar sér.	After prepared they ship theirs and held to sea, and is nothing said about voyage theirs, before but they came to Vinland, to Leif's-camp, and settled there about ship theirs and sat about still they winter and caught fish for food theirs.	They made their ship ready and put to sea, and nothing is said about their voyage before they came to Vinland, to Leif's camp, and they settled their ship, and stayed in place that winter and caught fish for their food.
En um vorið mælti Þorvaldur að þeir skyldu búa skip sitt og skyldi eftirbátur skipsins og nokkurir menn með fara fyrir vestan landið og kanna þar um sumarið.	But about spring said Thorvald, that they should prepare ship theirs and should boat ship's and some men with travel for western land and explore there about summer.	Then about spring Thorvald said that they should prepare their ship, and with the ship's boat some men should travel west of the land and explore there during the summer.

The Saga of the Greenlanders (Old Icelandic)

Old Icelandic	Literal	English
Þeim sýndist landið fagurt og skógótt, og skammt milli skógar og sjóvar, og hvítir sandar.	They seemed land beautiful and wooded and short between woods and sea and white sands.	To them the land seemed beautiful and well forested, and a short distance between the woods and the sea were white sands.
Þar var eyjótt mjög og grunnsævi mikið.	There were islands much and shallows much.	There were many islands and large stretches of shallow sea.
Þeir fundu hvergi mannavistir né dýra, en í eyju einni vestarlega fundu þeir kornhjálm af tré.	They found neither men food nor animals. But on island one westward found they corn-shed of wood.	The found neither sign of men nor animals. But on one of the westward islands they found a wooden corn shed.
Eigi fundu þeir fleiri mannaverk og fóru aftur og komu til Leifsbúða að hausti.	Not found they more men's-work and went back and came to Leif's-camp in autumn.	They did not find any more work by human hands and came back to Leif's camp in the autumn.
En að sumri öðru fór Þorvaldur fyrir austan með kaupskipið og hið nyrðra fyrir landið. Þá gerði að þeim veður hvasst fyrir andnesi einu og rak þá þar upp og brutu kjölinn undan skipinu og höfðu þar langa dvöl og bættu skip sitt.	But at summer the-next went Thorvald for eastward with ship and the north for land. Then was to them weather stormy before headland one, and driven then there up, and broke keel under ship and had there long dwelled and repaired ship theirs.	The next summer Thorvald journeyed eastwards with the ship and north around the land. Then they encountered stormy weather around one of the headlands, and they were driven ashore, and their keel brooke under their ship, and they stayed there a long time repairing their ship.
Þá mælti Þorvaldur við förunauta sína: "Nú vil eg að vér reisum hér upp kjölinn á nesinu og köllum Kjalarnes". Og svo gerðu þeir.	Then said Thorvald to companions his: "Now will I, that we raise here up keel on headland and call Kjalarnes". And so did they.	Then Thorvald said to his companions: "Now I wish that we raise the keel up on the headland and call it Keel Point". And so they did.
Síðan sigla þeir þaðan í braut og austur fyrir landið og inn í fjarðarkjafta þá er þar voru næstir og að höfða þeim er þar gekk fram.	Afterwards sailed they there to away and eastern for land and then into fjord-mouth then, which there was nearest, and to headland they, which there going from.	Afterwards they sailed away to the east of the land and then into the mouth of the next fjords, and then to a cape stretching out from there to the sea.
Hann var allur skógi vaxin.	It was all wood grown.	It was covered with forest.
Þá leggja þeir fram skip sitt í lægi og skjóta bryggjum á land og gengur Þorvaldur þar á land upp með alla förunauta sína.	There let they from ship theirs to lay and launched bridge to land, and went Thorvald there to land up with all companions his.	There they lay their ship and set out gangways to the land, and Thorvald and his companions went to shore.
Hann mælti þá: "Hér er fagurt og hér vildi eg bæ minn reisa".	He said then: "Here is beautiful, and here will I settlement mine raise",	Then he said: "It is beautiful here, and I wish to build a farm here",

The Saga of the Greenlanders (Old Icelandic)

Old Icelandic	Literal	English
Ganga síðan til skips og sjá á sandinum inn frá höfðanum þrjár hæðir og fóru til þangað og sjá þar húðkeipa þrjá og þrjá menn undir hverjum.	Went then to ship and saw on sands in from headland three heights, and went to there and saw there hide-boats three and three men under each.	Afterwards as they went back to the ship, they saw three hillocks on the beach inland from the cape, and saw three canoes with three men under each of them.
Þá skiptu þeir liði sínu og höfðu hendur á þeim öllum nema einn komst í burt með keip sinn.	Then divided they people theirs and had caught to they all, taken one came to away with canoe his.	They divided their forces and caught all of them, except one who escaped with his canoe.
Þeir drepa hina átta og ganga síðan aftur á höfðann og sjást þar um og sjá inn í fjörðinn hæðir nokkurar og ætluðu þeir það vera byggðir.	They killed the eight and went since back to headland and looked there about and saw that in fjord heights some, and supposed they that were dwellings.	They killed the other eight and afterwards went back to the cape, and they looked and saw that in some of the fjord heights, what they assumed to be settlements.
Eftir það sló á þá höfga svo miklum að þeir máttu eigi vöku halda og sofna þeir allir.	After that struck on then heaviness so much, that they may not awake keep, and slept they all.	After that they became so heavy with weariness, that they could not stay awake, and the all fell asleep.
Þá kom kall yfir þá svo að þeir vöknuðu allir.	Then came shout over then, so that they awoke all.	Then a voice called to them, and they all awoke.
Svo segir kallið: "Vaki þú Þorvaldur og allt föruneyti þitt ef þú vilt líf þitt hafa og far þú á skip þitt og allir menn þínir og farið frá landi sem skjótast".	So said call: "Wake you, Thorvald, and all companions yours, if you will lives yours have, and go you to ship yours and all men yours, and travel from land which quickly".	The voice called: "Wake up, Thorvald, and all your companions, if you wish to save your lives, get to your ship and all your men, and leave this land as quickly as you can".
Þá fór innan eftir firðinum ótal húðkeipa og lögðu að þeim.	Then went within behind fjord countless hide-boats, and lay at them.	Then from within the fjord came countless canoes heading towards them.
Þorvaldur mælti þá: "Vér skulum færa út á borð vígfleka og verjast sem best en vega lítt í mót".	Thorvald said then: "We should bring out to board battle and defend as best, but fight little to against".	Then Thorvald said: "We should bring out breastworks along the sides of the ship and defend as best we can, but fight back as little as we can".
Svo gera þeir en Skrælingjar skutu á þá um stund en flýja síðan í burt sem ákafast hver sem mátti.	So did they, but Skraelings shot towards then about awhile, but fled afterwards away as fast, each as may.	So they did, but the Skraelings shot at them for a while, they fled as rapidly as they could.
Þá spurði Þorvaldur menn sína ef þeir væru nokkuð sárir.	Then asked Thorvald men his, if they had any wounds.	Then Thorvald asked his men if any of them had been wounded.

The Saga of the Greenlanders (Old Icelandic)

Old Icelandic	Literal	English
Þeir kváðust eigi sárir vera.	They said not wounded were.	They said that they were not wounded.
Ég hef fengið sár undir hendi, segir hann, "og fló ör milli skipborðsins og skjaldarins undir hönd mér og er hér örin, en mun mig þetta til bana leiða.	"I have caught wound under arm", said he, "And flew arrow between ship's-berth and shield under arm to-me, and is here arrow, then should me this to death lead.	"I have been wounded under my arm", he said, "and an arrow flew between the ship's berth and the shield into my armpit, and this shall lead to my death.
Nú ræð ég að þér búið ferð yðra sem fljótast aftur á leið en þér skuluð færa mig á höfða þann er mér þótti byggilegast vera.	Now advise I, to you prepare travel depart as quickly return to journey, but you should bring me to headland that, which me thinks dwelling shall-be.	Now I advise you to prepare for your return journey as quickly as possible, but take me to that cape that I thought would make a good farm.
Má það vera að mér hafi satt á munn komið að eg muni þar búa á um stund.	May that be, by me have true to mouth come, that I should there dwell on for awhile.	Maybe the words I spoke shall prove true, that I shall dwell there for awhile.
Þar skuluð þér mig grafa og setja krossa að höfði mér og að fótum og kallið það Krossanes jafnan síðan".	There should you me engrave and set cross at head mine and at feet, and call that Krossanes ever after".	There you should bury me and put a cross at my head and feet, and call that Krossanes ever after".
Grænland var þá kristnað en þó andaðist Eiríkur rauði fyrir kristni.	Greenland was then Christian, but though died Erik the-Red before Christianity.	Greenland was then Christian, but Erik died before the conversion to Christianity.
Nú andaðist Þorvaldur en þeir gerðu allt eftir því sem hann hafði mælt og fóru síðan og hittu þar förunauta sína og sögðu hvorir öðrum slík tíðindi sem vissu og bjuggu þar þann vetur og fengu sér vínber og vínvið til skips síns.	Now died Thorvald, but they did all after according, which he had said, and went since and met their companions theirs, and said each other such tidings which knew and dwelt there that winter and gathered they grapes and vines to ship.	Now Thorvald died, and they did everything as he had said, and afterwards they went to meet their companions, and each group told its news to the others, and they stayed there that winter and gathered grapes and vines in their ship.
Nú búast þeir þaðan um vorið eftir til Grænlands og komu skipi sínu í Eiríksfjörð og kunnu Leifi að segja mikil tíðindi.	Now prepared they there about spring after to Greenland and came ship theirs in Eriksfjord and known Leif that said much tidings.	Now they prepared their ship about spring to return to Greenland, and their ship came in to Eriksfjord and had much news to tell Leif.
6	6	6
Það hafði gerst til tíðinda meðan á Grænlandi að Þorsteinn í Eiríksfirði hafði kvongast og fengið Guðríðar Þorbjarnardóttur er átt hafði Þórir austmaður er fyrr var frá sagt.	It had made to news meanwhile to Greenland, that Thorstein in Eriksfjord had married and married Guthrid Thorbjarnardottur, who had married Thorir Easterner, as before was from said.	Among the news meanwhile in Greenland was that Thorstein in Eriksfjord had married Gudrid Thorbjornadottir, who had previously been married to Thorir the Easterner who was spoken of earlier.

The Saga of the Greenlanders (Old Icelandic)

Old Icelandic	Literal	English
Nú fýstist Þorsteinn Eiríksson að fara til Vínlands eftir líki Þorvalds bróður síns og bjó skip hið sama og valdi hann lið að afli og vexti og hafði með sér hálfan þriðja tug manna og Guðríði konu sína og sigla í haf þegar þau eru búin og úr landsýn.	Now desired Thorstein Eriksson to travel to Vinland after body Thorvald's, brother his, and prepared ship the same, and chose he team in strength and well-built and had with him half third twenty men and Guthrid, wife his, and sailed to sea, then they were ready, and out-of land-sight.	Now Thorstein Eriksson wished to travel to Vinland and retrieve the body of his brother Thorvald, and made the same ship ready, and he chose his company for their strength and size, and had with him twenty five men and his wife Gudrid, and when they were ready the sailed to sea, and out of sight of land.
Þau velkti úti allt sumarið og vissu eigi hvar þau fóru.	They drove about all summer, and knew not, where they went.	They were driven about all summer, and they did not know where they went.
Og er vika var af vetri þá tóku þeir land í Lýsufirði á Grænlandi í hinni vestri byggð.	And when week was of winter, then took they land in Lysufjord in Greenland in the western settlement.	And when the first week of winter had passed, they made land in Lysufjord, in the Western Settlement of Greenland.
Þorsteinn leitaði þeim um vistir og fékk vistir öllum hásetum sínum.	Thorstein sought them about shelter and got lodging all crew his.	Thorstein found them shelter and got lodgings for all of his crew.
En hann var vistlaus og kona hans.	But he was without-lodging and wife his.	But he and his wife were without lodgings.
Nú voru þau eftir að skipi tvö nokkurar nætur.	Now were they remained in ship two some nights.	Now they remained on the ship for several nights.
Þá var enn ung kristni á Grænlandi.	Then was yet young Christianity in Greenland.	Then Christianity was still young in Greenland.
Það var einn dag að menn komu að tjaldi þeirra snemma.	It was one day, that people came by tent theirs early.	One day some men came early to their tent.
Sá spurði er fyrir þeim var hvað manna væri í tjaldinu.	So asked, who present they were, what men were in tent.	The asked what men were in the tent.
Þorsteinn svarar: "Tveir menn", segir hann, "eða hver spyr að?"	Thorstein answered: "Two people", said he, "But who asks to?"	Thorstein answered: "Two people", he said, "but who is asking?".
"Þorsteinn heiti eg og er eg kallaður Þorsteinn svartur.	"Thorstein called I, and am I called Thorstein-the-Black.	"I am called Thorstein, Thorstein the Black.
En það er erindi mitt hingað að eg vil bjóða ykkur báðum hjónum til vistar til mín".	But that is errand mine here, that I will bid you both couple to lodging to mine".	My reason for coming here is to invite you both to stay with me".

The Saga of the Greenlanders (Old Icelandic)

Old Icelandic	Literal	English
Þorsteinn kveðst vilja hafa umræði konu sinnar en hún bað hann ráða og nú játar hann þessu.	Thorstein said will have discussion wife his, but she bid he decide, and now accepted he this.	Thorstein said he wished to discuss this with his wife, but she asked him to decide, and he now accepted.
"Þá mun eg koma eftir ykkur á morgun með eyki því að mig skortir ekki til að veita ykkur vist en fásinni er mikið með mér að vera því að tvö erum við þar hjón því að eg er einþykkur mjög.	"Then should I come back to-you in morning with animals, for by shortage not to by supply you provisions, but remote is very with me by being, for that two we-are with there couple, because that I am solitary much".	"Then I shall come back to you in the morning with oxen, I have no shortage of supplies for you, but it is remote being here with me, because there are only two of us, my wife and I, and I am very much a solitary man.
Annan sið hefi eg og en þér hafið og ætla eg þann þó betra er þér hafið".	Another tradition have I and than you have, and suppose I that yet better, is you have".	Also I have another faith than you, but I suspect yours is the better of the two".
Nú kom hann eftir þeim um morguninn með eyki og fóru þau með Þorsteini svarta til vistar og veitti hann þeim vel.	Now came he after them about morning with animals, and went they with Thorstein the-Black to lodge, and supported he them well.	Now he came back to them around morning with oxen, and they went to stay with Thorstein the Black, and he provided for them generously.
Guðríður var sköruleg kona að sjá og vitur kona og kunni vel að vera með ókunnugum mönnum.	Guthrid was strong woman to see and wise woman and knew well at being with unknown people.	Gudrid was a strong woman, of striking appearance, and a wise woman who knew how to behave among strangers.
Það var snemma vetrar að sótt kom í lið Þorsteins Eiríkssonar og önduðust þar margir förunautar.	That was early winter, that sickness came to companions Thorstein's Eriksson, and died there many companions his.	It was early that winter that sickness came to Thorstein Eriksson's companions, and many of them died there.
Þorsteinn bað gera kistur að líkum þeirra er önduðust og færa til skips og búa þar um "því að eg vil láta flytja til Eiríksfjarðar að sumri öll líkin".	Thorstein asked made coffins for bodies theirs, who died, and brought to ship and laid there about, "For that I will lay carry to Eriksfjord in summer all bodies".	Thorstein asked that coffins be made for their bodies who had died, and brought back to the ship and laid there, "For I will carry all of them to Eriksfjord in the summer".
Nú er þess skammt að bíða að sótt kemur í híbýli Þorsteins og tók kona hans sótt fyrst er hét Grímhildur.	Now was this short to wait, that sickness came into dwelling Thorstein's, and took wife his sickness first, who called Grimhild.	It was not long until the sickness came to Thorstein the Black's house, and his wife Grimhild was the first to fall ill.
Hún var ákaflega mikil og sterk sem karlar en þó kom sóttin henni undir.	She was very large and strong as men, but yet came sickness her under.	She was a very large woman, strong as a man, yet she bowed to the sickness.

The Saga of the Greenlanders (Old Icelandic)

Old Icelandic	Literal	English
Og brátt eftir það tók sóttina Þorsteinn Eiríksson og lágu þau bæði senn og andaðist Grímhildur kona Þorsteins svarta.	And soon after that took sickness Thorstein Eriksson, and lay they both same, and died Grimhild, wife Thorstein the-Black's.	And soon after that Thorstein Eriksson was stricken, and both of them laid there, and Grimhild, the wife of Thorstein the Black died.
En er hún var dauð þá gekk Þorsteinn fram úr stofunni eftir fjöl að leggja á líkið.	But when she was dead, then went Thorstein from out room after plank to lay on body.	And when she had died, Thorstein the Black went from the main room to look for a plank to lay her body on.
Guðríður mælti þá: "Vertu litla hríð í brott Þorsteinn minn", segir hún.	Guthrid said then: "Be little time to away, Thorstein mine", said she.	Gudrid then spoke: "Don't be away long, dear Thorstein" she said.
Hann kvað svo vera skyldu.	He said so be should.	He said so it would be.
Þá mælti Þorsteinn Eiríksson: "Með undarlegum hætti er nú um húsfreyju vora því að nú örglast hún upp við ölnboga og þokar fótum sínum frá stokki og þreifar til skúa sinna".	Then said Thorstein Eriksson: "With strange way is now about housewife going, for that now rises she up with elbows and stretches feet hers from bed and feels for shoes hers".	Then Thorstein Eriksson said: "Strange are the actions of the mistress of the house now, she's struggling to raise herself up on her elbows, and stretches her feet from the bed and feels for her shoes".
Og í því kom Þorsteinn bóndi inn og lagðist Grímhildur niður í því og brakaði þá í hverju tré í stofunni.	And in for came Thorstein farmer the, and lay Grimhild down in for, and creaked then in each beam in room.	And in came Thorstein the farmer, and Grimhild fell back down, and every beam in the room creaked.
Nú gerir Þorsteinn kistu að líki Grímhildar og færði í brott og bjó um. Hann var bæði mikill maður og sterkur og þurfti hann þess alls áður hann kom henni burt af bænum.*	Now made Thorstein coffin for body Grimhild's and took it out and dwelling about. He was both large man and strong, and needed he this all, before he came her away out-of dwelling.	Thorstein then made a coffin for Grimhild's body and took it away from the house. He was a large and strong man, and he needed all his strenngth to carry her out of the house.
Nú elnaði sóttin Þorsteini Eiríkssyni og andaðist hann.	Now attacked sickness Thorstein Eriksson, and died he.	Now the sickness attacked Thorstein Eriksson, and he died.
Guðríður kona hans kunni því lítt.	Guthrid, wife his, knew therefore little.	Gudrid, his wife, was overtaken with grief and knew little else.
Þá voru þau öll í stofunni.	Then were they all in room.	All of them were in the main room.
Guðríður hafði setið á stóli frammi fyrir bekknum er hann hafði legið Þorsteinn bóndi hennar.	Guthrid had sat on stool from before bench, which he had laid, Thorstein, husband hers.	Gudrid sat on a stool in front of the bench where her husband Thorstein had lain.

The Saga of the Greenlanders (Old Icelandic)

Old Icelandic	Literal	English
Þá tók Þorsteinn bóndi Guðríði af stólinum í fang sér og settist í bekkinn annan með hana gegnt líki Þorsteins og taldi um fyrir henni marga vega og huggaði hana og hét henni því að hann mundi fara með henni til Eiríksfjarðar með líki Þorsteins bónda hennar og förunauta hans.	Then took Thorstein the-farmer Guthrid from stool into grasp his and sat on another bench with he opposite body Thorstein's and talked about before her many ways and comforted he and called her therefore, that he would go with her to Eriksfjord with body Thorstein's, husband hers, and companions his.	Thorstein the farmer then took Gudrid from the stool into his arms and sat with her on the bench across from her husband Thorstein's corpse and said many comforting things, consoling her and promising her that he would take her to Eriksfjord with her husband Thorstein's body, and those of his companions.
Og svo skal eg taka hingað hjón fleiri, segir hann, "þér til huggunar og skemmtanar".	"And so shall I take there couple more", said he, "You to comfort and entertain".	"And we'll invite other people to stay here", he said, "to provide you with solace and companionship".
Hún þakkaði honum.	She thanked him.	She thanked him.
Þorsteinn Eiríksson settist þá upp og mælti: "Hvar er Guðríður?"	Thorstein Eiriksson sat then up and said: "Where is Guthrid?"	Thorstein Eiriksson then sat up and said: "Where is Gudrid?"
Þrjá tíma mælti hann þetta en hún þagði.	Three times said he this, but she silent.	Three times he said this, but she remained silent.
Þá mælti hún við Þorstein bónda: "Hvort skal eg svör veita hans máli eða eigi?"	Then said she to Thorstein the-farmer: "However shall I answer know his speech or not?"	Then she said to Thorstein the farmer: "Shall I answer him or not?",
Hann bað hana eigi svara.	He bid she not answer.	He told her not to answer.
Þá gekk Þorsteinn bóndi yfir gólfið og settist á stólinn en Guðríður sat í knjám honum.	Then went Thorstein the-farmer over floor and sat on stool, but Guthrid sat on knees his.	Thorstein the farmer then crossed the floor and sat on the stool, and Gudrid on his knee.
Og þá mælti Þorsteinn bóndi: "Hvað viltu nafni?" segir hann.	And then said Thorstein the-farmer "What will-you, namesake?" said he.	Then Thorstein the farmer spoke: "What is it that you want, namesake?", he said.
Hann svarar er stund leið: "Mér er annt til þess að segja Guðríði forlög sín til þess að hún kunni þá betur andláti mínu því að eg er kominn til góðra hvíldarstaða.	He answered, at time way: "I who wish to this, to say Guthrid fortune hers, to this by she could then better death mine, for that I am come to good resting-place.	He answered after a short while: "I want to tell Gudrid her fate, to make it easier for her to deal with my death, for I have gone to a good resting place.

The Saga of the Greenlanders (Old Icelandic)

Old Icelandic	Literal	English
En það er þér að segja Guðríður að þú munt gift vera íslenskum manni og munu langar vera samfarir ykkar og mart manna mun frá ykkur koma, þroskasamt, bjart og ágætt, sætt og ilmað vel.	But this is you to say, Guthrid, that you shall married be Icelander man, and shall long be together you, and many people shall from you come, promising, bright and fine, settled and favoured well.	I say this to you, Gudrid, that you shall marry an Icelander, and you will long be together, and you shall have many descendants, promisinig, bright, and fine, sweet and well favoured.
Munuð þið fara af Grænlandi til Noregs og þaðan til Íslands og gera bú á Íslandi.	Shall you travel from Greenland to Norway and from-there to Iceland and make settlement on Iceland.	You will travel from Greenland to Norway, and from there to Iceland, and settle on Iceland.
Þar munuð þið lengi búa og muntu honum lengur lifa.	There shall you long live, and shall him longer live.	There you will live a long time, longer than your husband.
Þú munt utan fara og ganga suður og koma út aftur til Íslands til bús þíns og þá mun þar kirkja reist vera og muntu þar vera og taka nunnuvígslu og þar muntu andast".	You shall out travel and go south and come from return to Iceland to home yours, and then shall there church raised be, and shall there be and take nun's-vows, and there shall die".	You will travel and go south, and return to Iceland to your farm, and there a church will be raised, and there you will take a nun's vows, and there you will die".
Og þá hnígur Þorsteinn aftur og var búið um lík hans og fært til skips.	And then fell Thorstein back, and was prepared about body his and taken to ship.	And then Thorstein Eriksson fell back, and his corpse was prepared and taken to the ship.
Þorsteinn bóndi efndi vel við Guðríði allt það er hann hafði heitið.	Thorstein the-farmer kept well with Guthrid all that, which he had promised.	Thorstein the farmer kept all his promises to Gudrid.
Hann seldi um vorið jörð sína og kvikfé og fór til skips með Guðríði með allt sitt, bjó skipið og fékk menn til og fór síðan til Eiríksfjarðar.	He sold about spring land his and livestock and went to ship with Guthrid with all his, prepared ship and got men to and went then to Eriksfjord.	In the spring he sold his land and livestock, and went to the ship with all his posessions, prepared the ship, hired a crew, and sailed to Eriksfjord.
Voru nú líkin jörðuð að kirkju.	Were now bodies buried by church.	The bodies were now buried by a church.
Guðríður fór til Leifs í Brattahlíð en Þorsteinn svarti gerði bú í Eiríksfirði og bjó þar meðan hann lifði og þótti vera hinn vaskasti maður.	Guthrid travelled to Leif in Brattahlid, but Thorstein the-Black made dwelling at Eriksfjord and dwelt there, meantime he lived, and thought was he capable man.	Gudrid travlelled to Leif in Brattahlid, and Thorstein the Black built a farm in Eriksfjord and settled there as long as he lived, and he was thought of as a most capable man.

7

Það sama sumar kom skip af Noregi til Grænlands.	That same summer came ship from Norway to Greenland.	That same summer a ship came from Norway and arrived in Greenland.
Sá maður hét Þorfinnur karlsefni er því skipi stýrði.	The man called Thorfin Karlsefni, who for ship steered.	The captain of the ship was named Thorfin Karlsefni.

The Saga of the Greenlanders (Old Icelandic)

Old Icelandic	Literal	English
Hann var son Þórðar hesthöfða Snorrasonar, Þórðarsonar frá Höfða.	He was son-of Thord Horse-Head Snorrason, Thordarson from Hofdi.	He was the son of Thord Horse-Head, the son of Snorri Thordarson of Hofdi.
Þorfinnur karlsefni var stórauðigur að fé og var um veturinn í Brattahlíð með Leifi Eiríkssyni.	Thorfin Karlsefni was wealthy in cattle, and was about winter in Brattahlid with Leif Eriksson.	Thorfin Karlsefni was wealth in cattle, and he spent the winter in Brattahlid with Leif Eriksson.
Brátt felldi hann hug til Guðríðar og bað hennar en hún veik til Leifs svörum fyrir sig.	Soon fell he thoughts to Guthrid and asked her, but she referred to Leif's answer to him.	He was soon attracted to Gudrid and asked her to marry him, but she referred him to Leif for his answer.
Síðan var hún honum föstnuð og gert brúðhlaup þeirra á þeim vetri.	Afterwards was she to-him betrothed and was wedding theirs in that winter.	Afterwards she was engaged to him and their wedding was that winter.
Hin sama var umræða á Vínlandsför sem fyrr og fýstu menn Karlsefni mjög þeirrar ferðar, bæði Guðríður og aðrir menn.	The same was discussed to Vinland-voyage as before, and urged people Karlsefni much there to-journey, both Guthrid and other people.	The discussion of a voyage to Vinland continued as before, and people urged Karlsefni to make the journey, both Gudrid and others.
Nú var ráðin ferð hans og réð hann sér skipverja, sex tigi karla og konur fimm.	Now was agreed travel his, and hired he the crew six ten men and women five.	Now he was decided to travel, he hired a crew of sixty men and five women.
Þann máldaga gerðu þeir Karlsefni og hásetar hans að jöfnum höndum skyldu þeir hafa allt það er þeir fengju til gæða.	Then agreed was they Karlsefni and crew his, that even handed should they have all that, which they get to quality.	Then Karlsefni and his crew agreed that all goods they obtained would be divided equally among them.
Þeir höfðu með sér alls konar fénað því að þeir ætluðu að byggja landið ef þeir mættu það.	They have with them all-kinds livestock, for that they intended to settle land, if they may that.	They had with them all kinds of livestock, for they intended to settle the land if they could.
Karlsefni bað Leif húsa á Vínlandi en hann kveðst ljá mundu húsin en gefa eigi.	Karlsefni asked Leif houses in Vinland, but he said loan would houses, but give not.	Karlsefni asked Leif for his houses in Vinland, and Leif said he would lend them, but not give them to him.
Síðan héldu þeir í haf skipinu og komu til Leifsbúða með heilu og höldnu og báru þar upp húðföt sín.	Then held they to sea ship and came to Leif's-camp with whole and safe and carried there up skin-cots theirs.	Then they put the ship to sea and all arrived at Leif's camp safely and unloaded their sleeping-sacks.
Þeim bar brátt í hendur mikil föng og góð því að reyður var þar upp rekin, bæði mikil og góð, fóru til síðan og skáru hvalinn.	They bore soon to hand much provisions and good, for a rorqual was there up driven, both large and good, went to then and cut whale, shortage then not food.	They soon had plenty of good provisions, since a large and fine rorqual was driven up to shore, they had no shortage of food.
Skorti þá eigi mat.	Shortage then not food.	They had no shortage of food.

The Saga of the Greenlanders (Old Icelandic)

Old Icelandic	Literal	English
Fénaður gekk þar á land upp en það var brátt að graðfé varð úrigt og gerði mikið um sig.	Cattle went there to land up, but that was soon, the cattle were irritable and made greatly about themselves.	The livestock went inland, but the males were soon irritable and hard to handle.
Þeir höfðu haft með sér griðung einn.	They had had with them bull one.	They had with them a bull.
Karlsefni lét fella viðu og telgja til skips síns og lagði viðinn á bjarg eitt til þurrkanar.	Karlsefni let fell wood and hewn to ships theirs and lay trees on rock along to dry.	Karlsefni had trees felled and hewn for their ships, and lay the timber on a rock to dry.
Þeir höfðu öll gæði af landkostum þeim er þar voru, bæði af vínberjum og alls konar veiðum og gæðum.	They had all quality of land-benefits, they which there were, both of grapes and all kinds fish and quality.	They had all kinds of benefit from the land, which included grapes, all kinds of fish and game, and other quality things.
Eftir þann vetur hinn fyrsta kom sumar.	After that winter the first came summer.	After the first winter passed and summer came,
Þá urðu þeir varir við Skrælingja og fór þar úr skógi fram mikill flokkur manna.	Then became they aware with Skraelings, and went there out woods from large group men.	They became aware of the Skraelings, a large group of men came out of the woods.
Þar var nær nautfé þeirra en graðungur tók að belja og gjalla ákaflega hátt.	There was near cattle there, but bull took to bellowing and snorting very loudly.	There cattle were near, and the bull took to bellowing and snorting very loudly.
En það hræddust Skrælingjar og lögðu undan með byrðar sínar en það var grávara og safali og alls konar skinnavara og snúa til bæjar Karlsefnis og vildu þar inn í húsin en Karlsefni lét verja dyrnar.	But that frightened Skraelings and laid away with burdens theirs, but they were grey-skins and sables and all kinds furs, and turned towards farm Karlsefni's and willed there the into house, but Karlsefni laid protection door.	Then this frightened the Skraelings and they ran away with their burdens, which included grey skins, sables, and all kinds of fur, they turned towards Karlsefni's farm and wanted to get into the house, but Karlsefni had protected the door.
Hvorigir skildu annars mál.	Neither knew others' language.	Neither knew the others' language.
Þá tóku Skrælingjar ofan bagga sína og leystu og buðu þeim og vildu vopn helst fyrir en Karlsefni bannaði þeim að selja vopnin.	Then took Skraelings off bags theirs and loosened and offered they and willed weapons preferably for, but Karlsefni banned they to sell weapons.	Then the Skraelings took off their bags and opened them, offering their goods, preferably in exchange for weapons, but Karlsefni forbade them to trade weapons.
Og nú leitar hann ráðs með þeim hætti að hann bað konur bera út búnyt að þeim og þegar er þeir sáu búnyt þá vildu þeir kaupa það en ekki annað.	And now sought he solution with them to-stop, that he asked women bring out milk-products by them, and then when they saw milk-products, then willed they buy that, and nothing else.	And now he sought a solution to this, he asked the women to bring out milk-products, and when they saw these milk-products, they wanted to buy that and nothing else.

The Saga of the Greenlanders (Old Icelandic)

Old Icelandic	Literal	English
Nú var sú kaupför Skrælingja að þeir báru sinn varning í brott í mögum sínum en Karlsefni og förunautar hans höfðu eftir bagga þeirra og skinnavöru.	Now were their trading-with Skraelings, by them bearing their goods in away in stomachs theirs, but Karlsefni and companions his had after bags theirs and skin-wares.	The trading with the Skraelings resulted in them carrying away their purchases in their stomachs, leaving their packs and skins with Karlsefni.
Fóru þeir við svo búið í burt.	Went they with so settlement to away.	When this was done, they went away.
Nú er frá því að segja að Karlsefni lætur gera skíðgarð rammlegan um bæ sinn og bjuggust þar um.	Now was from therefore to say, that Karlsefni laid made fence strong about farm theirs, and prepared there about.	Now from this is to be told, that Karlsefni had a strong fence made around their farm to be prepared.
Í þann tíma fæddi Guðríður sveinbarn, kona Karlsefnis, og hét sá sveinn Snorri.	In that time bore Guthrid baby-boy, wife Karlsefni's, and called the boy Snorri.	At this time Karlsefni's wife Gudrid gave birth to a baby boy who was named Snorri.
Á öndverðum öðrum vetri þá komu Skrælingjar til móts við þá og voru miklu fleiri en fyrr og höfðu slíkan varnað sem fyrr.	The beginning next winter then came Skraelings to meet with then and were much more than before and had such wares as before.	At the beginning of the next winter the Skraelings came to meet with them in much greater numbers than before.
Þá mælti Karlsefni við konur: "Nú skuluð þér bera út slíkan mat sem fyrr var rífastur en ekki annað".	Then said Karlsefni to women: "Now should you bring out such food as before was demanded, but nothing else".	Karlsefni then spoke to the women: "Now you should bring out whatever food was most in demand, and nothing else".
Og er þeir sáu það þá köstuðu þeir böggunum sínum inn yfir skíðgarðinn.	And when they saw that, they threw they bags theirs the over fence.	And when the natives saw this, they cast their bags over the fence.
En Guðríður sat í dyrum inni með vöggu Snorra sonar síns.	But Guthrid sat in doorway in with cradle Snorri, son hers.	But Gudrid sat in the doorway with the cradle of her son Snorri.
Þá bar skugga í dyrin og gekk þar inn kona í svörtum námkyrtli, heldur lág, og hafði dregil um höfuð, og ljósjörp á hár, fölleit og mjög eygð svo að eigi hafði jafnmikil augu séð í einum mannshausi.	Then carried shadow in doorway, and going there the woman in dark gown, held tightly, and had shawl about head and bright-chestnut of hair, pale and much eyed, so that not had equal eyes seen in any people's-heads.	Then a shadow fell across the doorway, and there came a woman in a dark gown, held tightly, and had a shawl around her head of bright chestnut hair, pale and large eyes, such that no one had seen eyes like them in anyone's head.
Hún gekk þar er Guðríður sat og mælti: "Hvað heitir þú?" segir hún.	She went there by, was Guthrid sat, and spoke: "What called-are you?" said she.	She came to where Gudrud sat, and spoke: "What is your name?", she said.
"Ég heiti Guðríður eða hvert er þitt heiti?"	"I am-called Guthrid, but what is your name?".	"I am called Gudrid, but what is your name?".

The Saga of the Greenlanders (Old Icelandic)

Old Icelandic	Literal	English
"Ég heiti Guðríður", segir hún.	"I am-called Guthrid", said she.	"I am called Gudrid", she said.
Þá rétti Guðríður húsfreyja hönd sína til hennar að hún sæti hjá henni en það bar allt saman að þá heyrði Guðríður brest mikinn og var þá konan horfin og í því var og veginn einn Skrælingi af einum húskarli Karlsefnis því að hann hafði viljað taka vopn þeirra og fóru nú í brott sem tíðast en klæði þeirra lágu þar eftir og varningur.	Then extended Guthrid housewife hand hers to her, that she sit by her, but that bore all together, that then heard Guthrid crash great, and was then woman disappeared, and in therefore was also slain one Skraeling from one houseman Karlsefnis, because that he had willed take weapon theirs, and went now away that swiftly, but clothing theirs laid there left and goods.	Then Gudrid the housewife extended her hand to her, to sit by her, but then there was a great crash, and the woman disappeared, at that moment one of the natives had been killed by one of Karlsefni's men, because he had tried to take their weapons, and they went away swiftly, but their clothing lay there behind with other goods.
Engi maður hafði konu þessa séð utan Guðríður ein.	No man had woman this seen of Guthrid alone.	No one had seen the woman except for Gudrid.
Nú munum vér þurfa til ráða að taka, segir Karlsefni, "því að eg hygg að þeir muni vitja vor hið þriðja sinni með ófriði og fjölmenni.	"Now should we need to plan to take", said Karlsefni, "Because that I think, that they shall visit will the third they with warlike and many.	"Now we need to make a plan", said Karlsefni, "because I think that they will visit us a third time with hostility and in many numbers.
Nú skulum vér taka það ráð að tíu menn fari fram á nes þetta og sýni sig þar en annað lið vort skal fara í skóg og höggva þar rjóður fyrir nautfé vort þá er liðið kemur framúr skóginum.	Now should we take that plan, that ten men go from to headland this and show themselves there, while second team ours shall go into forest and strike there clearing for cattle ours, then as team come from out forest.	Now shall we follow this plan, that ten men will go out on this headland and show themselves there, while our second team will go into the forest and strike there a clearing for the cattle, then as a team come from out of the forest.
Vér skulum og taka griðung vorn og láta hann fara fyrir oss".	We shall also take bull ours and let him go ahead-of us".	We shall also take our bull and let him go before us".
En þar var svo háttað er fundur þeirra var ætlaður að vatn var öðru megin en skógur á annan veg.	But there was so the-way where battle theirs was intended, by water was the-other side, but forest on-the other way.	There where their battle was intended, there was water on one side, and a forest on the other.
Nú voru þessi ráð höfð er Karlsefni lagði til.	Now was this plan taken, as Karlsefni had to.	Now the followed the plan that Karlsefni had made.
Nú komu Skrælingjar í þann stað er Karlsefni hafði ætlað til bardaga.	Now came Skraelings to the place, where Karlsefni had intended to battle.	Now the Skraelings came to the place where Karlsefni had intended to battle.
Nú var þar bardagi og féll fjöldi af liði Skrælingja.	Now was there battle, and fell many of people Skraelings.	Now was there a battle, and many of the Skraeling people fell.

The Saga of the Greenlanders (Old Icelandic)

Old Icelandic	Literal	English
Einn maður var mikill og vænn í liði Skrælingja og þótti Karlsefni sem hann mundi vera höfðingi þeirra.	One man was tall and handsome in group Skraelings, and thought Karlsefni, that he would be leader theirs.	One of them men in their group was tall and handsome, and Karlsefni thought that he was probably their leader.
Nú hafði einn þeirra Skrælingja tekið upp öxi eina og leit á um stund og reiddi að félaga sínum og hjó til hans.	Now had one of-them Skraelings taken up axe one and looked to about awhile and aimed at companion his and struck to him.	Now one of the Skraelings took up an axe and looked around awhile and aimed at one of his companions and struck him.
Sá féll þegar dauður.	So fell then dead.	So he then fell dead.
Þá tók sá hinn mikli maður við öxinni og leit á um stund og varp henni síðan á sjóinn sem lengst mátti hann.	Then took so the tall man to axe and looked to about awhile and threw he then to sea, as long as-may he.	Then the tall man took the axe and looked around for awhile, and then he thew it into the sea as far as he could.
En síðan flýja þeir á skóginn svo hver sem fara mátti og lýkur þar nú þeirra viðskiptum.	But afterwards fled they to woods, so each as went may, and ended there now their dealings.	After that they fled into the woods as fast as they could, and they had no more dealings with them.
Voru þeir Karlsefni þar þann vetur allan.	Were they Karlsefni there that winter all.	Karlsefni and his companions were there all winter.
En að vori þá lýsir Karlsefni að hann vill eigi þar vera lengur og vill fara til Grænlands.	But at spring then declared Karlsefni, that he willed not there be longer and will travel to Greenland.	But in the spring, Karlsefni declared that he did not wish to be there any longer and wished to travel to Greenland.
Nú búa þeir ferð sína og höfðu þaðan mörg gæði í vínviði og berjum og skinnavöru.	Now prepared they journey theirs and had there many quality in vines and berries and skin-wares.	Now they prepared for their journey and they had much good quality vines, berries, and skins.
Nú sigla þeir í haf og komu til Eiríksfjarðar skipi sínu heilu og voru þar um veturinn.	Now sailed they to sea and came to Eriksfjord ship theirs whole and were there about winter.	Now they sailed to sea and their ship came safely to Eriksfjord and they stayed there over the winter.
8	8	8
Nú tekst umræða að nýju um Vínlandsferð því að sú ferð þykir bæði góð til fjár og virðingar.	Now took discussion that again about Vinland-voyage, since by that trip seemed both good to wealth and worthiness.	Now the discussion was taken to again about a Vinland voyage, since the trip seemed to bring both wealth and respect.
Það sama sumar kom skip af Noregi til Grænlands er Karlsefni kom af Vínlandi.	That same summer came ship of Norway to Greenland, when Karlsefni came of Vinland.	That same summer a ship came from Norway when Karlsefni came back from Vinland.

The Saga of the Greenlanders (Old Icelandic)

Old Icelandic	Literal	English
Því skipi stýrðu bræður tveir, Helgi og Finnbogi, og voru þann vetur á Grænlandi.	For ship steered brothers two, Helgi and Finnbogi, and were they wintered in Greenland.	The captains were two brothers, Helgi and Finnbogi, and they spent the winter in Greenland.
Þeir bræður voru íslenskir að kyni og úr Austfjörðum.	Those brothers were Icelanders by kin and from Austfjord.	The brothers were Icelanders, from the East Fjords.
Þar er nú til að taka að Freydís Eiríksdóttir gerði ferð sína heiman úr Görðum og fór til fundar við þá bræður Helga og Finnboga og beiddi þá að þeir færu til Vínlands með farkost sinn og hafa helming gæða allra við hana, þeirra er þar fengjust.	There is now to that take, that Freydis Eriksdottir made journey hers home from Gardar and went to meet with then brothers, Helgi and Finnbogi, and propose then, that they journey to Vinland with vessel theirs and have half quality everyone's with her, their which there caught.	Now we turn to Freydis Eriksdottir, who journeyed from here home at Gardar and then travelled to meet with the brothers, Helgi and Finnbogi, to invite them to travel to Vinland with their vessel and have a half share of any profits from it.
Nú játtu þeir því.	Now agreed they accordingly.	They agreed to this.
Þaðan fór hún á fund Leifs bróður síns og bað að hann gæfi henni hús þau er hann hafði gera látið á Vínlandi.	There travelled she to meet Leif, brother hers, and asked, to him give her houses those, which he had made laid in Vinland.	There she travelled to meet Leif, her brother, to ask him to give her those houses which he had made in Vinland.
En hann svarar hinu sama, kveðst ljá mundu hús en gefa eigi.	But he answered the same, said loan would houses, but give not.	But he answered the same as before, he said that he would loan the houses, but not give them to her.
Sá var máldagi með þeim bræðrum og Freydísi að hvorir skyldu hafa þrjá tigi vígra manna á skipi og konur umfram.	So were matters with they brothers and Freydis, that each should have three ten fighting men on ship and women about from.	So were matters between the brothers and Freydis, that each should have thirty fighting men on their ships and women in addition.
En Freydís brá af því þegar og hafði fimm mönnum fleira og leyndi þeim og urðu þeir bræður eigi fyrri við þá varir en þeir komu til Vínlands.	But Freydis drew off for already and had five men more and concealed them, and became they brothers not before to then foreseen but they came to Vinland.	But Freydis broke the agreement straight away and had five extra men, concealing them so that the brothers would not be aware of this until they came to Vinland.
Nú létu þau í haf og höfðu til þess mælt áður að þau mundu samflota hafa ef svo vildi verða, og þess var lítill munur.	Now laid they to sea and had to this said before, that they should together have, if so will be, and this was little difference.	Now they put to sea and had said before that they should be together if they could, which they almost did.
En þó komu þeir bræður nokkuru fyrri og höfðu upp borið föng sín til húsa Leifs.	But though came they brothers sometime before and had up carried possessions theirs to houses Leif's.	Though the brothers arrived sometime before and carried their possessions to Leif's houses.

The Saga of the Greenlanders (Old Icelandic)

Old Icelandic	Literal	English
En er Freydís kom að landi þá ryðja þeir skip sitt og bera upp til húss föng sín.	But when Freydis came to land, then cleared they ship theirs and carried up to houses possessions theirs.	Then when Freydis came to land, they cleared their ship and carried their possessions up to their houses.
Þá mælti Freydís: "Hví báruð þér inn hér föng yður?"	Then spoke Freydis: "Why carried you in here possessions yours?"	Then Freydis spoke: "Why have you carried your posessions in here?".
Því að vér hugðum, segja þeir, "að haldast muni öll ákveðin orð með oss".	"Because that we thought", said they, "That hold would all agreed word with us".	"Because we thought", they said, "that you would keep your agreement with us".
Mér léði Leifur húsanna, segir hún, "en eigi yður".	"To-me lent Leif houses", said she, "But not you".	"Leif lent the houses to me", she said, "not you".
Þá mælti Helgi: "Þrjóta mun okkur bræður illsku við þig".	Then said Helgi: "Scarcely would-be we brothers ill-will with you",	Then Helgi said: "We brothers would scarcely be a match for your ill-will".
Báru nú út föng og gerðu sér skála og settu þann skála firr sjónum á vatnsströndu og bjuggu vel um.	Carried now out possessions and made they cabin and placed they cabin further-from the-sea towards a-lake and settled well about.	They removed their posessions and they made a longhouse further from the sea towards a lake, and settled in well.
En Freydís lét fella viðu til skips síns.	Then Freydis had wood felled for ship hers.	Then Freydis had wood cut to make a load for her ship.
Nú tók að vetra og töluðu þeir bræður að takast mundu upp leikar og væri höfð skemmtan.	Now took in winter, and talked they brothers, that take should up games and would have amusement.	Now winter took, and the brothers talked of taking up games that would bring entertainment.
Svo var gert um stund þar til er menn bárust verra í milli.	So was done about awhile, there until were men brought worse in between.	And so they did for a while, until disagreements arose between them.
Og þá gerðist sundurþykki með þeim og tókust af leikar og öngar gerðust komur milli skálanna. *Og fór svo fram lengi vetrar.*	And then made disagreement with them, and took of games, and none did come between cabins and went so from long winter.	And then was a rift between them, and the activities ceased, and none came or went between their cabins, and so it went all winter long.
Það var einn morgun snemma að Freydís stóð upp úr rúmi sínu og klæddist og fór eigi í skóklæðin en veðri var svo farið að dögg var fallin mikil.	It was one morning early, that Freydis stood up out-of room theirs and dressed and went not in shoes, but weather was such going, that dew was fallen much.	It was early one morning, that Freydis got up and dressed, but did not wear any shoes, but the weather had left much dew fallen on the ground.

The Saga of the Greenlanders (Old Icelandic)

Old Icelandic	Literal	English
Hún tók kápu bónda síns og fór í en síðan gekk hún til skála þeirra bræðra og til dyra.	She took cape husband hers and went into, but then went she to cabin theirs brothers and to door.	She took her husband's cape and went out, and then she went to the door of the brothers' cabin.
En maður einn hafði út gengið litlu áður og lokið hurð aftur á miðjan klofa.	But man one had out gone little before and left door back to middle gap.	One of the men had gone out shortly before and left the door half open.
Hún lauk upp hurðinni og stóð í gáttum stund þá og þagði.	She closed up door and stood in doorway awhile then and silent.	She closed the door and stood silently in the doorway awhile.
En Finnbogi lá innstur í skálanum og vakti.	But Finnbogi lay inside in cabin and awoke.	Finnbogi lay inside the cabin and awoke.
Hann mælti: "Hvað viltu hingað Freydís?"	He said: "What will-you here, Freydis?".	He said: "What do you want here Freydis?".
Hún svarar: "Eg vil að þú standir upp og gangir út með mér og vil eg tala við þig".	She answered: "I will, that you stand up and go out with me, and will I speak with you".	She answered: "I want you to get up and come outside, and I want to speak with you".
Svo gerir hann.	So did he.	So he did.
Þau ganga að tré er lá undir skálavegginum og settust þar niður.	They went to tree, that lay near cabins, and sat there down.	They went to a tree that lay near the cabins, and there sat down.
"Hversu líkar þér?" segir hún.	"How like you?" said she.	"How do you like it here?" she said.
Hann svarar: "Góður þykir mér landskostur en illur þykir mér þústur sá er vor í milli er því að eg kalla ekki hafa til orðið".	He answered: "Good think me land-benefits, but ill think me discord so, that sprung to between as, for I call not have to word".	He answered: "I think the land here has much benefit, but I don't like the ill feeling that has arisen between us, as I have no words for it".
Þá segir þú sem er, segir hún,	"Then say you as is", said she,	"What you say is true", she said,
"og svo þykir mér. En það er erindi mitt á þinn fund að eg vildi kaupa skipum við ykkur bræður því að þið hafið meira skip en eg og vildi eg í brott héðan".	"And so think I. But that which business mine to you find, that I will purchase ship with you brothers, because that you have more ship than I, and will I to away hence".	"And I agree. But my purpose in meeting with you, is that I wish to buy yours and your brother's ship, because you have more ship than I, and I wish to leave soon".
Það mun eg láta gangast, segir hann, "ef þér líkar þá vel".	"That should I let go", said he, "If you like then well".	"That I could agree to", he said, "If that pleases you".
Nú skilja þau við það.	Now separated they with that,	Now with that they separated,

The Saga of the Greenlanders (Old Icelandic)

Old Icelandic	Literal	English
Gengur hún heim en Finnbogi til hvílu sinnar.	went she home, and Finnbogi to bed his.	and she went home, and Finnbogi to his bed.
Hún stígur upp í rúmið köldum fótum og vaknar hann Þorvarður við og spyr hví að hún væri svo köld og vot.	She climbed up into room cold feet, and awoke he Thorvald to and asked, why that she was so cold and wet.	She climbed up into the room with cold feet, and Thorvard woke and asked why she was so cold and wet.
Hún svarar með miklum þjósti: "Eg var gengin", segir hún, "til þeirra bræðra að fala skip að þeim og vildi eg kaupa meira skip. En þeir urðu við það svo illa að þeir börðu mig og léku sárlega en þú, vesæll maður, munt hvorki vilja reka minnar skammar né þinnar og mun eg það nú finna að eg er í brottu af Grænlandi og mun eg gera skilnað við þig utan þú hefnir þessa".	She answered with much vehemence: "I was gone", said she, "To the brothers to bargain ship of them, and wished I purchase bigger ship. But they became with that so bad, that they beat me and played woundingly, but you, miserable man, would neither will expel my shame nor yours, and should I that now find, that I am in gone from Greenland, and should I make separate with you, outside-of you avenge this".	She answered vehemently: "I was gone", she said, "to the brothers to purchase their ship from them, and wished I to buy a bigger ship. With that they became so angry, that they beat me, and struck me woundingly, but you, miserable man, will neither expel my shame or yours, and if that's the case, then I will leave Greenland, and divorce you, unless you avenge this".
Og nú stóðst hann eigi átölur hennar og bað menn upp standa sem skjótast og taka vopn sín. Og svo gera þeir og fara þegar til skála þeirra bræðra og gengu inn að þeim sofundum og tóku þá og færðu í bönd og leiddu svo út hvern sem bundinn var en Freydís lét drepa hvern sem út kom.	And now stood he not reproaches hers and ordered men up stand while quickly and take weapons theirs, And so did they and went straightaway to cabin they brothers and went in by them sleeping and took then and went in binding and lead so out each, who bound was. Then Freydis had killled each, who out came.	And now, unable to withstand her reproaches, he ordered that the men get up quickly and get their weapons, And so they did, travelling straightaway to the brothers' cabin, and went in while they were sleeping, took them, bound them, and led them outside as they were bound. Then Freydis had each one killed as they came out.
Nú voru þar allir karlar drepnir en konur voru eftir og vildi engi þær drepa.	Now were there all men killed, but women were left, and willed none they kill.	Now all the men were killed, there remained the women, but no one wanted to kill them.
Þá mælti Freydís: "Fái mér öxi í hönd".	Then said Freydis: "Give me axe into hand".	Then Freydis said: "Give me the axe in my hand".
Svo var gert. Síðan vegur hún að konum þeim fimm er þar voru og gekk af þeim dauðum.	So was done. Then slayed she that women they five, who there were, and went of them dead.	So was it done. Then she slayed the five women who were there, and all of them were dead.

The Saga of the Greenlanders (Old Icelandic)

Old Icelandic	Literal	English
Nú fóru þau til skála síns eftir það hið illa verk og fannst það eitt á að Freydís þóttist allvel hafa um ráðið og mælti við félaga sína: "Ef oss verður auðið að koma til Grænlands", segir hún, "þá skal eg þann mann ráða af lífi er segir frá þessum atburðum.	Now went they to cabin theirs after that the evil work, and found that one all, that Freydis thought all-well have about resolved, and said to companions hers: "If we worth fated to come to Greenland", said she, "Then shall I then men rule of life, who says from these events.	Now they went back to their cabin after that evil work, and they all found that Freydis thought all was well done, and she spoke to her companions: "If we are fated to return to Greenland", she said, "Then I shall have killed any man who says anything about these events.
Nú skulum vér það segja að þau búi hér eftir þá er vér förum í brott".	Now should we this say, that they remained here behind, when were we travelling to away".	Now shall we say of this that they remained here, when we travelled away".
Nú bjuggu þeir skipið snemma um vorið, það er þeir bræður höfðu átt, með þeim öllum gæðum er þau máttu til fá og skipið bar, sigla síðan í haf og urðu vel reiðfara og komu í Eiríksfjörð skipi sínu snemma sumars.	Now readied they ship early about spring, that was the brothers had had, with them all quality, that they may to get and ship carry, sailed after to sea and became well voyage and came to Eriksfjord ship theirs early summer.	Early in the spring they prepared the ship which the brothers had owned, with all the goods that the ship could carry, then afterwards sailed to sea and they had a good voyage and their ship came into Eriksfjord early in the summer.
Nú var þar Karlsefni fyrir og hafði albúið skip sitt til hafs og beið byrjar og er það mál manna að eigi mundi auðgara skip gengið hafa af Grænlandi en það er hann stýrði.	Now was there Karlsefni already and had prepared ship his to sea and waited begin, and is that said men, that not would richer ship go sea off Greenland but that, which he steered.	Karlsefni was there already, and had his ship all prepared for sea, waiting for a favourable wind, and it was said that none would go to sea with a richer ship from Greenland than that which he captained.
9	9	9
Freydís fór nú til bús síns því að það hafði staðið meðan óskatt.	Freydis travelled now to dwelling hers, for as that had stood meantime uninjured.	Freydis travelled now to her farm, which withstood her absence without injury.
Hún fékk mikinn feng fjár öllu föruneyti sínu því að hún vildi leyna láta ódáðum sínum.	She gave great gifts wealth all companions hers, for that she would conceal let dishonour hers.	She gave great gifts of wealth to all her companions, so that she could conceal her dishonour.
Situr hún nú í búi sínu.	Sat she now in house hers.	She remained at her farm.
Eigi urðu allir svo haldinorðir að þegðu yfir ódáðum þeirra eða illsku að eigi kæmi upp um síðir.	Not became all so held-words, by silence over dishonour theirs or evil, that not came up about eventually.	Not all words were held in silence over their dishonour or evil, that didn't come up eventually.
Nú kom þetta upp um síðir fyrir Leif bróður hennar og þótti honum þessi saga allill.	Now came this up about eventually before Leif, brother hers, and thought he this story evil.	Now this came up before Leif, her brother, and he thought this story was most evil.

The Saga of the Greenlanders (Old Icelandic)

Old Icelandic	Literal	English
Þá tók Leifur þrjá menn af liði þeirra Freydísar og píndi þá til sagna um þenna atburð allan jafnsaman og var með einu móti sögn þeirra.	Then took Leif three men of band theirs Freydis and tortured then to say about these events all equally, and was with one towards story theirs.	Then Leif took three men from Freydis's company and tortured them to talk about those events, they were all equal and as one in their telling.
"Eigi nenni eg", segir Leifur, "að gera það að við Freydísi systur mína sem hún væri verð en spá mun eg þeim þess að þeirra afkvæmi mun lítt að þrifum verða".	"Not bother I", said Leif, "To do that to Freydis, sister mine, which she would deserve, but prophecy should I that these, by their offspring should little by thriving be".	"I am not the one", said Leif, "to do to Freydis, my sister, that which she deserves, but I should prophecise this, that their offspring shall little thriving become".
Nú leið það svo fram að öngum þótti um þau vert þaðan í frá nema ills.	Now laid that so from, that none thought about them worthy there in from taking ill.	Now as it happened, none thought anything of them except evil.
Nú er að segja frá því er Karlsefni býr skip sitt og sigldi í haf. Honum fórst vel og kom til Noregs með heilu og höldnu og sat þar um veturinn og seldi varning sinn og hafði þar gott yfirlæti og þau bæði hjón af hinum göfgustum mönnum í Noregi. En um vorið eftir bjó hann skip sitt til Íslands.	Now is to say from therefore, when Karlsefni prepared ship his and sailed to sea. He travelled well and came to Norway with whole and safe and sat there about winter and sold wares his and had there benefit respectable and they both couple of the respectable people in Norway, but about spring after prepared he ship his to Iceland.	Now to turn to Karlsefni, he prepared his ship and sailed to sea. He travelled well and came to Norway safe an well, and remained there over the winter and sold his goods, and both him and his wife were treated well by the noble people in Norway, and after about spring, he prepared his ship for Iceland.
Og er hann var albúinn og skip hans lá til byrjar fyrir bryggjunum þá kom þar að honum Suðurmaður einn, ættaður af Brimum úr Saxlandi. Hann falar af Karlsefni húsasnotru hans.	And when he was ready and ship his lay to fair-wind for bridge, then came there to him southern-man one, descended from Bremen of Saxony. He bargained-for that Karlsefni carved decoration his.	And when he was ready and his ship waited for a fair wind on the gangways, then came a southern man, descended from Bremen of Saxony. He asked Karlsefni to sell him the carved decoration on the prow.
"Eg vil eigi selja", sagði hann.	"I will not sell", said he.	"I don't care to sell it", he said.
"Eg mun gefa þér við hálfa mörk gulls", segir Suðurmaður.	"I would give you to half mark gold", said southern-man.	"I'll give you half a mark of gold for it", said the southern man.
Karlsefni þótti vel við boðið og keyptu síðan.	Karlsefni thought well with offer, and sold afterwards.	Karlsefni thought this was a good offer, and then sold it.

The Saga of the Greenlanders (Old Icelandic)

Old Icelandic	Literal	English
Fór Suðurmaður í burt með húsasnotruna en Karlsefni vissi eigi hvað tré var.	Went southern-man to away with carved-decoration, but Karlsefni knew not, what wood was.	The southern man went away with his carved decoration, but Karlsefni did not know what wood it was made of.
En það var mösur kominn af Vínlandi.	But that was burl-wood, coming from Vinland.	But it was made of burl wood, which came from Vinland.
Nú siglir Karlsefni í haf og kom skipi sínu fyrir norðan land í Skagafjörð og var þar upp sett skip hans um veturinn.	Now sailed Karlsefni to sea and came ship his for north land to Skagafjord, and was there up set ship his about winter.	Now Karlsefni sailed to sea and his ship came to the north of the land to Skagafjord, and he set up his ship there for the winter.
En um vorið keypti hann Glaumbæjarland og gerði bú á og bjó þar meðan hann lifði og var hið mesta göfugmenni og er mart manna frá honum komið og Guðríði konu hans og góður ættbogi.	Then about spring bought he Glaumbær and made dwelling on and lived there, long-as he lived, and was the most greatest, and which many people from him came and Guthrid, wife his, and good descendents.	Then in the spring he purchased land at Glaumbaer and made a farm there, as long as he lived, and was the the most respected, and many pepople are came from him and his wife Gudrid, with good descendents.
Og er Karlsefni var andaður tók Guðríður við búsvarðveislu og Snorri son hennar er fæddur var á Vínlandi.	And when Karlsefni was dead, took Guthrid to farming and Snorri, son hers, who born was in Vinland.	And when Karlsefni died, Gudrid took over the farm with her son Snorri, who had been born in Vinland.
Og er Snorri var kvongaður þá fór Guðríður utan og gekk suður og kom út aftur til bús Snorra sonar síns og hafði hann þá látið gera kirkju í Glaumbæ.	And when Snorri was married, then went Guthrid out and went south and came out returning to house Snorri, son hers, and had he then caused made church in Glaumbær.	And when Snorri was married, Gudrid travelled abroad, and went south, returning to her son Snorri's farm, and he had built a church in Glaumbaer.
Síðan varð Guðríður nunna og einsetukona og var þar meðan hún lifði.	Afterwards was Guthrid a-nun and recluse and was there, long-as she lived.	Later Gudrid became a nun and an anchoress and remained there as long as she lived.
Snorri átti son þann er Þorgeir hét.	Snorri had son that, was Thorgeir named.	Snorri has a son who was named Thorgeir.
Hann var faðir Yngveldar móður Brands biskups.	He was father-of Yngvild, mother Brand Bishop's	He was the father of Yngvild, who was mother to Bishop Brand.
Dóttir Snorra Karlsefnissonar hét Hallfríður.	Daughter Snorri Karlsefnison's was-called Hallfrid.	Snorri Karlsefnison's daughter was called Hallfrid.
Hún var kona Runólfs föður Þorláks biskups.	She was wife Runolf's, father Thorlak Bishop's	She was the wife of Runolf, father of Bishop Thorlak.
Björn hét sonur Karlsefnis og Guðríðar.	Bjorn was-called son-of Karlsefni's and Guthrid's.	Karlsefni and Gudrid had a son called Bjorn.
Hann var faðir Þórunnar móður Bjarnar biskups.	He was father-of Thorun, mother Bjarn Bishop's	He was the father of Thorun, mother to Bishop Bjorn.

The Saga of the Greenlanders (Old Icelandic)

Old Icelandic	Literal	English
Fjöldi manna er frá Karlsefni komið og er hann kynsæll maður orðinn.	Many people were from Karlsefni come, and was he kin-blessed man become.	Many people are descended from Karlesfni, and his was a prosperous clan.
Og hefir Karlsefni gerst sagt allra manna atburði um farar þessar allar er nú er nokkuð orði á komið.	And has Karlsefni made said every people's events about voyages these all, which now is somewhat recited to came.	It was Karlsefni who told of people's events about these voyages, some of which came to words.

Word List *(Norse to English)*

OI = Old Icelandic   ON = Old Norse

Norse	English
A, a	
að	a OI, as OI, at OI, by OI, for OI, from OI, in OI, it OI, of OI, that OI, the OI, to OI
aðrir	other OI, other ON
af	from OI, from OI, from ON, from ON, of OI, of ON, of ON, off OI, off ON, that OI
afkvæmi	offspring OI, offspring ON
afli	strength OI, strength ON
aftr	after ON, back ON, return ON, returning ON
aftur	after OI, back OI, return OI, returning OI
akkeri	anchor OI, anchor ON
akkerum	anchor OI, anchor OI, anchor ON, anchor ON
albúið	all-prepared OI
albúinn	ready OI, ready ON
albúit	all-prepared ON
aldr	age ON
aldri	age OI, age ON
aldur	age OI
alla	all OI, all OI, all ON, all ON
allan	all OI, all ON
allar	all OI, all ON
allill	evil OI, evil ON
allir	all OI, all OI, all ON, all ON
allr	all ON
allra	every OI, every ON, everyone's OI, everyone's ON
alls	all OI, all OI, all ON, all ON
allskonar	all-kinds ON
allt	all OI, all OI, all ON, all ON
allur	all OI
allvel	all-well OI, all-well ON
andaðist	died OI, died OI, died ON, died ON
andaðr	dead ON
andaður	dead OI
andast	die OI, die ON
andist	died ON
andláti	death OI, death ON
andliti	face OI, face ON
andnesi	headland OI, headland ON
annað	another OI, else OI
annan	another OI, another ON, other OI, other ON, second OI, second ON
annar	another OI
annarr	another ON
annars	others' OI, others' ON
annat	another ON, else ON
annt	wish OI, wish ON
arnlaugr	Arnlaug (a name) ON
arnlaugsfjörð	Arnlaugsfjord (a place) OI, Arnlaugsfjord (a place) ON
arnlaugur	Arnlaug (a name) OI
at	a ON, as ON, at ON, by ON, for ON, in ON, it ON, of ON, that ON, the ON, to OI, to ON
atburð	events OI, events ON
atburði	events OI, events ON
atburðum	events OI, events ON
auðgara	richer OI, richer ON
auðið	fated OI
auðit	fated ON
augu	eyes OI, eyes ON
augunum	eyes OI, eyes ON
austan	east OI, east ON
austfjörðum	Austfjord (a place) OI, Austfjord (a place) ON
austmaðr	eastern-man ON
austmaður	eastern-man OI
austr	eastern ON
austur	eastern OI

Word List (Norse to English)

Norse	English

Á, á

Norse	English
á	all OI, all ON, at OI, at ON, at-the OI, at-the ON, by ON, for OI, for ON, have OI, have ON, in OI, in ON, of OI, of ON, on OI, on ON, on-the ON, the OI, the ON, then OI, then ON, to OI, to ON, towards OI, towards ON
áðr	before ON, return ON
áður	before OI, return OI
ágætt	fine OI, fine ON
ákafast	fast OI, fast ON
ákaflega	extremely OI
ákafliga	extremely ON, very ON
ákveðin	agreed OI, agreed ON
álftafirði	Alftafjord (a place) OI, Alftafjord (a place) ON
álftafjörð	Alftafjord (a place) OI, Alftafjord (a place) ON
ámæli	reproach OI, reproach OI, reproach ON, reproach ON
ána	river OI, river ON
ánni	river OI, river ON
ásvalds	Asvald (a name) OI, Asvald (a name) ON
átölur	reproaching OI, reproaching ON
átt	had OI, had ON
átta	eight OI, eight ON
átti	had OI, had ON, married OI, married ON
áttir	direction OI

Æ, æ

Norse	English
ætla	suppose OI, suppose ON, supposed OI, supposed ON
ætlað	intend OI, intended OI
ætlaði	intended OI, intended ON, supposed OI, supposed ON
ætlaðr	intended ON
ætlaður	intended OI
ætlat	intend ON, intended ON
ætluðu	intended OI, intended ON, supposed OI, supposed ON
ættaðr	descended ON
ættaður	descended OI
ættbogi	descendents OI, descendents ON
ættir	direction ON

B, b

Norse	English
bað	asked OI, asked ON, bid OI, bid ON
báðum	both OI, both ON
bæ	dwelling OI, dwelling ON
bæði	both OI, both ON
bæjar	farm OI, farm ON
bænum	dwelling OI, dwelling ON
bærist	bearing OI, bearing ON
bættu	repaired OI, repaired ON
bagga	bags OI, bags ON
bakborða	larboard-side OI, larboard-side ON
baki	back OI, back ON
bana	death OI, death ON
bannaði	banned OI, banned ON
bar	bear OI, bear ON, boar OI, bore OI, bore ON, carried ON
bardaga	battle OI, battle ON
bardagar	battle OI, battle ON
bardagi	battle OI, battle ON
bárðarson	Son-of-Bard (a name) OI, Son-of-Bard (a name) ON
barnæsku	childhood OI, childhood ON

Word List (Norse to English)

Norse	English
báru	bearing OI, bearing ON, bore OI, bore ON, brought OI, brought ON
báruð	carried OI, carried ON
bárust	bore OI, bore ON
báti	boat OI, boat ON, boats OI, boats ON
bátinn	boat OI, boat ON
bátr	boat ON
bauð	bid ON, invited OI
beið	waited OI, waited ON
beiddi	propose OI, propose ON
beina	assist OI, assist ON
beitim	apply ON
beitum	apply OI
bekkinn	bench OI, bench ON
bekknum	bench OI, bench ON
belja	bellowing OI, bellowing ON
bera	bear OI, bear ON, bore OI, bore ON, unload OI, unload ON
berjum	berries OI, berries ON
best	best OI
betr	better ON
betra	better OI, better ON
betur	better OI
bezt	best ON
bið	bid OI
bíða	wait OI, wait ON
biðk	bid ON
biskup	bishop OI, bishop ON
biskups	the-bishop OI, the-bishop ON
biskupsstóll	bishop's-seat OI, bishop's-seat ON
bjarg	rock OI, rock ON
bjarna	Bjarni (a name) OI, Bjarni (a name) ON
bjarnar	Bear's (a name) OI, Bear's (a name) ON
bjarni	Bjarni (a name) OI, Bjarni (a name) ON
bjart	bright OI, bright ON
bjó	dwelt OI, dwelt ON, lived OI, lived ON, prepared OI, prepared ON
bjóða	bid OI, bid ON, invite OI, invite ON
björn	Bjorn (a name) OI, Bjorn (a name) ON
bjóst	prepared OI, prepared OI, prepared ON, prepared ON
bjuggu	dwelt OI, dwelt ON, lived OI, lived ON, prepared OI, prepared ON, settled OI, settled ON, settles OI
bjuggust	prepared OI, prepared ON
bláserkr	Blaserkur (a place) ON
bláserkur	Blaserkur (a place) OI
boðið	bid OI
boðit	bid ON
böggunum	bags OI, bags ON
bönd	binding OI, binding ON
bónda	hunsband's ON, husband OI, husband ON, husband's OI, the-Farmer OI, the-farmer ON
bóndi	Farmer (a nickname) OI, Farmer ON, husband OI, husband ON, the-Farmer OI, the-Farmer ON
borð	board OI, board ON
börðu	beat OI, beat ON
borgarfirði	Borgafjord (a place) OI, Borgafjord (a place) ON
borið	bore OI
borit	bore ON
börn	children OI, children ON
botn	bottom-of OI, bottom-of ON
brá	drew OI, drew ON, prepared OI, prepared ON
bræðr	brothers ON
bræðra	brothers OI, brothers ON
bræðrum	brothers OI, brothers ON
bræður	brothers OI

Word List (Norse to English)

Norse	English	Norse	English
brakaði	creaked OI, creaked ON	búi	farm OI, farm ON, settled OI, settled ON, settlement OI, settlement ON
brands	Brand (a name) OI, Brand (a name) ON		
brátt	soon OI, soon OI, soon ON, soon ON	búið	prepare OI, prepare ON, prepared OI, settlement OI
brattahlíð	Brattahlid (a place) OI, Brattahlid (a place) ON	búin	ready OI, ready ON
brattahlíðar	Brattahlid (a place) OI, Brattahlid (a place) ON	búinn	ready OI, ready ON
brattleitr	steep-looking ON	búit	prepared ON, settlement ON
brattleitur	steep-looking OI	bundinn	bound OI, bound ON
braut	away OI, away ON	búnir	prepared OI, prepared ON, ready OI, ready ON
breiðabólstað	upholstery OI, upholstery ON		
breiðafirði	Breidafjord (a place) OI, Breidafjord (a place) ON	búnyt	milk-products OI, milk-products ON
breiðafjarðar	Breidafjord (a place) OI, Breidafjord (a place) ON	burt	away OI, away ON
		bús	home OI, home ON, settlement OI, settlement ON
breiðafjörð	Breidafjord (a place) OI, Breidafjord (a place) ON	bústað	abode OI, abode ON
		búsvarðveislu	farming OI
		búsvarðveizlu	farming ON
brest	crash OI, crash ON	byggð	settlement OI, settlement ON
brimum	Bremen (a place) OI, Bremen (a place) ON	byggðir	dwellings OI, dwellings ON
bróðir	brother OI, brother ON	byggilegast	dwelling OI
bróður	brother OI, brother ON	byggiligast	dwelling ON
brot	away ON	byggja	settle OI, settle ON
brott	away OI, away ON	byggjanda	habitable ON
brottu	gone OI, gone ON	byggjandi	habitable OI
brúðhlaup	wedding OI	byggjum	inhabit OI, inhabit ON
brúðlaup	wedding ON	byggt	settled OI, settled ON
brugðu	brought OI, brought ON	byr	fair-wind OI, fair-wind ON, wind ON
brutu	broke OI, broke ON		
bryggjum	bridge OI, bridge ON	býr	prepared OI, prepared ON
bryggjunum	bridge OI, bridge ON	byrðar	burdens OI, burdens ON
bú	settlement OI, settlement ON	byri	fair-wind OI, fair-wind ON
búa	dwell OI, dwell ON, laid OI, laid ON, prepare OI, prepare ON, prepared OI, prepared ON	byrina	fair-wind OI, fair-wind ON
		byrjar	begin OI, begin ON, fair-wind OI, fair-wind ON
búast	prepared OI, prepared ON, stay OI, stay ON		
búðir	booths OI, booths ON		
buðu	offered OI, offered ON		

D, d

Word List (Norse to English)

Norse	English
dægr	days ON
dægrum	days OI, days ON
dægur	days OI
dag	day OI, day ON
daga	days OI, days ON
dagmála	morning ON
dagmálastað	morning OI
dags	day ON
dauð	dead OI, dead ON
dauðr	dead ON
dauðum	dead OI, dead ON
dauður	dead OI
deila	share OI, share ON
deilur	disputes OI, disputes ON
dögg	dew OI, dew ON
döggina	dew OI, dew ON
dóttir	daughter OI, daughter ON
dóttur	daughter-of OI, daughter-of ON
dregil	pulled OI, pulled ON
drepa	kill ON, killed OI, killed ON
drepnir	killed OI, killed ON
drepr	failed ON
drepstokki	Drepstokk (a place) OI, Drepstokk (a place) ON
drepur	failed OI
dröngum	Drangar (a place) OI, Drangar (a place) ON
drottinn	master OI
dróttinn	master ON
duga	help OI, help ON
dura	door ON
durum	doorway ON
dvöl	dwelled OI, dwelled ON
dygði	enough OI, enough ON
dyra	door OI
dýra	animals OI, animals ON
dyrin	doorway OI
dyrnar	doors OI
dyrrin	doorway ON
dyrrnar	doors ON
dyrum	doorway OI

E, e

Norse	English
eða	but OI, but ON, or OI, or ON
eðr	or ON
ef	if OI, if ON
efndi	kept OI, kept ON
efnilegsti	promising OI
efniligsti	promising ON
efra	over OI, over ON
eftir	after OI, after ON, behind OI, behind ON, left OI, left ON, remained OI, remained ON
eftirbátr	boat ON, boats ON
eftirbátur	boat OI, boats OI
eg	I OI
eigi	not OI, not ON, not-be OI, not-be ON
eigum	own OI, own ON
ein	a OI, a ON, alone OI, alone ON, one OI, one ON
eina	one OI, one ON
einarr	Einar (a name) ON
einarsfjörð	Einarsfjord (a place) ON
einhverju	one-such OI, one-such ON, some ON
einn	one OI, one ON
einni	one OI, one ON
einsetukona	recluse OI, recluse ON
einþykkr	solitary ON
einþykkur	solitary OI
einu	one OI, one ON
einum	any OI, any ON, one OI, one ON
eirík	Erik (a name) OI, Erik (a name) ON
eiríki	Erik (a name) OI, Erik (a name) ON
eiríkr	Erik (a name) ON
eiríks	Erik (a name) OI, Erik (a name) ON
eiríksdóttir	Eriksdottir (a name) OI, Eriksdottir (a name) ON

Word List (Norse to English)

Norse	English
eiríksey	Eriksey (a place) OI, Eriksey (a place) ON
eiríksfirði	Eriksfjord (a place) OI, Eriksfjord (a place) ON
eiríksfjarðar	Eriksfjord (a place) OI, Eriksfjord (a place) ON
eiríksfjörð	Eriksfjord (a place) OI, Eriksfjord (a place) ON
eiríksson	Son-of-Erik (a name) OI, Son-of-Erik (a name) ON
eirikssonar	Son-of-Erik (a name) OI, Son-of-Erik (a name) ON
eiríksstöðum	Eriksstadir (a place) OI, Eriksstadir (a place) ON
eirikssyni	Eriksson (a name) OI, Eriksson (a name) ON
eiríksvági	Eriksvog (a place) ON
eiríksvogi	Eriksvog (a place) OI
eiríkur	Erik (a name) OI
eitt	along OI, along ON, one OI, one ON
ek	I ON
ekki	not OI, not ON, nothing OI, nothing ON
elnaði	attacked OI, attacked ON
elskað	loved OI
elskat	loved ON
em	am ON
en	and OI, and ON, as OI, as ON, but OI, but ON, than OI, than ON, that OI, that ON, then OI, then ON, while OI, while ON
engar	none ON
engi	no OI, no ON, none OI, none ON, not OI, not ON, nothing OI, nothing ON
engu	nothing ON
engum	none ON
enn	but OI, but ON, still OI, still ON, was OI, was ON, yet OI, yet ON
er	a OI, a ON, am OI, are OI, are ON, as OI, as ON, at OI, at ON, is OI, is ON, that OI, that ON, then OI, then ON, was OI, was ON, were OI, were ON, when OI, when ON, where OI, where ON, which OI, which ON, who OI, who ON
erendi	errand ON
erindi	errand OI
ertu	are-you OI, are-you ON
eru	are OI, are ON, were OI, were ON
eruð	are OI, are ON
erum	we-are OI, we-are ON
ey	island OI, island ON
eygð	eyed OI, eyed ON
eyjar	the-island OI, the-island ON
eyjarinnar	island OI, island ON
eyjólfr	Eyjolf (a name), Eyolf (a name) ON
eyjólfs	Eyolf's (a name) OI, Eyolf's (a name) ON
eyjólfur	Eyjolf (a name) OI
eyjótt	islands OI, islands ON
eyju	island OI, island ON
eyki	animals OI, animals ON
eyktar	mid-afternoon ON
eyktarstað	mid-afternoon OI
eyland	island OI, island ON
eyrar	islands OI, islands ON
eystri	eastern OI, eastern ON

É, é

Norse	English
ég	I OI

F, f

Norse	English
fá	get OI, get ON
faðir	father OI, father ON, father-of OI, father-of ON

Word List (Norse to English)

Norse	English
fæddi	bore OI, bore ON
fæddr	fathered ON
fæddur	fathered OI
færa	bring OI, bring ON, brought OI, brought ON
færði	took OI, took ON
færðu	travelled OI, travelled ON
færi	travel ON
fært	taken OI, taken ON
færu	travel OI
fæti	feet OI, feet ON
fagnað	welcomed OI
fagnat	welcomed ON
fagrt	beautiful ON
fagurt	beautiful OI
fái	give OI, give ON
fala	bargain OI, bargain ON
falar	bargained-for OI, bargained-for ON
fallin	fallen OI, fallen ON
fang	grasp OI, grasp ON
fann	found OI, found ON
fannst	found OI, found ON
far	go OI, go ON
fara	go OI, go ON, travel OI, travel ON, travelled OI, travelled ON
farar	travel OI, travel ON, voyages OI, voyages ON
fari	go OI, go ON, travel OI, travel ON
farið	going OI, travel OI
farit	going ON, travel ON
farkost	vessel OI, vessel ON
farmi	cargo OI, cargo ON
farminn	cargo OI, cargo ON
farmr	cargo ON
farmur	cargo OI
fásinni	remote OI, remote ON
fé	cattle OI, cattle ON
feðgum	father-and-son OI, father-and-son ON
feðr	father ON
fekk	gave ON, got ON, married OI, married ON
fékk	gave OI, got OI
félaga	companion OI, companion ON, companions ON
félagar	comrades OI, comrades ON
fell	fell ON, mountain ON
féll	fell OI, mountain OI
fella	fell OI, fell ON
felldi	fell OI, fell ON
felli	rising ON
félli	rising OI
félögum	companions OI, companions ON
fémunum	goods OI, goods ON
fénað	cattle OI, cattle ON
fénaðr	cattle ON
fénaður	cattle OI
feng	gifts OI, gifts ON
fengi	got ON
fengið	caught OI, got OI
fengist	caught ON
fengit	caught ON, got ON
fengju	got OI
fengjust	caught OI
fengu	gathered OI, gathered ON
ferð	journey OI, journey ON, travel OI, travel ON, voyage OI, voyage ON
ferðar	go OI, go ON, journey OI, journey ON, voyage OI, voyage ON
ferðum	voyages OI, voyages ON
fimm	five OI, five ON
fimmtán	fifteen OI, fifteen ON
finna	find OI, find ON
finnboga	Finnbogi (a name) OI, Finnbogi (a name) ON
finnbogi	Finnbogi (a name) OI, Finnbogi (a name) ON
firðinum	Fjord (a place) OI, Fjord (a place) ON
firr	further OI, further ON
fiska	fish OI, fish ON
fjár	wealth OI, wealth ON
fjarðarkjafta	Fjord-Mouth (a place) OI, Fjord-Mouth (a place) ON

Word List (Norse to English)

Norse	English	*Norse*	English
fjóði	fourth OI	förum	travel OI, travel ON, travelling OI
fjögr	four ON	förunauta	companions OI, companions ON
fjögur	four OI	förunautar	companions OI, companions ON
fjöl	plank OI, plank ON	förunautum	travelling-men OI, travelling-men ON
fjöldi	many OI	föruneyti	companions OI, companions ON
fjölði	many ON	föruneytinu	companions OI, companions ON
fjöll	mountains OI, mountains ON	forvitni	curiosity OI, curiosity ON
fjöllótt	mountainous OI, mountainous ON	föstnuð	betrothed OI, betrothed ON
fjölmenni	many OI, many ON	fóstra	foster-father OI, foster-father ON
fjórða	fourth OI, fourth ON	fóstri	foster OI, foster ON
fjórði	fourth OI, fourth ON	fótr	foot ON
fjörðinn	Fjord (a place) OI, Fjord (a place) ON	fótum	feet OI, feet ON
fjórtán	fourteen OI, fourteen ON	fótur	foot OI
fjöru	tide OI, tide ON	frá	from OI, from ON
fleira	more OI, more ON	frændi	kinsman OI, kinsman ON
fleiri	more OI, more ON	frændum	kinsmen OI, kinsmen ON
fljótast	immediately OI, immediately ON, quickly OI, quickly ON	fram	from OI, from ON, from ON
fló	fled OI, fled ON	framar	from OI, from ON
flokkr	group ON	frammi	from OI, from ON
flokkur	group OI	framstafn	prow OI, prow ON
fluttu	floated OI, floated ON	framúr	from OI
flýja	fled OI, fled ON	fráskili	separated OI, separated ON
flytja	carry OI, carry ON	frásögn	said OI, said ON
fóðr	fodder ON	freydís	Freydis (a name) OI, Freydis (a name) ON
fóður	fodder OI	freydísar	Freydis (a name) OI, Freydis (a name) ON
föður	father OI, father ON, father-of OI, father-of ON	freydísi	Freydis (a name) OI, Freydis (a name) ON
foldar	folds OI, folds ON	friðmenn	peaceful-men OI, peaceful-men ON
fólk	folk OI, folk ON	friðrekr	Fridrek (a name) ON
fölleit	pale OI, pale ON	friðrekur	Fridrek (a name) OI
föng	possessions OI, possessions ON	fróðir	wise OI, wise ON
fór	returned ON, travelled OI, travelled ON	frost	frost OI, frost ON
förinni	voyage OI, voyage ON	fund	meet OI, meet ON, visit OI, visit ON
forlög	fortune OI, fortune ON		
fórst	travelled OI, travelled ON		
fóru	travelled OI, travelled ON		
fórum	travelling ON		

Word List (Norse to English)

Norse	English
fundar	meet OI, meet ON
fundi	meet OI, meet ON
fundið	found OI
fundit	found ON
fundr	battle ON
fundu	found OI, found ON
fundur	battle OI
fylgd	follow OI
fylgð	follow ON
fylgdu	followed OI
fylgðu	followed ON
fylgja	follow OI, follow ON
fylldr	filled ON
fylltur	filled OI
fyndi	found OI, found ON
fyrir	ahead-of OI, ahead-of ON, at-hand OI, at-hand ON, because-of-a OI, because-of-a ON, before OI, before ON, for OI, for ON, for-the OI, for-the ON, present OI, present ON
fyrr	before OI, before ON
fyrra	first OI, first ON
fyrri	before OI, before ON
fyrst	first OI, first ON
fyrsta	first OI, first ON
fýsa	attract OI, attract ON
fýstist	desired OI, desired ON
fýstu	urged OI, urged ON

G, g

Norse	English
gæða	quality OI, quality ON
gæðalaust	without-quality OI, without-quality ON
gæði	quality OI, quallty ON
gæðum	quality OI, quality ON
gæfi	give OI, give ON
gaf	gave OI, gave ON
ganga	go OI, go ON, went OI, went ON
gangast	go OI, go ON
gangir	go OI, go ON
gáttum	doorway OI, doorway ON
gefa	give OI, give ON
gefin	married OI, married ON
gegnt	opposite OI, opposite ON
gekk	going OI, going ON, went OI, went ON
gellis	Gellir (a name), howler OI, Gellir (a name), howler ON
gengið	go OI, gone OI
gengin	gone OI, gone ON
genginn	going OI, going ON
gengit	go ON, gone ON
gengr	went ON
gengu	went OI, went ON
gengur	went OI
gera	did OI, did ON, do OI, do ON, made OI, made ON, make OI, make ON
gerði	did OI, did ON, made OI, made ON, was OI, was ON
gerðist	became OI, became ON, made OI, made ON
gerðu	did OI, did ON, made OI, made ON, make OI, make ON
gerður	made OI
gerðust	did OI, did ON, made OI, made ON
gerir	did OI, did ON, made OI, made ON
gerr	made ON
gerst	made OI, made ON
gert	done OI, done ON, was OI, was ON
gerzt	made ON
gift	married OI, married ON
gjalla	snorting OI, snorting ON
glaumbæ	Glaumbaer (a place) OI
glaumbæjarland	Glaumbaer (a place) OI, Glaumbaer (a place) ON
glaunbæ	Glaumbaer (a place) ON
glóra	The-Sensible (a name) ON

Word List (Norse to English)

Norse	English
góð	good OI, good ON
góðr	good ON
góðra	good OI, good ON
góðu	good OI, good ON
góður	good OI
göfgasti	respectable OI, respectable ON
göfgustum	respectable OI, respectable ON
göfugmenni	greatest OI, greatest ON
gólfið	floor OI
gólfit	floor ON
görðum	Gardar (a place), realm OI, Gardar (a place), realm ON
gott	benefit OI, benefit ON, benefited ON, benefitted OI, good OI, good ON
graðfé	cattle OI, cattle ON
graðungr	bull ON
graðungur	bull OI
grænland	Greenland (a place) OI, Greenland (a place) ON
grænlandi	Greenland (a place) OI, Greenland (a place) ON
grænlands	Greenland (a place) OI, Greenland (a place) ON
grænlandsferðar	Greenland-voyage OI, Greenland-voyage ON
grænlandshaf	Greenland-Sea (a place) OI, Greenland-Sea (a place) ON
grafa	engrave OI, engrave ON
gras	grass OI, grass ON
grasinu	grass OI, grass ON
grávara	grey-skins OI, grey-skins ON
gretti	frowned OI, frowned ON
griðung	bull OI, bull ON
grímhildar	Grimhild's OI
grímhildr	Grimhild (a name) ON
grímhildur	Grimhild (a name) OI
grös	grass OI, grass ON
grunnsævi	shallows OI, shallows ON
guðríðar	Guthrid (a name) OI, Guthrid (a name) ON
guðríði	Guthrid (a name) OI, Guthrid (a name) ON
guðríðr	Guthrid (a name) ON
guðríður	Guthrid (a name) OI
gulls	gold OI, gold ON
gunnbjarnarsker	Gunnbjarnarsker (a place) OI, Gunnbjarnarsker (a place) ON
gunnbjörn	Gunnbjorn (a name) OI, Gunnbjorn (a name) ON

H, h

Norse	English
hæðir	heights OI, heights ON
hætti	stop OI, stop ON, way OI, way ON
hættir	gave-up ON
haf	sea OI, sea ON
hafa	have OI, have ON, having OI, having ON, sea OI, sea ON
hafði	had OI, had ON, had-been OI, had-been ON, married ON
hafgerðingadrápu	sea-poem OI, sea-poem ON
hafgrímr	Hafgrim (a name) ON
hafgrímsfjörð	Hafgrimsfjord (a place) OI, Hafgrimsfjord (a place) ON
hafgrímur	Hafgrim (a name) OI
hafi	have OI, have ON
hafið	have OI, have ON
hafim	have ON
hafs	sea OI, sea ON
haft	had OI, had ON
hagleik	sports OI, sports ON
halda	held OI, held ON, hold OI, hold ON, keep OI, keep ON
haldast	hold OI, hold ON

Word List (Norse to English)

Norse	English
haldi	hold OI, hold ON
haldinorðir	held-words OI, held-words ON
hálfa	half OI, half ON
hálfan	half OI, half ON
hálfr	half ON, half-of ON
hálfur	half OI, half-of OI
hallar	hall OI, hall ON
hallfríðr	Hallfrid (a name) ON
hallfríður	Hallfrid (a name) OI
han	he ON
hana	her OI, her ON, him OI, him ON, she OI, she ON
hann	he OI, he ON, him OI, him ON, it OI, it ON
hans	he OI, he ON, him OI, him ON, his OI, his ON
hár	hair OI, hair ON
hárar	high ON
hárrar	high OI
háseta	men OI, men ON
hásetar	sailors OI, sailors ON
hásetum	sailors OI, sailors ON
hátt	high OI, high ON, loudly OI, loudly ON
háttað	the-way OI
háttat	the-way ON
haukadal	Haukadal (a place) OI, Haukadal (a place) ON
haukdælski	Haukadal (a place) OI, Haukadal (a place) ON
hausti	autumn OI, autumn ON
heðan	hence ON
héðan	hence OI
hef	have OI
hefði	have ON
hefðu	had OI
hefi	have OI, have ON
hefir	has OI, has ON, have OI, have ON
hefnir	avenge OI, avenge ON
heiðið	heathen OI
heiðis	heath OI, heath ON
heiðit	heathen ON
heill	luck OI, luck ON
heilu	whole OI, whole ON
heim	home OI, home ON
heima	home OI, home ON
heiman	home OI, home ON
heita	named OI, named ON
heiti	am-named ON, name OI, name ON, named OI, named ON
heitið	pledged OI
heitir	is-named OI, is-named ON, named OI, named ON
heitit	pledged ON
heldr	held ON, rather ON
heldu	held ON
héldu	held OI
heldur	held OI, rather OI
helga	Helga (a name), holy OI, Helga (a name), holy ON
helgi	Helgi (a name) OI, Helgi (a name) ON
hella	stone-slab OI, stone-slab ON
helluland	Helluland (a place) OI, Helluland (a place) ON
helming	half OI, half ON
helmingr	half ON
helmingur	half OI
helst	preferably OI
helzt	preferably ON
hendi	arm OI, arm ON
hendr	caught ON, hand ON
hendur	caught OI, hand OI
hennar	her OI, her ON, hers OI, hers ON
henni	he OI, he ON, her OI, her ON
heppni	lucky OI, lucky ON
hér	here OI, here ON
herjólfi	Herjolf (a name) ON
herjólfr	Herjolf (a name) ON
herjólfsfjörð	Herjolfsfjord (a place) OI, Herjolfsfjord (a place) ON
herjólfsnes	Herjolfsnes (a place) ON
herjólfsnesi	Herjolfsnes (a place) OI, Herjolfsnes (a place) ON

Word List (Norse to English)

Norse	English
herjólfsson	Son-of-Herjolf (a name) ON
herjólfssonar	Son-of-Herjolf (a name), Son-of-Herjolf's (a name) ON
herjólfur	Herjolf (a name) OI
herjúlfi	Herjolf (a name) OI
herjúlfsnesi	Herjolfsness (a place) OI
herjúlfsson	Son-of-Herjolf OI
herjúlfssonar	Son-of-Herjolf OI
herjúlfur	Herjolf (a name) OI
hesthöfða	Horse-Head (a name) OI, Horse-Head (a name) ON
hestrinn	horse's ON
hesturinn	horse's OI
hét	named OI, named ON, was-named OI, was-named ON
héti	was-named OI, was-named ON
heyrði	heard OI, heard ON
híbýli	dwelling OI
hið	the OI
hin	the OI
hina	the OI, the ON
hingað	here OI
hingat	here ON
hinn	a OI, he OI, of OI, the OI
hinni	of-the OI, the OI
hinu	the OI
hinum	the OI
hirðmaðr	court-man ON
hirðmaður	court-man OI
hítardal	Hitardal (a place) OI, Hitardal (a place) ON
hittu	met OI, met ON
hjá	near OI, near ON
hjó	struck OI, struck ON
hjón	couple OI, couple ON
hjónum	couple OI
hjónunum	couple ON
hluti	part-of OI, part-of ON, things OI, things ON
hniginn	declining OI, declining ON
hnígr	fell ON
hnígur	fell OI
höfð	have OI, have ON, taken OI, taken ON
höfða	headland OI, headland ON
höfðann	headland OI, headland ON
höfðanum	headland OI, headland ON
höfði	head OI, head ON
höfðingi	leader OI, leader ON
höfðu	had OI, had ON
höfga	heaviness OI, heaviness ON
hófsmaðr	moderate-man ON
hófsmaður	moderate-man OI
höfuð	head OI, head ON
höfum	have OI
hogginn	cut-down OI
höggva	fell OI, fell ON, strike OI, strike ON
höggvinn	cut-down ON
höldnu	safe OI, safe ON
hólmgöngu-hrafns	Raven-The-Dueller (a name) OI, Raven-The-Dueller (a name) ON
hólmum	Holm (a place) OI, Holm (a place) ON
hon	she ON
hönd	arm OI, arm ON, hand OI, hand ON
höndum	handed OI, handed ON, hands OI, hands ON
honum	he OI, he ON, him OI, him ON, his OI, his ON, to-him OI, to-him ON
horfa	turn OI, turn ON
horfin	disappeared OI, disappeared ON
hornströndum	Hornstrandir (a place) OI, Hornstrandir (a place) ON
hræddust	frightened OI, frightened ON
hrafn	Hrafn (a name) OI, Hrafn (a name) ON
hrafnsfjörð	Hrafnsfjord (a place) OI, Hrafnsfjord (a place) ON

Word List (Norse to English)

Norse	English
hríð	time OI, time ON
húðföt	skin-cots OI, skin-cots ON
húðkeipa	skin-boats OI, skin-boats ON
hug	thoughts OI, thoughts ON
hugðum	thought OI, thought ON
huggaði	comforted OI, comforted ON
hugganar	comfort ON
huggunar	comfort OI
hún	she OI, she ON
hurð	door OI, door ON
hurðinni	door OI, door ON
hús	houses OI, houses ON
húsa	houses OI, houses ON
húsanna	houses OI, houses ON
húsasnotru	house-besom OI, house-besom ON
húsasnotruna	house-besom OI, house-besom ON
húsfreyja	housewife OI, housewife ON
húsfreyju	housewife OI, housewife ON
húsgerð	house-building OI, house-building ON
húsin	house ON, houses OI, houses ON
húskarli	houseman OI, houseman ON
húss	houses OI, houses ON
hvað	what OI
hvalinn	whale OI, whale ON
hvar	where OI, where ON
hvarf	disappeared OI, disappeared ON
hvarfsgnípu	Hvarfsgnipu (a place) OI, Hvarfsgnipu (a place) ON
hvárigir	neither ON
hvárir	each ON
hvárki	neither ON
hvárt	either ON, how ON, if ON, whether ON
hvasst	stormy OI, stormy ON
hvat	what ON
hver	each OI, who OI
hvergi	neither OI, neither ON
hverju	each OI, each ON
hverjum	each OI, each ON
hvern	each OI, each ON
hverr	each ON, who ON
hversu	how OI, how ON
hvert	where OI, where ON, which OI, which ON
hví	why OI, why ON
hvíldarstaða	resting-place OI
hvíldastaða	resting-place ON
hvílu	bed OI, bed ON
hvítir	white OI, white ON
hvorigir	neither OI
hvorir	each OI
hvorki	neither OI
hvort	either OI, how OI, if OI, whether OI
hýbýli	dwelling ON
hygg	think OI, think ON
hyggja	thought OI, thought ON

I, i

Norse	English
i	to ON
illa	bad OI, bad ON, evil OI, evil ON
illr	ill ON
ills	ill OI, ill ON
illsku	ill-will OI, ill-will ON
illur	ill OI
ilmað	favoured OI
ilmat	favoured ON
in	the ON
ina	the ON
ingólfr	Ingolf (a name) ON
ingólfs	Ingolf's (a name) OI, Ingolf's (a name) ON
ingólfur	Ingolf (a name) OI
inn	a ON, he ON, in OI, in ON, of ON, that OI, that ON, the OI, the ON, then OI, then ON
innan	within OI, within ON
inni	in OI, in ON, of-the ON, the ON

Word List (Norse to English)

Norse	English	Norse	English
innstr	inside ON	jöklanna	mountains OI, mountains ON
innstur	inside OI	jöklar	glaciers OI, glaciers ON
inu	the ON	jöklum	glaciers OI, glaciers ON
inum	the ON	jökull	glaciers OI, glaciers ON
it	the ON	jörð	land OI, land ON
		jörðuð	buried OI, buried ON
		jörundar	Jorund (a name) OI, Jorund (a name) ON

Í, í

í	among OI, among ON, at OI, at ON, ay ON, in OI, in ON, into OI, into ON, is OI, is ON, it OI, it ON, on OI, on ON, to OI, to ON		

K, k

Norse	English
kæmi	came OI, came ON
ísland	Iceland (a place) OI, Iceland (a place) ON
kall	shout OI, shout ON
íslandi	Iceland (a place), Icelander OI, Iceland (a place), Icelander ON
kalla	call OI, call ON
kallaði	called OI, called ON
kallaðr	called ON
íslands	Iceland (a place) OI, Iceland (a place) ON
kallaður	called OI
kallat	called ON
íslenskir	Icelanders OI
kallið	call OI, call ON
íslenskum	Icelander OI
kallim	call ON
íslenzkir	Icelanders ON
kallit	call ON
íslenzkum	Icelander ON
kann	know OI, know ON
íþróttamaðr	excellent ON
kanna	explore OI, explore ON
íþróttamaður	excellent OI
kannað	explored OI
		kannat	explored ON
		kápu	cape OI, cape ON

J, j

		karla	men OI, men ON
		karlar	men OI, men ON
jaðri	Jaeren (a place) OI, Jaeren (a place) ON	karlsefni	Karlsefni (a name) OI, Karlsefni (a name) ON
jafnan	ever OI, ever ON	karlsefnis	Karlsefni's (a name) OI, Karlsefni's (a name) ON
jafndægri	equal-day OI, equal-day ON	karlsefnissonar	Son-of-Karlesfni (a name), Son-of-Karlsefni (a name) OI, Son-of-Karlsefni (a name), Son-of-Karlsefni (a name) ON
jafnmikil	equal OI, equal ON
jafnsætt	as-sweet OI, as-sweet ON
jafnsaman	equally OI, equally ON
jarl	earl OI, earl ON
jarls	earl OI, earl ON, earl's OI, earl's ON	kasta	cast OI, cast ON
játar	accepted OI, accepted ON	kaupa	buy OI, buy ON, purchase ON
játtu	agreed OI, agreed ON	kaupför	purchases OI, purchases ON
jöfnum	even OI, even ON	kaupskipið	merchant-ship OI
		kaupskipit	merchant-ship ON

90

Word List (Norse to English)

Norse	English	Norse	English
keip	canoe OI, canoe ON	*kona*	wife OI, wife ON, woman OI, woman ON
kemr	came ON, come ON	*konan*	woman OI, woman ON
kemur	came OI, come OI	*konar*	all-kinds OI, kinds OI, kinds ON, kinds-of OI, kinds-of ON
kennt	known OI, known ON		
ketill	Ketil (a name) OI, Ketil (a name) ON	*konu*	wife OI, wife ON, woman OI, woman ON
ketilsfjörð	Ketilsfjord (a place) OI, Ketilsfjord (a place) ON	*konum*	women OI, women ON
keypti	bought OI, bought ON	*konur*	women OI, women ON
keyptu	sold OI, sold ON	*kornhjálm*	corn-shed OI, corn-shed ON
kirkja	church OI, church ON	*kost*	advantage OI, advantage ON, choice OI, choice ON
kirkju	church OI, church ON		
kistu	coffin OI, coffin ON		
kistur	coffins OI, coffins ON	*köstuðu*	cast OI, cast ON, threw ON
kjalarnes	Kjalarnes (a place) OI, Kjalarnes (a place) ON	*kostum*	benefit OI, benefit ON
kjölinn	keel OI, keel ON	*kráku*	Crow (a name) OI, crow ON
klæddist	dressed OI, dressed ON	*kristinn*	christian OI, christian ON
klæði	clothing OI, clothing ON	*kristnað*	Christian OI
klofa	gap OI, gap ON	*kristnat*	Christian ON
knarrarbringu	Knarrarbringu (a name) OI, Knarrarbringu (a name) ON	*kristni*	christianity OI, christianity ON
		krossa	cross OI, cross ON
knjám	knees OI, knees ON	*krossanes*	Krossanes (a place) OI, Krossanes (a place) ON
koðránsson	Son-of-Kodran (a name) OI, Son-of-Kodran (a name) ON		
		kunni	could OI, could ON, knew OI, knew ON
köld	cold OI, cold ON	*kunnu*	known OI, known ON
köldum	cold OI, cold ON	*kvað*	said OI, said ON
köllum	call OI	*kvaðst*	said OI, said ON
kom	came OI, came ON	*kváðu*	said OI, said ON
koma	came OI, came ON, come OI, come ON	*kváðust*	said OI, said ON
komi	come OI, come ON	*kvámur*	come ON
komið	came OI, come OI	*kvángaðr*	married ON
kominn	come OI, come ON, coming OI, coming ON	*kvángazt*	married ON
		kveðr	said ON
komit	came ON, come ON	*kveðst*	said OI, said ON, saying OI, saying ON
komnir	coming OI, coming ON		
komst	came OI, came ON	*kveður*	said OI
komu	came OI	*kveldi*	evening OI, evening ON
kómu	came ON		
komur	come OI	*kvikfé*	livestock OI, livestock ON
komust	arrived OI	*kvongaður*	married OI
kómust	arrived ON	*kvongast*	married OI

Word List (Norse to English)

Norse	English
kyni	kin OI, kin ON
kynsæll	kin-blessed OI, kin-blessed ON
kyrrt	still OI, still ON

L, l

Norse	English
lá	lay OI, lay ON
lægðu	lowered OI, lowered ON
lægi	lay OI, lay ON
lætr	laid ON
lætur	laid OI
lág	low OI, low ON
lagði	laid ON, lay OI, lay ON
lagðist	lay OI, lay ON
lágu	laid OI, laid ON, lay OI, lay ON
land	land OI, land ON
landaleitan	land-exploring OI, land-exploring ON
landi	land OI, land ON
landið	land OI, lands OI, the-land OI
landinu	land OI, land ON
landit	land ON, lands ON, the-land ON
landkostr	land-benefits ON
landkostum	land-benefits OI, land-benefits ON
landnámamanns	land-taking-man OI, land-taking-man ON
landnyrðingsveðr	North-East-Wind ON
landnyrðingsveður	North-East-Wind OI
lands	land OI, land ON, lands OI, lands ON
landsins	land OI, land ON
landskostr	land-benefits ON
landskostur	land-benefits OI
landsýn	land-sight OI, land-sight ON
langa	long OI, long ON
langar	long OI, long ON
langt	long OI, long ON
láta	lay OI, lay ON, let OI, let ON, put OI, put ON
látið	laid OI, let OI
látit	laid ON, let ON
lauk	closed OI, closed ON
lauseygr	loose-eyed ON
lauseygur	loose-eyed OI
lax	salmon OI, salmon ON
léði	lent OI, lent ON
leggja	lay OI, lay ON, let OI, let ON
legið	laid OI
legit	laid ON
leið	journey OI, journey ON, laid OI, laid ON, way OI, way ON
leiða	lead OI, lead ON
leiddu	lead OI, lead ON
leif	Leif (a name) OI, Leif (a name) ON
leifi	Leif (a name) OI, Leif (a name) ON
leifr	Leif (a name) ON
leifs	Leif (a name) OI, Leif (a name) ON, Leif's OI, Leif's ON
leifsbúða	Leif's-Camp (a place) OI, Leif's-Camp (a place) ON
leifur	Leif (a name) OI
leikar	sports OI, sports ON
leit	looked OI, looked ON
leita	search OI, search ON, seek OI, seek ON
leitaði	sought OI, sought ON
leitar	sought OI, sought ON
léku	played OI, played ON
lengi	long OI, long ON
lengr	longer ON
lengra	further OI, further ON
lengst	long OI, long ON
lengur	longer OI
lesa	gather OI, gather ON
lestist	injured OI, injured ON
lét	allowed OI, allowed ON, laid OI, laid ON, let OI, let ON
létu	laid OI, laid ON, left OI, left ON, let OI, let ON
leyna	conceal OI, conceal ON

Word List (Norse to English)

Norse	English
leyndi	concealed OI, concealed ON
leystu	loosened OI, loosened ON
lið	company OI, company ON, team OI, team ON
liði	company OI, company ON
liðið	team OI
liðit	team ON
liðs	company OI, company ON
líf	lives OI, lives ON
lifa	live OI, live ON
lifði	lived OI, lived ON
lífi	life OI, life ON
lík	body OI, body ON
líkar	like OI, like ON
líkast	like OI, like ON
líki	body OI, body ON
líkið	body OI
líkin	bodies OI, bodies ON
líkit	body ON
líkum	bodies OI, bodies ON
líst	appears OI
lítill	little OI, little ON
lítilmenni	little-man OI, little-man ON
litla	little OI, little ON
litlu	little OI, little ON
litlum	little OI, little ON
lítt	little OI, little ON
lízt	appears ON
ljá	loan OI, loan ON
ljósjörp	bright-chestnut OI, bright-chestnut ON
lögðu	laid OI, laid ON, lay OI, lay ON
lögtekin	law-taken OI, law-taken ON
lokið	ended OI, left OI
lokit	ended ON, left ON
lönd	land OI, land ON
löndum	lands OI, lands ON
lutu	lent OI, lent ON
lýkr	ended ON
lýkur	ended OI
lýsir	declared OI, declared ON
lýsufirði	Lysufjord (a place) OI, Lysufjord (a place) ON

M, m

Norse	English
má	may OI, may ON
maðr	a-man ON, man ON
maður	a-man OI, man OI
mælt	said OI, said ON
mælti	said OI, said ON, spoke OI, spoke ON, talked OI, talked ON
mætti	may ON
mættu	may OI
mál	language OI, language ON, said OI, said ON
máldaga	agreement OI, agreement ON
máldagi	matters OI, matters ON
máli	speech OI, speech ON
máls	speak OI, speak ON
málum	the-matter OI, the-matter ON
mann	men OI, men ON
manna	man OI, man ON, man's OI, men OI, men ON, men's ON
mannaverk	men's-work OI, men's-work ON
mannavistir	habitation OI
manni	a-man OI, a-man ON, man OI, man ON
manns	man OI, man ON
mannshausi	men's-heads OI, men's-heads ON
mannvirðingar	man-worthiness OI, man-worthiness ON, worthiness OI, worthiness ON
marga	many OI, many ON
margir	many OI, many ON
margt	many ON
markland	Markland (a place) OI, Markland (a place) ON
mart	many OI
mat	food OI, food ON
matar	food OI, food ON

Word List (Norse to English)

Norse	English	Norse	English
mátti	as-may OI, as-may ON, may OI, may ON	mína	mine OI, mine ON
máttu	could OI, could ON, may OI, may ON	mínar	my OI, my ON
		minn	mine OI, mine ON
með	along OI, along ON, between OI, between ON, with OI, with ON	minna	less OI, less ON
		minnar	my OI, my ON
		minni	less OI, less ON
meðan	awhile OI, awhile ON, long-as OI, long-as ON, meantime ON, while OI, while ON	míns	mine OI, mine ON
		mínu	mine OI, mine ON
		mitt	mine OI, mine ON, my OI, my ON
mega	able OI, able ON	mjög	much OI, very OI
megin	side OI, side ON	mjök	much ON, very ON
meinalausan	harmlessly OI, harmlessly ON	móður	mother-of OI, mother-of ON
meira	greater OI, greater ON, more OI, more ON	mögum	stomachs OI, stomachs ON
menn	men OI, men ON	mönnum	men OI, men ON
mér	me OI, me ON, mine OI, mine ON, to-me OI, to-me ON	mörg	many OI, many ON
		morgin	morning ON
		morgininn	morning ON
mesta	most OI, most ON	mörgum	many OI, many ON
mestri	most OI, most ON	morgun	morning OI
miðjan	middle OI, middle ON	morguninn	morning OI, morning ON
miðjökul	Midjokul (a place) OI, Midjokul (a place) ON	mörk	mark OI, mark ON
miðri	middle OI, middle ON	mörkina	trees OI, trees ON
mig	me OI, my OI	mösur	maple OI
mik	me ON	mösurr	maple ON
mikið	great OI, greatly OI, much OI, very OI	mót	against OI, against ON, meet OI, meet ON
mikil	great OI, great ON, large OI, large ON, much OI, much ON	móti	towards OI, towards ON
		móts	meet OI, meet ON
mikill	big OI, big ON, great OI, great ON, large OI, large ON, much OI, much ON, very OI, very ON	mun	could OI, could ON, shall OI, shall ON, should OI, should ON, will OI, will ON, would OI, would ON, would-be OI, would-be ON
mikinn	great OI, great ON		
mikit	great ON, greatly ON, much ON, very ON	mundi	could OI, could ON, would OI, would ON
mikli	large OI, large ON	mundu	should OI, would OI, would ON
miklir	great OI, great ON, large OI, large ON	muni	shall OI, shall ON, should OI, should ON, would OI
miklu	much OI, much ON		
miklum	much OI, much ON		
milli	between OI, between ON	munka	monks OI, monks ON
mín	mine OI, mine ON	munn	mouth OI, mouth ON, mouths OI, mouths ON

Word List (Norse to English)

Norse	English
munr	difference ON
munt	shall OI, shall ON
muntu	shall OI, shall ON
munu	shall OI, shall ON
munuð	shall OI, shall ON
munum	should OI, should ON
munur	difference OI
myndi	should ON
mynni	the-inlet OI, the-inlet ON

N, n

Norse	English
ná	near OI, near ON
náði	got OI, got ON
nær	near OI, near ON, near-the OI, near-the ON
næst	next OI, next ON
næstir	nearest OI, nearest ON
nætr	nights ON
nætur	nights OI
nafn	name OI, name ON, named ON
nafni	namesake OI, namesake ON
náim	near ON
nálguðust	approached OI, approached ON
námkyrtli	gown OI, gown ON
námu	took OI, took ON
nánd	close OI, close ON
nauðsyn	necessity OI, necessity ON
náum	near OI
nautfé	cattle OI, cattle ON
né	nor OI, nor ON
nema	taken OI, taken ON, taking OI, taking ON
nenni	bother OI, bother ON
nenntu	bothered OI, bothered ON
nes	headland OI, headland ON
nesi	headland ON
nesið	headland OI
nesinu	headland OI, headland ON
nesit	headland ON
ness	headland OI, headland ON
niðr	down ON
niður	down OI
nokkuð	any OI, few OI, some OI
nokkur	something OI
nökkur	something ON
nokkurar	some OI
nökkurar	some ON
nokkurir	some OI
nökkurir	some ON
nokkuru	sometime OI
nökkuru	sometime ON
nökkut	any ON, few ON, some ON
noræmn	Nordic OI
norðan	north OI, north ON, northwards OI, northwards ON
norðr	north ON
norður	North OI
noregi	Norway OI
nóregi	Norway (a place) ON
noregs	Norway OI
nóregs	Norway (a place) ON
norrænn	Nordic ON
norrænu	norse OI, norse ON
norrænur	north-wind OI, north-wind ON
nótt	night OI, night ON
nú	now OI, now ON
nunna	a-nun OI, a-nun ON
nunnuvígslu	nun's-vows OI, nun's-vows ON
nýju	again OI, again ON
nýnæmi	new OI, new ON
nyrðra	north OI, north ON

O, o

Norse	English
of	of OI, of ON
ofan	off OI, off ON, on OI, on ON
og	also OI, and OI
ok	also ON, and OI, and ON
okkr	we ON

Word List (Norse to English)

Norse	English
okkur	we OI
orð	word OI, word ON
orði	words OI, words ON
orðið	word OI
orðinn	become OI, become ON
orðit	word ON
orti	wrote OI, wrote ON
oss	us OI, us ON, we OI, we ON

Ó, ó

Norse	English
óbirgir	without-supplies OI, without-supplies ON
óbyggð	settlement OI, settlement ON
ódáðum	dishonour OI, dishonour ON
ófjöllótt	without-mountains OI, without-mountains ON
óforvitinn	no-curiosity OI, no-curiosity ON
ófriði	warlike OI, warlike ON
ógagnvænlegt	uninviting OI
ógagnvænligt	uninviting ON
ókunnugum	strangers OI
ókunnum	strangers ON
ór	from ON, of ON, out ON, out-of ON
ósæbratt	unbroken-sea OI, unbroken-sea ON
óskatt	uninjured OI, uninjured ON
ótal	countless OI, countless ON
óvíða	little-wide OI, little-wide ON
óvitrlig	unwise ON
óviturleg	unwisely OI
óx	grew OI, grew ON

Ö, ö

Norse	English
öðru	other OI, other ON
öðrum	next OI, next ON, other OI, other ON
öll	all OI, all ON
öllu	all OI, all ON
öllum	all OI, all ON
ölnboga	elbows OI, elbows ON
önduðust	died OI, died ON
öndverðum	beginning OI, beginning ON
öngar	none OI
öngu	nothing OI
öngum	none OI
ör	arrow OI, arrow ON
örglast	rises OI, rises ON
örin	arrow OI, arrow ON
örnefni	place-names OI, place-names ON
öxi	axe OI, axe ON
öxinni	axe OI, axe ON
öxna-Þórissonar	Son-of-Oxna-Thori (a name) OI, Son-of-Oxna-Thori (a name) ON
öxney	Oxney (a place) OI, Oxney (a place) ON

P, p

Norse	English
píndi	tortured OI, tortured ON

R, r

Norse	English
ráð	advice OI, advice ON, advised OI, advised ON, counsel OI, counsel ON, plan OI, plan ON
ráða	decide OI, decide ON, plan OI, plan ON, rule OI, rule ON
ráðið	resolved OI
ráðin	agreed OI, agreed ON
ráðit	resolved ON
ráðs	counsel OI, counsel ON
ráðum	counsel OI, counsel ON
ræð	advise OI, advise ON

Word List (Norse to English)

Norse	English
ræddu	advised OI, advised ON, discussed OI, discussed ON
rak	driven OI, driven ON
rammlegan	strong OI
rammligan	strong ON
rauða	the-Red OI, the-Red ON
rauði	Red (a name) OI, red ON, the-Red OI, the-red ON
réð	appointed OI, appointed ON, hired OI, hired ON
réði	leader OI, leader ON
réðst	rode OI, rode ON, went OI, went ON
reið	riding OI, riding ON
reiða	decided OI, decided ON
reiddi	aimed OI, aimed ON
reiðfara	voyage OI, voyage ON
reisa	raise OI, raise ON
reisim	raise ON
reist	raised OI, raised ON
reisum	raise OI
reka	expel OI, expel ON
rekin	driven OI, driven ON
rénuðu	receded OI, receded ON
reru	rowed ON
réru	rowed OI
rétti	extended OI, extended ON
reyðr	rorqual ON
reyður	rorqual OI
reykjaness	Reykjanes (a place) OI, Reykjanes (a place) ON
reyni	tester OI, tester ON
riðr	rode ON
ríður	rode OI
rífastr	demanded ON
rífastur	demanded OI
rjóðr	clearing ON
rjóður	clearing OI
rúmi	room OI, room ON
rúmið	room OI
rúmit	room ON
runnu	ran OI, ran ON
runólfs	Runolf'S (a name) OI, Runolf'S (a name) ON
ryðja	cleared OI, cleared ON

S, s

Norse	English
sá	saw OI, saw ON, so OI, so ON, that OI, that ON, the OI, the ON, this OI, this ON
sækja	sought OI, sought ON
sæti	sit OI, sit ON
sætt	settled OI, settled ON
sætti	agreed OI, agreed ON
safali	sables OI, sables ON
saga	story OI, story ON
sagði	said OI, said OI, said ON, said ON, told OI, told ON
sagðir	said OI, said ON
sagna	say OI, say ON
sagt	said OI, said OI, said ON, said ON
sakir	conviction OI, conviction ON
sama	same OI, same ON
saman	together OI, together ON
samfarir	together OI, together ON
samflota	together OI, together ON
samt	together OI, together ON
sandar	sands OI, sands ON, sands ON
sandinum	sands OI, sands ON
sár	wound OI, wound ON
sárir	wounded OI, wounded ON, wounds OI, wounds ON
sárlega	woundingly OI
sárliga	woundingly ON
sást	looked ON
sat	sat OI, sat OI, sat ON, sat ON
satt	true OI, true ON
sátu	sat OI, sat ON

97

Word List (Norse to English)

Norse	English	Norse	English
sáu	saw OI	síðan	after OI, after ON, afterwards OI, afterwards ON, since OI, since ON, then OI, then ON
saurs	the-Foul OI, the-foul ON		
sáust	looked OI		
saxlandi	Saxony (a place) OI, Saxony (a place) ON		
sé	see OI, see ON, so ON	síðast	last OI, last ON
séð	seen OI	síðasta	last OI, last ON
segir	said OI, said ON, say OI, say ON, says OI, says ON	síðir	eventually OI, eventually ON
		siðvenju	custom OI, custom ON
segja	said OI, said ON, say OI, say ON	sig	herself OI, himself OI, themselves OI
		sigla	sail OI, sail ON, sailed OI, sailed ON, sailing OI, sailing ON
segl	sails OI, sails ON		
seinn	late OI, late ON		
sekr	outlawed ON	sigldi	sailed OI, sailed ON
sekur	outlawed OI	sigldu	sailed OI, sailed ON
seldi	sold OI, sold ON	siglingum	sailing ON
selja	sell OI, sell ON	siglir	sailed OI, sailed ON
sem	as OI, as ON, since OI, since ON, that OI, that ON, which OI, which ON, while ON, who OI, who ON	siglt	sailed OI, sailed ON
		siglufjörð	Siglefjord (a place) ON
		sik	herself ON, himself ON, themselves ON
		sín	hers OI, hers ON, theirs OI, theirs ON, them OI, them ON
senn	same OI, same ON		
sér	he OI, he ON, him OI, him ON, his OI, his ON, the ON, theirs OI, theirs ON, them OI, them ON, they OI, they ON	sína	hers OI, hers ON, his OI, his ON, theirs OI, theirs ON
		sínar	theirs OI, theirs ON
		sinn	he OI, he ON, his OI, his ON, the OI, the ON, their OI, their ON, theirs OI, theirs ON, they ON
sét	seen ON		
setið	sat OI		
setit	sat ON		
setja	set OI, set ON	sinna	hers OI, hers ON, his OI, his ON
setstokka	seat-posts OI, seat-posts ON		
		sinnar	his OI, his ON
sett	set OI, set ON	sinni	his OI, his ON, theirs OI, theirs ON, they OI
settist	sat OI, sat ON		
settu	sat OI, sat ON, set OI, set ON, turned OI, turned ON	síns	hers OI, hers ON, his OI, his ON, theirs OI, theirs ON
settust	sat OI, sat ON	sínu	hers OI, hers ON, his OI, his ON, theirs OI, theirs ON
séu	so OI		
sex	six OI, six ON		
sið	tradition OI, tradition ON	sínum	hers OI, hers ON, his OI, his ON, theirs OI, theirs ON
		sitr	sat ON

Word List (Norse to English)

Norse	English	Norse	English
sitt	his OI, his ON, theirs OI, theirs ON, these OI, these ON	skiljist	separate OI
		skilnað	separate OI, separate ON
situr	sat OI	skinnavara	furs OI, furs ON
sjá	looked OI, looked ON, saw OI, saw ON, see OI, see ON	skinnavöru	skin-wares OI
		skinnvöru	skin-wares ON
		skip	ship OI, ship ON
sjáið	see OI, see ON	skipa	ships OI, ships ON
sjást	looked OI, looked ON	skipborðsins	ship's-berth OI, ship's-berth ON
sjávar	sea ON		
sjóinn	sea OI, sea ON	skipi	ship OI, ship ON, ships OI, ships ON
sjónum	sea OI, sea ON, the-sea OI, the-sea ON	skipið	ship OI
		skipinu	ship OI, ship ON, the-ship OI, the-ship ON
sjór	sea OI, sea ON		
sjóvar	sea OI	skipit	ship ON
skagafjörð	Skagafjord (a place) OI, Skagafjord (a place) ON	skips	ship OI, ship ON, ships OI, ships ON
		skipsins	ship OI, ship ON, ship's OI, ship's ON, ships-his ON
skal	shall OI, shall ON		
skála	cabin OI, cabin ON		
skálanna	cabins OI, cabins ON	skipta	divide OI, divide ON
skálanum	cabin OI, cabin ON	skipti	time OI, time ON
skálavegginum	cabins OI, cabins ON	skiptu	divided OI, divided ON
skalt	shall OI, shall ON	skipum	ship OI, ship ON
skammar	shame OI, shame ON	skipverja	crew OI, crew ON
skammdegi	short-time-of-day OI, short-time-of-day ON	skjaldarins	shield OI, shield ON
		skjóta	launched OI, launched ON
skammt	short OI, short ON		
skapgott	well-tempered OI, well-tempered ON	skjótast	quickly OI, quickly ON
		skkutu	launched ON
skáru	cut OI, cut ON	skóg	forest OI, forest ON
skaut	shot OI, shot ON, stern OI, stern ON	skógar	forests OI, forests ON
		skógi	forest OI, forest ON, forests OI, forests ON
skemmtan	amusement OI, amusement ON		
skemmtanar	entertain OI, entertain ON	skóginn	woods OI, woods ON
		skóginum	forest OI, forest ON
sker	rock OI, rock ON	skógótt	forested OI, forested ON
skerið	rock OI		
skerinu	rock OI, rock ON	skógr	forest ON
skerit	rock ON	skógur	forest OI
skíðgarð	fence OI, fence ON	skóklæðin	shoes OI, shoes ON
skíðgarðinn	fence OI, fence ON	skorti	shortage OI, shortage ON
skildu	knew OI	skortir	shortage OI, shortage ON
skilðu	knew ON		
skilist	separate ON	sköruleg	strong OI
skilja	separated OI, separated ON	skörulegastur	striking OI
		skörulig	strong ON

Word List (Norse to English)

Norse	English	Norse	English
sköruligastr	striking ON	sölvi	Sölvi (a name) OI, Sölvi (a name) ON
skrælinga	skraelings ON	son	son OI, son ON, son-of OI
skrælingar	skraelings ON	sonar	son OI, son ON
skrælingi	Skraeling OI	sonr	son ON, son-of ON
skrælingja	Skraelings OI	sonur	son OI, son-of OI
skrælingjar	Skraelings OI	sótt	sickness OI, sickness ON
skrælingr	skraeling ON	sóttin	sickness OI, sickness ON
skúa	shoes OI, shoes ON	sóttina	sickness OI, sickness ON
skugga	shadow OI, shadow ON	spá	prophecy OI, prophecy ON
skuluð	should OI, should ON	spurði	asked OI, asked ON
skulum	shall OI, shall ON, should OI, should ON	spurðu	asked OI, asked ON
skutu	launched OI, launched ON	spyr	asked OI, asks OI
skyldi	should OI, should ON	spyrja	asked OI, asked ON
skyldu	should OI, should ON	spyrr	asked ON, asks ON
slétt	flat OI, flat ON	stað	place OI, place ON, stood ON
slík	such OI, such ON	staði	parts OI, parts ON
slíkan	such OI, such ON	staðið	stood OI
sló	struck OI, struck ON	staðit	stood ON
smár	small OI, small ON	stærra	larger OI, larger ON
smáskitlegr	dirty ON	stafn	stern OI, stern ON
smáskitlegur	dirty OI	stalli	altar OI, altar ON
snæfells	Snaefell (a place) OI, Snaefell (a place) ON	standa	stand OI, stand ON
snæfellsjökli	Snaefellsjokli (a place) OI, Snaefellsjokli (a place) ON	standir	stand OI, stand ON
snemma	early OI, early ON	stef	stave OI, stave ON
snorra	Snorri (a name) OI, Snorri (a name) ON	stefndu	steered OI, steered ON
snorrasonar	Son-of-Snorri (a name) OI, Son-of-Snorri (a name) ON	sterk	strong OI, strong ON
		sterkr	strong ON
		sterkur	strong OI
		stígr	climbed ON
		stígur	climbed OI
snorri	Snorri (a name) OI, Snorri (a name) ON	stjórn	steering OI, steering ON
snúa	turned OI, turned ON	stóð	stood OI, stood ON
sofna	slept OI, slept ON	stóðst	stood OI, stood ON
soföndum	sleeping ON	stofunni	room OI, room ON
sofundum	sleeping OI	stokki	bed OI, bed ON
sögðu	said OI, said ON	stóli	stool OI, stool ON
sögn	story OI, story ON	stólinn	stool OI, stool ON
sögu	saga OI, saga ON	stólinum	stool OI, stool ON
sól	sun OI, sun ON, the-sun OI, the-sun ON	stórauðigr	wealthy ON
sölvadal	Solvadal (a place) OI, Solvadal (a place) ON	stórauðigur	wealthy OI

100

Word List (Norse to English)

Norse	English
stórilla	greatly OI, greatly ON
stund	awhile OI, awhile ON, time ON, while OI, while ON
stýra	steer OI, steer ON
stýrði	steered OI, steered ON
stýrðu	steered OI, steered ON
stýrir	steer OI, steer ON
styrr	Styrr (a name) OI, Styrr (a name) ON
sú	their OI, their ON
suðr	south ON
suðreyskr	south-islander ON
suðrmaðr	southern-man ON
suður	south OI
suðureyskur	south-islander OI
suðurmaður	southern-man OI
sum	some OI, some ON
sumar	summer OI, summer ON
sumarið	summer OI
sumarit	summer ON
sumars	summer OI, summer ON
sumir	some OI, some ON
sumri	summer OI, summer ON
sund	strait OI, strait ON
sundrþykki	discord ON
sundurþykki	discord OI
svá	so ON, such ON
sváfu	slept OI, slept ON
svara	answer OI, answer ON
svaraði	answered OI
svarar	answered OI, answered ON
svarri	haughty OI, haughty ON
svarta	the-Black (a name) OI, the-Black ON, the-Black's ON
svarti	the-Black (a name) OI, The-Black (a name) ON
svartr	the-Black ON
svartur	the-Black (a name) OI
sveinbarn	baby-boy OI, baby-boy ON
sveinn	boy OI, boy ON
svíney	Sviney (a place) OI, Sviney (a place) ON
svipta	shorten OI, shorten ON
svo	so OI, such OI
svör	answer OI, answer ON
svörtum	dark OI, dark ON
svörum	answer OI, answer ON
sýndist	seemed OI, seemed ON
sýni	show OI, show ON
synir	sons OI, sons ON
sýslur	pursuits OI, pursuits ON
systur	sister OI, sister ON

T, t

Norse	English
taka	take OI, take ON, took ON
takast	take OI, take ON
tala	talk OI, talk ON
talaði	talked OI, talked ON
taldi	talked OI, told OI, told ON
talði	talked ON
taldist	told OI
talðist	told ON
tekið	taken OI
tekit	taken ON
tekst	took OI, took ON
telgja	told OI, told ON
tíðast	swiftly OI, swiftly ON
tíðenda	news ON
tíðendi	tidings ON
tíðinda	news OI
tíðindi	tidings OI
tíðindum	news OI, news ON
tigi	tens OI
tigu	tens ON
til	for OI, for ON, to OI, to ON, towards OI, towards ON, until OI, until ON
tíma	time OI, time ON, times OI, times ON
tíu	ten OI, ten ON
tjaldi	tent OI, tent ON

101

Word List (Norse to English)

Norse	English
tjaldinu	tent OI, tent ON
tög	twenty ON
tögr	twenty ON
tók	took OI, took ON
tóku	took OI, took ON
tókust	took OI, took ON
tólf	twelve OI, twelve ON
töluðu	told OI, told ON
tré	beam OI, beam ON, tree OI, tree ON, wood OI, wood ON
tug	twenty OI
tugur	twenty OI
tvá	two ON
tvau	two ON
tveir	two OI, two ON
tvennar	two OI, two ON
tvo	two OI
tvö	two OI
týndust	lost OI, lost ON
tyrkir	Tyrkir (a name) OI, Tyrkir (a name) ON

Þ, þ

Norse	English
þá	them OI, them ON, then OI, then ON, there OI, there ON, they OI, they ON, when OI, when ON
það	it OI, than OI, that OI, they OI, this OI
þaðan	from-there OI, from-there ON, there OI, there ON
þær	they OI, they ON
þagði	silent OI, silent OI, silent ON, silent ON
þágu	accepted OI, accepted ON
þakkaði	thanked OI, thanked ON
þangað	there OI, there OI
þangat	there ON, there ON
þann	that OI, that ON, the OI, the ON, then OI, then ON, then ON, they OI, they ON, this OI, this OI, this ON
þar	their OI, their ON, there OI, there OI, there ON, there ON, they OI
þat	it ON, it ON, than ON, that ON, they ON, this ON
þau	them OI, them ON, these OI, these ON, they OI, they ON, those OI, those ON
þegar	already OI, already ON, straightaway OI, straightaway ON, then OI, then ON, when OI, when ON
þegði	silence ON
þegðu	silence OI
þeim	that OI, that ON, them OI, them ON, these OI, these ON, they OI, they ON, to ON, to-them OI, to-them ON
þeir	the ON, them OI, them ON, there OI, there ON, they OI, they ON, those OI, those ON
þeira	of-them ON, the ON, their ON, theirs ON, them ON, there ON
þeirar	their ON, there ON
þeirra	of-them OI, the OI, their OI, theirs OI, them OI, there OI
þeirrar	their OI, there OI
þenna	these OI, these ON
þér	to-you OI, to-you ON, you OI, you ON
þess	these OI, these ON, this OI, this ON
þessa	this OI, this ON
þessar	these OI, these ON
þessi	these OI, these ON, this OI, this ON
þessir	these OI, these ON
þessu	this OI, this ON

Word List (Norse to English)

Norse	English
þessum	these OI, these ON
þetta	that OI, that ON, this OI, this ON, thus OI, thus ON
þette	this ON
þið	you OI, you-two OI
þig	you OI
þiggja	receive OI, receive ON
þik	you ON, yours ON
þínir	yours OI, yours ON
þinn	you OI, you ON
þinnar	yours OI, yours ON
þíns	yours OI, yours ON
þit	you ON, you-two ON
þitt	your OI, your ON, yours OI, yours ON
þjóðhildar	Thjodhild (a name) OI, Thjodhild (a name) ON
þjósti	vehemence OI, vehemence ON
þó	though OI, though ON, yet OI, yet ON
þokar	stretches OI, stretches ON
þokur	fog OI, fog ON
þorbjargar	Thorbjorg (a name) OI, thorbjorg ON
þorbjarnardóttur	Thorbjarnardottur (a name) OI, Thorbjarnardottur (a name) ON
þorbjörn	Thorbjorn (a name) OI, Thorbjorn (a name) ON
þorbrands	Thorbrand (a name) OI, Thorbrand (a name) ON
þorbrandsson	Son-of-Thorbrand (a name) OI, Son-of-Thorbrand (a name) ON
þórðar	Son-of-Thord (a name) OI, Son-of-Thord (a name) ON
þórðarsonar	Son-of-Thord (a name) OI, Son-of-Thord (a name) ON
þorfinnr	Thorfin (a name), Thorfin (a name) ON
þorfinnur	Thorfin (a name) OI
þorgeir	Thorgeir (a name) OI
þorgeirr	Thorgeir (a name) ON
þorgerðr	Thorgerd (a name) ON
þorgerður	Thorgerd (a name) OI
þorgesti	Thorgest (a name) OI, Thorgest (a name) ON
þorgestlingum	Thorgest's-Sons (a name) OI, Thorgest's-Sons (a name) ON
þorgrímsson	Son-of-Thorgrim (a name) OI, Son-of-Thorgrim (a name) ON
þóri	Thori (a name) OI, Thori (a name) ON
þórir	Thorir (a name) OI, Thorir (a name) ON
þóris	Thori (a name) OI, Thori (a name) ON
þorláks	Thorlak (a name) OI, Thorlak (a name) ON
þórsnessþingi	Thorsnes-Assembly (a name) OI, Thorsnes-Assembly (a name) ON
þorstein	Thorstein (a name) OI, Thorstein (a name) ON
þorsteini	Thorstein (a name) OI, Thorstein (a name) ON
þorsteinn	Thorstein (a name) OI, Thorstein (a name) ON
þorsteins	Thorstein (a name) OI, Thorstein's OI, Thorstein's ON
þórunnar	Thorun (a name) OI, Thorun (a name) ON
þorvald	Thorvald (a name) OI, Thorvald (a name) ON
þorvaldi	Thorvald (a name) OI, Thorvald (a name) ON
þorvaldr	Thorvald (a name) ON
þorvalds	Thorvald's (a name) OI, Thorvald's (a name) ON
þorvaldur	Thorvald (a name) OI
þorvarðr	Thorvald (a name), Thorvard (a name) ON
þorvarður	Thorvard (a name) OI
þótti	thinks OI, thinks ON, thought OI, thought ON
þóttist	thought OI, thought ON

Word List (Norse to English)

Norse	English
þóttu	thought OI, thought ON
þóttust	thought OI, thought ON
þreifar	feels OI, feels ON
þrem	three OI
þremr	three ON
þriði	thirty OI, thirty ON
þriðja	third OI, third ON
þrifum	thriving OI, thriving ON
þrjá	three OI, three ON
þrjár	three OI, three ON
þrjóta	exhausted OI, exhausted ON
þrjú	three OI, three ON
þroskasamt	developed OI, developed ON
þú	you OI, you ON
þurfa	need OI, need ON, needed OI, needed ON
þurfti	needed OI, needed ON
þurftugir	in-need OI, in-need ON
þurrkanar	dry OI
þurrkunar	dry ON
þústr	discord ON
þústur	discord OI
því	according OI, according ON, accordingly OI, accordingly ON, because OI, because ON, before OI, before ON, for OI, for ON, since OI, since ON, that OI, that ON, therefore OI, therefore ON
þykir	seemed OI, seems OI
þykja	seem OI
þykkir	seemed ON, seems ON
þykkja	seem ON
þýsku	German OI
þýzku	german ON

U, u

Norse	English
um	about OI, about ON, among OI, among ON, at OI, at ON, for OI, for ON
umfram	about-from OI
umráði	counsel OI, counsel ON
umræða	discussed OI, discussed ON, discussion OI, discussion ON, talk OI, talk ON
umræði	discussion OI, discussion ON
undan	away OI, away ON, from OI, from ON, under ON
undarlegum	strange OI
undarligum	strange ON
undir	near OI, near ON, under OI, under ON, up-to OI, up-to ON
ung	young OI, young ON
unga	young OI, young ON
upp	up OI, up ON
uppi	up OI, up ON
urðu	became OI, became ON
utan	except-for OI, out OI, out-of OI, out-travel OI

Ú, ú

Norse	English
úlfs	Ulf (a name) OI, ulf ON
úlfssonar	Son-of-Ulf (a name) OI, Son-of-Ulf (a name) ON
úr	from OI, of OI, out OI, out-of OI
úrigt	irritable OI, irritable ON
út	out OI, out ON, out-of OI, out-of ON
útan	except-for ON, out ON, out-of ON, out-travel ON
úti	about OI, about ON, out OI, out ON
útsynnings	South-West (a place) ON
útsynningsbyr	south-west-wind OI

V, v

104

Word List (Norse to English)

Norse	English
vænn	handsome OI, handsome ON
væri	had ON, was OI, was ON, were OI, were ON, would OI, would ON
væru	had OI
vágs	Vog (a place) ON
vakði	awoke ON
vaki	wake OI, wake ON
vaknar	awoke OI, awoke ON
vakti	awoke OI
valdi	chose OI
valði	chose ON
vant	missing OI, missing ON
vápn	weapon ON, weapons ON
vápnin	weapons ON
var	was OI, was ON, were OI, were ON
vár	been ON, our ON, sprung ON, will ON
vára	going ON
várar	spring ON
varð	was OI, was ON, were OI, were ON
vári	spring ON
varir	aware OI, aware ON, foreseen OI, foreseen ON
várit	spring ON
várn	ours ON
varnað	wares OI, wares ON
varning	goods OI, goods ON, wares OI, wares ON
varningr	goods ON
varningur	goods OI
varp	threw OI, threw ON
varstu	was OI, was ON
várt	ours ON
váru	ours ON, was ON, were ON
várum	we ON
vási	cold-and-wet ON
vaskasti	valiant OI, valiant ON
vát	wet ON
vatn	water OI, water ON
vatnað	water-taken OI
vatnahverfi	Vatnahverfi (a place) OI, Vatnahverfi (a place) ON
vatnat	water-taken ON
vatni	river OI, river ON
vatnið	lake OI
vatninu	lake OI, lake ON
vatnit	lake ON
vatnshorni	Vatnshorn (a place) OI, Vatnshorn (a place) ON
vatnsströndu	beach OI, beach ON
vaxið	growing OI, grown OI
vaxin	grown OI
vaxinn	grown ON
vaxit	growing ON, grown ON
veðr	weather ON, winds ON
veðri	weather OI, weather ON
veðrið	wind OI
veðrit	wind ON
veður	weather OI, winds OI
veg	way OI, way ON
vega	fight OI, fight ON, ways OI, ways ON
veginn	away OI, away ON
vegr	slayed ON
vegur	slayed OI
veiddu	caught OI, caught ON
veiðum	hunting OI, hunting ON
veik	referred OI, referred ON
veit	know OI, know ON
veita	know OI, know ON, lead OI, lead ON, supply OI, supply ON
veitti	supported OI, supported ON
veittu	supported OI, supported ON
vel	well OI, well ON
velkði	drove ON
velkti	drove OI
vér	we OI, we ON
vera	be OI, be ON, being OI, being ON, shall-be OI, shall-be ON, was OI, was ON, were OI, were ON

Word List (Norse to English)

Norse	English
verð	deserve OI, deserve ON
verða	be OI, be ON
verði	be OI, be ON
verðr	worth ON
verður	worth OI
verið	been OI, had-been OI
verit	been ON, had-been ON
verja	protection OI, protection ON
verjast	defend OI, defend ON
verk	work OI, work ON
verra	worse OI, worse ON
vert	worthy OI, worthy ON
vertu	be OI, be ON
vesæll	wretched OI
vesall	wretched ON
vesallegr	poor-wretch ON
vesallegur	poor-wretch OI
vestan	western OI, western ON
vestarlega	westward OI
vestarliga	westward ON
vestr	west ON
vestrætt	westwards ON
vestri	western OI, western ON
vestribyggðar	Vestribyggd (a place) OI, Vestribyggd (a place) ON
vestur	west OI
vesturátt	westwards OI
vetr	winter ON, wintered ON
vetra	winter OI, winter ON
vetrar	winter OI, winter ON
vetri	winter OI, winter ON
vetrinn	winter ON
vetrum	winter OI, winter ON, winters OI, winters ON
vetrvist	winter ON
vetur	winter OI, wintered OI
veturinn	winter OI
veturvist	winter OI
vexti	grown OI, grown ON, well-built OI, well-built ON
við	by ON, in OI, in ON, to OI, to ON, with OI, with ON, wood OI, wood ON
víða	many OI, many ON, widely OI, widely ON
viði	wood OI, wood ON, woods OI, woods ON
viðinn	trees OI, trees ON
viðskiptum	dealings OI, dealings ON
viðu	wood OI, wood OI, wood ON, wood ON
vífilsson	Son-of-Vifil (a name) OI, Son-of-Vifil (a name) ON
víg	killing-of OI, killing-of ON
víga	killing OI, killing ON
vígfleka	battle OI, battle ON
vígra	fighting OI, fighting ON
vika	week OI, week ON
vil	will OI, will ON
vilda	will ON, wished ON
vildi	will OI, will ON, willed OI, willed ON
vildu	willed OI, willed ON
vilið	will ON
vilja	will OI, will ON, willed OI, willed ON, would OI, would ON
viljað	willed OI
viljat	willed ON
viljið	will OI
vill	will ON, willed OI, willed ON, wished OI, wished ON
villtu	will-you ON
vilt	will OI
viltu	will-you OI, will-you ON
vina	friends OI, friends ON
vínber	grapes OI, grapes ON
vínberjum	grapes OI, grapes ON
vinda	wind OI, wind ON
vínland	Vinland (a place) OI, Vinland (a place) ON
vínlandi	Vinland (a place) OI, Vinland (a place) ON
vínlands	Vinland (a place) OI, Vinland (a place) ON

Word List (Norse to English)

Norse	English
vínlandsferð	Vinland-voyage OI, vinland-voyage ON
vínlandsför	Vinland-voyage OI, Vinland-voyage ON
vínvið	vines OI, vines ON
vínviði	vines OI, vines ON
virðingar	worthiness OI, worthiness ON
virðingu	worthiness OI, worthiness ON
vissi	knew OI, knew ON
vissu	knew OI, knew ON
vist	provisions OI, provisions ON
vistar	lodge OI, lodge ON, lodging OI, lodging ON, stay OI, stay ON
vistir	lodging ON, lodgings OI, provisions OI, provisions ON
vistlaus	homeless OI
vistlauss	homeless ON
vísu	know OI, know ON
vit	with ON
vitja	visit OI, visit ON
vitr	wise ON
vitur	wise OI
vöggu	cradle OI, cradle ON
vogs	Vogs (a place) OI
vöknuðu	awoke OI, awoke ON
vöku	awake OI, awake ON
vopn	weapon OI, weapons OI
vopnin	weapons OI
vor	been OI, our OI, sprung OI, will OI
vora	going OI
vorar	spring OI
vori	spring OI
vorið	spring OI
vorn	ours OI
vort	ours OI
voru	ours OI, was OI, were OI
vorum	ours OI
vosi	cold-and-wet OI
vot	wet OI

Y, y

Norse	English
yðr	you ON
yðra	depart OI, depart ON
yður	you OI, yours OI, yours ON
yfir	over OI, over ON
yfirlæti	respectable OI, respectable ON
ykkar	you OI
ykkr	you ON
ykkrar	you ON
ykkur	you OI, you ON, your OI
yngveldar	Yngvild (a name) OI
yngvildar	Yngvild (a name) ON

Ý, ý

Norse	English
ýmisst	either ON
ýmist	either OI

Word List *(English to Norse)*

OI = Old Icelandic ON = Old Norse

English	*Norse*
A, a	
a	*að* OI, *at* ON, *ein* OI, *ein* ON, *er* OI, *er* ON, *hinn* OI, *inn* ON
able	*mega* OI, *mega* ON
abode	*bústað* OI, *bústað* ON
about	*um* OI, *um* ON, *úti* OI, *úti* ON
about-from	*umfram* OI
accepted	*játar* OI, *játar* ON, *þágu* OI, *þágu* ON
according	*því* OI, *því* ON
accordingly	*því* OI, *því* ON
advantage	*kost* OI, *kost* ON
advice	*ráð* OI, *ráð* ON
advise	*ræð* OI, *ræð* ON
advised	*ráð* OI, *ráð* ON, *ræddu* OI, *ræddu* ON
after	*aftr* ON, *aftur* OI, *eftir* OI, *eftir* ON, *síðan* OI, *síðan* ON
afterwards	*síðan* OI, *síðan* ON
again	*nýju* OI, *nýju* ON
against	*mót* OI, *mót* ON
age	*aldr* ON, *aldri* OI, *aldri* ON, *aldur* OI
agreed	*ákveðin* OI, *ákveðin* ON, *játtu* OI, *játtu* ON, *ráðin* OI, *ráðin* ON, *sætti* OI, *sætti* ON
agreement	*máldaga* OI, *máldaga* ON
ahead-of	*fyrir* OI, *fyrir* ON
aimed	*reiddi* OI, *reiddi* ON
Alftafjord (a place)	*álftafirði* OI, *álftafirði* ON, *álftafjörð* OI, *álftafjörð* ON
all	*á* OI, *á* ON, *alla* OI, *alla* ON, *allan* OI, *allan* ON, *allar* OI, *allar* ON, *allir* OI, *allir* ON, *allr* ON, *alls* OI, *alls* ON, *allt* OI, *allt* ON, *allur* OI, *öll* OI, *öll* ON, *öllu* OI, *öllu* ON, *öllum* OI, *öllum* ON
all-kinds	*allskonar* ON, *konar* OI
allowed	*lét* OI, *lét* ON
all-prepared	*albúið* OI, *albúit* ON
all-well	*allvel* OI, *allvel* ON
alone	*ein* OI, *ein* ON
along	*eitt* OI, *eitt* ON, *með* OI, *með* ON
already	*þegar* OI, *þegar* ON
also	*og* OI, *ok* ON
altar	*stalli* OI, *stalli* ON
am	*em* ON, *er* OI
a-man	*maðr* ON, *maður* OI, *manni* OI, *manni* ON
am-named	*heiti* ON
among	*í* OI, *í* ON, *um* OI, *um* ON
amusement	*skemmtan* OI, *skemmtan* ON
anchor	*akkeri* OI, *akkeri* ON, *akkerum* OI, *akkerum* ON
and	*en* OI, *en* ON, *og* OI, *ok* OI, *ok* ON
animals	*dýra* OI, *dýra* ON, *eyki* OI, *eyki* ON
another	*annað* OI, *annan* OI, *annan* ON, *annar* OI, *annarr* ON, *annat* ON
answer	*svara* OI, *svara* ON, *svör* OI, *svör* ON, *svörum* OI, *svörum* ON
answered	*svaraði* OI, *svarar* OI, *svarar* ON
a-nun	*nunna* OI, *nunna* ON
any	*einum* OI, *einum* ON, *nokkuð* OI, *nökkut* ON
appears	*líst* OI, *lízt* ON
apply	*beitim* ON, *beitum* OI

Word List (English to Norse)

English	Norse	English	Norse
appointed	réð OI, réð ON	awoke	vakði ON, vaknar OI, vaknar ON, vakti OI, vöknuðu OI, vöknuðu ON
approached	nálguðust OI, nálguðust ON		
are	er OI, er ON, eru OI, eru ON, eruð OI, eruð ON	axe	öxi OI, öxi ON, öxinni OI, öxinni ON
are-you	ertu OI, ertu ON	ay	í ON
arm	hendi OI, hendi ON, hönd OI, hönd ON		
Arnlaug (a name)	arnlaugr ON, arnlaugur OI		
Arnlaugsfjord (a place)	arnlaugsfjörð OI, arnlaugsfjörð ON		

B, b

English	Norse
arrived	komust OI, kómust ON
arrow	ör OI, ör ON, örin OI, örin ON
as	að OI, at ON, en OI, en ON, er OI, er ON, sem OI, sem ON
asked	bað OI, bað ON, spurði OI, spurði ON, spurðu OI, spurðu ON, spyr OI, spyrja OI, spyrja ON, spyrr ON
asks	spyr OI, spyrr ON
as-may	mátti OI, mátti ON
assist	beina OI, beina ON
as-sweet	jafnsætt OI, jafnsætt ON
Asvald (a name)	ásvalds OI, ásvalds ON
at	á OI, á ON, að OI, at ON, er OI, er ON, í OI, í ON, um OI, um ON
at-hand	fyrir OI, fyrir ON
attacked	elnaði OI, elnaði ON
at-the	á OI, á ON
attract	fýsa OI, fýsa ON
Austfjord (a place)	austfjörðum OI, austfjörðum ON
autumn	hausti OI, hausti ON
avenge	hefnir OI, hefnir ON
awake	vöku OI, vöku ON
aware	varir OI, varir ON
away	braut OI, braut ON, brot ON, brott OI, brott ON, burt OI, burt ON, undan OI, undan ON, veginn OI, veginn ON
awhile	meðan OI, meðan ON, stund OI, stund ON

English	Norse
baby-boy	sveinbarn OI, sveinbarn ON
back	aftr ON, aftur OI, baki OI, baki ON
bad	illa OI, illa ON
bags	bagga OI, bagga ON, böggunum OI, böggunum ON
banned	bannaði OI, bannaði ON
bargain	fala OI, fala ON
bargained-for	falar OI, falar ON
battle	bardaga OI, bardaga ON, bardagar OI, bardagar ON, bardagi OI, bardagi ON, fundr ON, fundur OI, vígfleka OI, vígfleka ON
be	vera OI, vera ON, verða OI, verða ON, verði OI, verði ON, vertu OI, vertu ON
beach	vatnsströndu OI, vatnsströndu ON
beam	tré OI, tré ON
bear	bar OI, bar ON, bera OI, bera ON
bearing	bærist OI, bærist ON, báru OI, báru ON
Bear's (a name)	bjarnar OI, bjarnar ON
beat	börðu OI, börðu ON
beautiful	fagrt ON, fagurt OI
became	gerðist OI, gerðist ON, urðu OI, urðu ON
because	því OI, því ON
because-of-a	fyrir OI, fyrir ON
become	orðinn OI, orðinn ON
bed	hvílu OI, hvílu ON, stokki OI, stokki ON

Word List (English to Norse)

English	*Norse*	English	*Norse*
been	*vár* ON, *verið* OI, *verit* ON, *vor* OI	bodies	*líkin* OI, *líkin* ON, *líkum* OI, *líkum* ON
before	*áðr* ON, *áður* OI, *fyrir* OI, *fyrir* ON, *fyrr* OI, *fyrr* ON, *fyrri* OI, *fyrri* ON, *því* OI, *því* ON	body	*lík* OI, *lík* ON, *líki* OI, *líki* ON, *líkið* OI, *líkit* ON
		booths	*búðir* OI, *búðir* ON
		bore	*bar* OI, *bar* ON, *báru* OI, *báru* ON, *bárust* OI, *bárust* ON, *bera* OI, *bera* ON, *borið* OI, *borit* ON, *fæddi* OI, *fæddi* ON
begin	*byrjar* OI, *byrjar* ON		
beginning	*öndverðum* OI, *öndverðum* ON		
behind	*eftir* OI, *eftir* ON		
being	*vera* OI, *vera* ON	Borgafjord (a place)	*borgarfirði* OI, *borgarfirði* ON
bellowing	*belja* OI, *belja* ON		
bench	*bekkinn* OI, *bekkinn* ON, *bekknum* OI, *bekknum* ON	both	*báðum* OI, *báðum* ON, *bæði* OI, *bæði* ON
		bother	*nenni* OI, *nenni* ON
		bothered	*nenntu* OI, *nenntu* ON
benefit	*gott* OI, *gott* ON, *kostum* OI, *kostum* ON	bottom-of	*botn* OI, *botn* ON
		bought	*keypti* OI, *keypti* ON
benefited	*gott* ON	bound	*bundinn* OI, *bundinn* ON
benefitted	*gott* OI		
berries	*berjum* OI, *berjum* ON	boy	*sveinn* OI, *sveinn* ON
best	*best* OI, *bezt* ON		
betrothed	*föstnuð* OI, *föstnuð* ON	Brand (a name)	*brands* OI, *brands* ON
better	*betr* ON, *betra* OI, *betra* ON, *betur* OI	Brattahlid (a place)	*brattahlíð* OI, *brattahlíð* ON, *brattahlíðar* OI, *brattahlíðar* ON
between	*með* OI, *með* ON, *milli* OI, *milli* ON		
bid	*bað* OI, *bað* ON, *bauð* ON, *bið* OI, *biðk* ON, *bjóða* OI, *bjóða* ON, *boðið* OI, *boðit* ON	Breidafjord (a place)	*breiðafirði* OI, *breiðafirði* ON, *breiðafjarðar* OI, *breiðafjarðar* ON, *breiðafjörð* OI, *breiðafjörð* ON
big	*mikill* OI, *mikill* ON		
binding	*bönd* OI, *bönd* ON	Bremen (a place)	*brimum* OI, *brimum* ON
bishop	*biskup* OI, *biskup* ON	bridge	*bryggjum* OI, *bryggjum* ON, *bryggjunum* OI, *bryggjunum* ON
bishop's-seat	*biskupsstóll* OI, *biskupsstóll* ON		
Bjarni (a name)	*bjarna* OI, *bjarna* ON, *bjarni* OI, *bjarni* ON	bright	*bjart* OI, *bjart* ON
Bjorn (a name)	*björn* OI, *björn* ON	bright-chestnut	*ljósjörp* OI, *ljósjörp* ON
Blaserkur (a place)	*bláserkr* ON, *bláserkur* OI	bring	*færa* OI, *færa* ON
		broke	*brutu* OI, *brutu* ON
boar	*bar* OI	brother	*bróðir* OI, *bróðir* ON, *bróður* OI, *bróður* ON
board	*borð* OI, *borð* ON		
boat	*báti* OI, *báti* ON, *bátinn* OI, *bátinn* ON, *bátr* ON, *eftirbátr* ON, *eftirbátur* OI	brothers	*bræðr* ON, *bræðra* OI, *bræðra* ON, *bræðrum* OI, *bræðrum* ON, *bræður* OI
boats	*báti* OI, *báti* ON, *eftirbátr* ON, *eftirbátur* OI	brought	*báru* OI, *báru* ON, *brugðu* OI, *brugðu* ON, *færa* OI, *færa* ON

Word List (English to Norse)

English	*Norse*	English	*Norse*
bull	*graðungr* ON, *graðungur* OI, *griðung* OI, *griðung* ON	caught	*fengið* OI, *fengist* ON, *fengit* ON, *fengjust* OI, *hendr* ON, *hendur* OI, *veiddu* OI, *veiddu* ON
burdens	*byrðar* OI, *byrðar* ON	childhood	*barnæsku* OI, *barnæsku* ON
buried	*jörðuð* OI, *jörðuð* ON	children	*börn* OI, *börn* ON
but	*eða* OI, *eða* ON, *en* OI, *en* ON, *enn* OI, *enn* ON	choice	*kost* OI, *kost* ON
buy	*kaupa* OI, *kaupa* ON	chose	*valdi* OI, *valði* ON
by	*á* ON, *að* OI, *at* ON, *við* ON	christian	*kristinn* OI, *kristinn* ON, *kristnað* OI, *kristnat* ON
		christianity	*kristni* OI, *kristni* ON

C, c

English	*Norse*	English	*Norse*
cabin	*skála* OI, *skála* ON, *skálanum* OI, *skálanum* ON	church	*kirkja* OI, *kirkja* ON, *kirkju* OI, *kirkju* ON
cabins	*skálanna* OI, *skálanna* ON, *skálavegginum* OI, *skálavegginum* ON	cleared	*ryðja* OI, *ryðja* ON
		clearing	*rjóðr* ON, *rjóður* OI
		climbed	*stígr* ON, *stígur* OI
call	*kalla* OI, *kalla* ON, *kallið* OI, *kallið* ON, *kallim* ON, *kallit* ON, *köllum* OI	close	*nánd* OI, *nánd* ON
		closed	*lauk* OI, *lauk* ON
		clothing	*klæði* OI, *klæði* ON
		coffin	*kistu* OI, *kistu* ON
called	*kallaði* OI, *kallaði* ON, *kallaðr* ON, *kallaður* OI, *kallat* ON	coffins	*kistur* OI, *kistur* ON
		cold	*köld* OI, *köld* ON, *köldum* OI, *köldum* ON
came	*kæmi* OI, *kæmi* ON, *kemr* ON, *kemur* OI, *kom* OI, *kom* ON, *koma* OI, *koma* ON, *komið* OI, *komit* ON, *komst* OI, *komst* ON, *komu* OI, *kómu* ON	cold-and-wet	*vási* ON, *vosi* OI
		come	*kemr* ON, *kemur* OI, *koma* OI, *koma* ON, *komi* OI, *komi* ON, *komið* OI, *kominn* OI, *kominn* ON, *komit* ON, *komur* OI, *kvámur* ON
		comfort	*hugganar* ON, *huggunar* OI
canoe	*keip* OI, *keip* ON	comforted	*huggaði* OI, *huggaði* ON
cape	*kápu* OI, *kápu* ON		
cargo	*farmi* OI, *farmi* ON, *farminn* OI, *farminn* ON, *farmr* ON, *farmur* OI	coming	*kominn* OI, *kominn* ON, *komnir* OI, *komnir* ON
		companion	*félaga* OI, *félaga* ON
carried	*bar* ON, *báruð* OI, *báruð* ON	companions	*félaga* ON, *félögum* OI, *félögum* ON, *förunauta* OI, *förunauta* ON, *förunautar* OI, *förunautar* ON, *föruneyti* OI, *föruneyti* ON, *föruneytinu* OI, *föruneytinu* ON
carry	*flytja* OI, *flytja* ON		
cast	*kasta* OI, *kasta* ON, *köstuðu* OI, *köstuðu* ON		
cattle	*fé* OI, *fé* ON, *fénað* OI, *fénað* ON, *fénaðr* ON, *fénaður* OI, *graðfé* OI, *graðfé* ON, *nautfé* OI, *nautfé* ON	company	*lið* OI, *lið* ON, *liði* OI, *liði* ON, *liðs* OI, *liðs* ON
		comrades	*félagar* OI, *félagar* ON

Word List (English to Norse)

English	*Norse*	English	*Norse*
conceal	*leyna* OI, *leyna* ON	dealings	*viðskiptum* OI, *viðskiptum* ON
concealed	*leyndi* OI, *leyndi* ON	death	*andláti* OI, *andláti* ON, *bana* OI, *bana* ON
conviction	*sakir* OI, *sakir* ON	decide	*ráða* OI, *ráða* ON
corn-shed	*kornhjálm* OI, *kornhjálm* ON	decided	*reiða* OI, *reiða* ON
could	*kunni* OI, *kunni* ON, *máttu* OI, *máttu* ON, *mun* OI, *mun* ON, *mundi* OI, *mundi* ON	declared	*lýsir* OI, *lýsir* ON
		declining	*hniginn* OI, *hniginn* ON
		defend	*verjast* OI, *verjast* ON
		demanded	*rífastr* ON, *rífastur* OI
counsel	*ráð* OI, *ráð* ON, *ráðs* OI, *ráðs* ON, *ráðum* OI, *ráðum* ON, *umráði* OI, *umráði* ON	depart	*yðra* OI, *yðra* ON
		descended	*ættaðr* ON, *ættaður* OI
		descendents	*ættbogi* OI, *ættbogi* ON
		deserve	*verð* OI, *verð* ON
countless	*ótal* OI, *ótal* ON	desired	*fýstist* OI, *fýstist* ON
couple	*hjón* OI, *hjón* ON, *hjónum* OI, *hjónunum* ON	developed	*þroskasamt* OI, *þroskasamt* ON
court-man	*hirðmaðr* ON, *hirðmaður* OI	dew	*dögg* OI, *dögg* ON, *döggina* OI, *döggina* ON
cradle	*vöggu* OI, *vöggu* ON		
crash	*brest* OI, *brest* ON	did	*gera* OI, *gera* ON, *gerði* OI, *gerði* ON, *gerðu* OI, *gerðu* ON, *gerðust* OI, *gerðust* ON, *gerir* OI, *gerir* ON
creaked	*brakaði* OI, *brakaði* ON		
crew	*skipverja* OI, *skipverja* ON		
cross	*krossa* OI, *krossa* ON		
crow	*kráku* ON		
Crow (a name)	*kráku* OI	die	*andast* OI, *andast* ON
curiosity	*forvitni* OI, *forvitni* ON	died	*andaðist* OI, *andaðist* ON, *andist* ON, *önduðust* OI, *önduðust* ON
custom	*siðvenju* OI, *siðvenju* ON		
cut	*skáru* OI, *skáru* ON	difference	*munr* ON, *munur* OI
cut-down	*hogginn* OI, *höggvinn* ON	direction	*ættir* ON, *áttir* OI
		dirty	*smáskitlegr* ON, *smáskitlegur* OI
		disappeared	*horfin* OI, *horfin* ON, *hvarf* OI, *hvarf* ON

D, d

English	*Norse*	English	*Norse*
dark	*svörtum* OI, *svörtum* ON	discord	*sundrþykki* ON, *sundurþykki* OI, *þustr* ON, *þustur* OI
daughter	*dóttir* OI, *dóttir* ON		
daughter-of	*dóttur* OI, *dóttur* ON	discussed	*ræddu* OI, *ræddu* ON, *umræða* OI, *umræða* ON
day	*dag* OI, *dag* ON, *dags* ON		
days	*dægr* ON, *dægrum* OI, *dægrum* ON, *dægur* OI, *daga* OI, *daga* ON	discussion	*umræða* OI, *umræða* ON, *umræði* OI, *umræði* ON
		dishonour	*ódáðum* OI, *ódáðum* ON
dead	*andaðr* ON, *andaður* OI, *dauð* OI, *dauð* ON, *dauðr* ON, *dauðum* OI, *dauðum* ON, *dauður* OI	disputes	*deilur* OI, *deilur* ON
		divide	*skipta* OI, *skipta* ON
		divided	*skiptu* OI, *skiptu* ON

112

Word List (English to Norse)

English	Norse	English	Norse
do	*gera* OI, *gera* ON	eastern-man	*austmaðr* ON, *austmaður* OI
done	*gert* OI, *gert* ON	eight	*átta* OI, *átta* ON
door	*dura* ON, *dyra* OI, *hurð* OI, *hurð* ON, *hurðinni* OI, *hurðinni* ON	Einar (a name)	*einarr* ON
		Einarsfjord (a place)	*einarsfjörð* ON
doors	*dyrnar* OI, *dyrrnar* ON	either	*hvárt* ON, *hvort* OI, *ýmisst* ON, *ýmist* OI
doorway	*durum* ON, *dyrin* OI, *dyrrin* ON, *dyrum* OI, *gáttum* OI, *gáttum* ON	elbows	*ölnboga* OI, *ölnboga* ON
down	*niðr* ON, *niður* OI	else	*annað* OI, *annat* ON
Drangar (a place)	*dröngum* OI, *dröngum* ON	ended	*lokið* OI, *lokit* ON, *lýkr* ON, *lýkur* OI
Drepstokk (a place)	*drepstokki* OI, *drepstokki* ON	engrave	*grafa* OI, *grafa* ON
		enough	*dygði* OI, *dygði* ON
dressed	*klæddist* OI, *klæddist* ON	entertain	*skemmtanar* OI, *skemmtanar* ON
drew	*brá* OI, *brá* ON	equal	*jafnmikil* OI, *jafnmikil* ON
driven	*rak* OI, *rak* ON, *rekin* OI, *rekin* ON	equal-day	*jafndægri* OI, *jafndægri* ON
drove	*velkði* ON, *velkti* OI	equally	*jafnsaman* OI, *jafnsaman* ON
dry	*þurrkanar* OI, *þurrkunar* ON	Erik (a name)	*eirík* OI, *eirík* ON, *eiríki* OI, *eiríki* ON, *eiríkr* ON, *eiríks* OI, *eiríks* ON, *eiríkur* OI
dwell	*búa* OI, *búa* ON		
dwelled	*dvöl* OI, *dvöl* ON		
dwelling	*bæ* OI, *bæ* ON, *bænum* OI, *bænum* ON, *byggilegast* OI, *byggiligast* ON, *híbýli* OI, *hýbýli* ON	Eriksdottir (a name)	*eiríksdóttir* OI, *eiríksdóttir* ON
		Eriksey (a place)	*eiríksey* OI, *eiríksey* ON
		Eriksfjord (a place)	*eiríksfirði* OI, *eiríksfirði* ON, *eiríksfjarðar* OI, *eiríksfjarðar* ON, *eiríksfjörð* OI, *eiríksfjörð* ON
dwellings	*byggðir* OI, *byggðir* ON		
dwelt	*bjó* OI, *bjó* ON, *bjuggu* OI, *bjuggu* ON		
		Eriksson (a name)	*eiríkssyni* OI, *eiríkssyni* ON

E, e

English	Norse	English	Norse
		Eriksstadir (a place)	*eiríksstöðum* OI, *eiríksstöðum* ON
each	*hvárir* ON, *hver* OI, *hverju* OI, *hverju* ON, *hverjum* OI, *hverjum* ON, *hvern* OI, *hvern* ON, *hverr* ON, *hvorir* OI	Eriksvog (a place)	*eiríksvági* ON, *eiríksvogi* OI
		errand	*erendi* ON, *erindi* OI
		even	*jöfnum* OI, *jöfnum* ON
earl	*jarl* OI, *jarl* ON, *jarls* OI, *jarls* ON	evening	*kveldi* OI, *kveldi* ON
earl's	*jarls* OI, *jarls* ON	events	*atburð* OI, *atburð* ON, *atburði* OI, *atburði* ON, *atburðum* OI, *atburðum* ON
early	*snemma* OI, *snemma* ON		
east	*austan* OI, *austan* ON	eventually	*síðir* OI, *síðir* ON
eastern	*austr* ON, *austur* OI, *eystri* OI, *eystri* ON	ever	*jafnan* OI, *jafnan* ON
		every	*allra* OI, *allra* ON

113

Word List (English to Norse)

English	*Norse*	English	*Norse*
everyone's	*allra* OI, *allra* ON	feet	*fæti* OI, *fæti* ON, *fótum* OI, *fótum* ON
evil	*allill* OI, *allill* ON, *illa* OI, *illa* ON	fell	*féll* OI, *fell* ON, *fella* OI, *fella* ON, *felldi* OI, *felldi* ON, *hnígr* ON, *hnígur* OI, *höggva* OI, *höggva* ON
excellent	*íþróttamaðr* ON, *íþróttamaður* OI		
except-for	*utan* OI, *útan* ON		
exhausted	*þrjóta* OI, *þrjóta* ON	fence	*skíðgarð* OI, *skíðgarð* ON, *skíðgarðinn* OI, *skíðgarðinn* ON
expel	*reka* OI, *reka* ON		
explore	*kanna* OI, *kanna* ON		
explored	*kannað* OI, *kannat* ON	few	*nokkuð* OI, *nökkut* ON
extended	*rétti* OI, *rétti* ON	fifteen	*fimmtán* OI, *fimmtán* ON
extremely	*ákaflega* OI, *ákafliga* ON		
		fight	*vega* OI, *vega* ON
eyed	*eygð* OI, *eygð* ON	fighting	*vígra* OI, *vígra* ON
eyes	*augu* OI, *augu* ON, *augunum* OI, *augunum* ON	filled	*fylldr* ON, *fylltur* OI
		find	*finna* OI, *finna* ON
		fine	*ágætt* OI, *ágætt* ON
Eyjolf (a name)	*eyjólfur* OI	Finnbogi (a name)	*finnboga* OI, *finnboga* ON, *finnbogi* OI, *finnbogi* ON
Eyjolf (a name), Eyolf (a name)	*eyjólfr* ON		
Eyolf's (a name)	*eyjólfs* OI, *eyjólfs* ON	first	*fyrra* OI, *fyrra* ON, *fyrst* OI, *fyrst* ON, *fyrsta* OI, *fyrsta* ON

F, f

English	*Norse*	English	*Norse*
		fish	*fiska* OI, *fiska* ON
		five	*fimm* OI, *fimm* ON
face	*andliti* OI, *andliti* ON	Fjord (a place)	*firðinum* OI, *firðinum* ON, *fjörðinn* OI, *fjörðinn* ON
failed	*drepr* ON, *drepur* OI		
fair-wind	*byr* OI, *byr* ON, *byri* OI, *byri* ON, *byrina* OI, *byrina* ON, *byrjar* OI, *byrjar* ON	Fjord-Mouth (a place)	*fjarðarkjafta* OI, *fjarðarkjafta* ON
		flat	*slétt* OI, *slétt* ON
fallen	*fallin* OI, *fallin* ON	fled	*fló* OI, *fló* ON, *flýja* OI, *flýja* ON
farm	*bæjar* OI, *bæjar* ON, *búi* OI, *búi* ON		
		floated	*fluttu* OI, *fluttu* ON
Farmer	*bóndi* ON	floor	*gólfið* OI, *gólfit* ON
Farmer (a nickname)	*bóndi* OI	fodder	*fóðr* ON, *fóður* OI
farming	*búsvarðveislu* OI, *búsvarðveizlu* ON	fog	*þokur* OI, *þokur* ON
		folds	*foldar* OI, *foldar* ON
fast	*ákafast* OI, *ákafast* ON	folk	*fólk* OI, *fólk* ON
fated	*auðið* OI, *auðit* ON	follow	*fylgd* OI, *fylgð* ON, *fylgja* OI, *fylgja* ON
father	*faðir* OI, *faðir* ON, *feðr* ON, *föður* OI, *föður* ON		
		followed	*fylgdu* OI, *fylgðu* ON
father-and-son	*feðgum* OI, *feðgum* ON	food	*mat* OI, *mat* ON, *matar* OI, *matar* ON
fathered	*fæddr* ON, *fæddur* OI		
father-of	*faðir* OI, *faðir* ON, *föður* OI, *föður* ON	foot	*fótr* ON, *fótur* OI
		for	*á* OI, *á* ON, *að* OI, *at* ON, *fyrir* OI, *fyrir* ON, *því* OI, *því* ON, *til* OI, *til* ON, *um* OI, *um* ON
favoured	*ilmað* OI, *ilmat* ON		
feels	*þreifar* OI, *þreifar* ON		

Word List (English to Norse)

English	Norse	English	Norse
foreseen	*varir* OI, *varir* ON	gap	*klofa* OI, *klofa* ON
forest	*skóg* OI, *skóg* ON, *skógi* OI, *skógi* ON, *skóginum* OI, *skóginum* ON, *skógr* ON, *skógur* OI	Gardar (a place), realm	*görðum* OI, *görðum* ON
		gather	*lesa* OI, *lesa* ON
		gathered	*fengu* OI, *fengu* ON
		gave	*fékk* OI, *fekk* ON, *gaf* OI, *gaf* ON
forested	*skógótt* OI, *skógótt* ON	gave-up	*hættir* ON
forests	*skógar* OI, *skógar* ON, *skógi* OI, *skógi* ON	Gellir (a name), howler	*gellis* OI, *gellis* ON
for-the	*fyrir* OI, *fyrir* ON	German	*þýsku* OI, *þýzku* ON
fortune	*forlög* OI, *forlög* ON	get	*fá* OI, *fá* ON
foster	*fóstri* OI, *fóstri* ON	gifts	*feng* OI, *feng* ON
foster-father	*fóstra* OI, *fóstra* ON	give	*fái* OI, *fái* ON, *gæfi* OI, *gæfi* ON, *gefa* OI, *gefa* ON
found	*fann* OI, *fann* ON, *fannst* OI, *fannst* ON, *fundið* OI, *fundit* ON, *fundu* OI, *fundu* ON, *fyndi* OI, *fyndi* ON		
		glaciers	*jöklar* OI, *jöklar* ON, *jöklum* OI, *jöklum* ON, *jökull* OI, *jökull* ON
four	*fjögr* ON, *fjögur* OI		
fourteen	*fjórtán* OI, *fjórtán* ON	Glaumbaer (a place)	*glaumbæ* OI, *glaumbæjarland* OI, *glaumbæjarland* ON, *glaunbæ* ON
fourth	*fjóði* OI, *fjórða* OI, *fjórða* ON, *fjórði* OI, *fjórði* ON		
		go	*far* OI, *far* ON, *fara* OI, *fara* ON, *fari* OI, *fari* ON, *ferðar* OI, *ferðar* ON, *ganga* OI, *ganga* ON, *gangast* OI, *gangast* ON, *gangir* OI, *gangir* ON, *gengið* OI, *gengit* ON
Freydis (a name)	*freydís* OI, *freydís* ON, *freydísar* OI, *freydísar* ON, *freydísi* OI, *freydísi* ON		
Fridrek (a name)	*friðrekr* ON, *friðrekur* OI		
friends	*vina* OI, *vina* ON		
frightened	*hræddust* OI, *hræddust* ON		
from	*að* OI, *af* OI, *af* ON, *frá* OI, *frá* ON, *fram* OI, *fram* ON, *framar* OI, *framar* ON, *frammi* OI, *frammi* ON, *framúr* OI, *ór* ON, *undan* OI, *undan* ON, *úr* OI	going	*farið* OI, *farit* ON, *gekk* OI, *gekk* ON, *genginn* OI, *genginn* ON, *vára* ON, *vora* OI
		gold	*gulls* OI, *gulls* ON
		gone	*brottu* OI, *brottu* ON, *gengið* OI, *gengin* OI, *gengin* ON, *gengit* ON
from-there	*þaðan* OI, *þaðan* ON	good	*góð* OI, *góð* ON, *góðr* ON, *góðra* OI, *góðra* ON, *góðu* OI, *góðu* ON, *góður* OI, *gott* OI, *gott* ON
frost	*frost* OI, *frost* ON		
frowned	*grelli* OI, *gretti* ON		
furs	*skinnavara* OI, *skinnavara* ON		
further	*firr* OI, *firr* ON, *lengra* OI, *lengra* ON	goods	*fémunum* OI, *fémunum* ON, *varning* OI, *varning* ON, *varningr* ON, *varningur* OI

G, g

English	Norse
got	fékk OI, fekk ON, fengi ON, fengið OI, fengit ON, fengju OI, náði OI, náði ON
gown	námkyrtli OI, námkyrtli ON
grapes	vínber OI, vínber ON, vínberjum OI, vínberjum ON
grasp	fang OI, fang ON
grass	gras OI, gras ON, grasinu OI, grasinu ON, grös OI, grös ON
great	mikið OI, mikil OI, mikil ON, mikill OI, mikill ON, mikinn OI, mikinn ON, mikit ON, miklir OI, miklir ON
greater	meira OI, meira ON
greatest	göfugmenni OI, göfugmenni ON
greatly	mikið OI, mikit ON, stórilla OI, stórilla ON
Greenland (a place)	grænland OI, grænland ON, grænlandi OI, grænlandi ON, grænlands OI, grænlands ON
Greenland-Sea (a place)	grænlandshaf OI, grænlandshaf ON
Greenland-voyage	grænlandsferðar OI, grænlandsferðar ON
grew	óx OI, óx ON
grey-skins	grávara OI, grávara ON
Grimhild (a name)	grímhildr ON, grímhildur OI
Grimhild's	grímhildar OI
group	flokkr ON, flokkur OI
growing	vaxið OI, vaxit ON
grown	vaxið OI, vaxin OI, vaxinn ON, vaxit ON, vexti OI, vexti ON
Gunnbjarnarsker (a place)	gunnbjarnarsker OI, gunnbjarnarsker ON
Gunnbjorn (a name)	gunnbjörn OI, gunnbjörn ON
Guthrid (a name)	guðríðar OI, guðríðar ON, guðríði OI, guðríði ON, guðríðr ON, guðríður OI

H, h

English	Norse
habitable	byggjanda ON, byggjandi OI
habitation	mannavistir OI
had	átt OI, átt ON, átti OI, átti ON, hafði OI, hafði ON, haft OI, haft ON, hefðu OI, höfðu OI, höfðu ON, væri ON, væru OI
had-been	hafði OI, hafði ON, verið OI, verit ON
Hafgrim (a name)	hafgrímr ON, hafgrímur OI
Hafgrimsfjord (a place)	hafgrímsfjörð OI, hafgrímsfjörð ON
hair	hár OI, hár ON
half	hálfa OI, hálfa ON, hálfan OI, hálfan ON, hálfr ON, hálfur OI, helming OI, helming ON, helmingr ON, helmingur OI
half-of	hálfr ON, hálfur OI
hall	hallar OI, hallar ON
Hallfrid (a name)	hallfríðr ON, hallfríður OI
hand	hendr ON, hendur OI, hönd OI, hönd ON
handed	höndum OI, höndum ON
hands	höndum OI, höndum ON
handsome	vænn OI, vænn ON
harmlessly	meinalausan OI, meinalausan ON
has	hefir OI, hefir ON
haughty	svarri OI, svarri ON
Haukadal (a place)	haukadal OI, haukadal ON, haukdælski OI, haukdælski ON

Word List (English to Norse)

English	*Norse*	English	*Norse*
have	*á* OI, *á* ON, *hafa* OI, *hafa* ON, *hafi* OI, *hafi* ON, *hafið* OI, *hafið* ON, *hafim* ON, *hef* OI, *hefði* ON, *hefi* OI, *hefi* ON, *hefir* OI, *hefir* ON, *höfð* OI, *höfð* ON, *höfum* OI	Herjolf (a name)	*herjólfi* ON, *herjólfr* ON, *herjólfur* OI, *herjúlfi* OI, *herjúlfur* OI
		Herjolfsfjord (a place)	*herjólfsfjörð* OI, *herjólfsfjörð* ON
		Herjolfsnes (a place)	*herjólfsnes* ON, *herjólfsnesi* OI, *herjólfsnesi* ON
having	*hafa* OI, *hafa* ON	Herjolfsness (a place)	*herjúlfsnesi* OI
he	*han* ON, *hann* OI, *hann* ON, *hans* OI, *hans* ON, *henni* OI, *henni* ON, *hinn* OI, *honum* OI, *honum* ON, *inn* ON, *sér* OI, *sér* ON, *sinn* OI, *sinn* ON	hers	*hennar* OI, *hennar* ON, *sín* OI, *sín* ON, *sína* OI, *sína* ON, *sinna* OI, *sinna* ON, *síns* OI, *síns* ON, *sínu* OI, *sínu* ON, *sínum* OI, *sínum* ON
head	*höfði* OI, *höfði* ON, *höfuð* OI, *höfuð* ON	herself	*sig* OI, *sik* ON
headland	*andnesi* OI, *andnesi* ON, *höfða* OI, *höfða* ON, *höfðann* OI, *höfðann* ON, *höfðanum* OI, *höfðanum* ON, *nes* OI, *nes* ON, *nesi* ON, *nesið* OI, *nesinu* OI, *nesinu* ON, *nesit* ON, *ness* OI, *ness* ON	high	*hárar* ON, *hárrar* OI, *hátt* OI, *hátt* ON
		him	*hana* OI, *hana* ON, *hann* OI, *hann* ON, *hans* OI, *hans* ON, *honum* OI, *honum* ON, *sér* OI, *sér* ON
		himself	*sig* OI, *sik* ON
		hired	*réð* OI, *réð* ON
heard	*heyrði* OI, *heyrði* ON	his	*hans* OI, *hans* ON, *honum* OI, *honum* ON, *sér* OI, *sér* ON, *sína* OI, *sína* ON, *sinn* OI, *sinn* ON, *sinna* OI, *sinna* ON, *sinnar* OI, *sinnar* ON, *sinni* OI, *sinni* ON, *síns* OI, *síns* ON, *sínu* OI, *sínu* ON, *sínum* OI, *sínum* ON, *sitt* OI, *sitt* ON
heath	*heiðis* OI, *heiðis* ON		
heathen	*heiðið* OI, *heiðit* ON		
heaviness	*höfga* OI, *höfga* ON		
heights	*hæðir* OI, *hæðir* ON		
held	*halda* OI, *halda* ON, *heldr* ON, *héldu* OI, *heldu* ON, *heldur* OI		
held-words	*haldinorðir* OI, *haldinorðir* ON	Hitardal (a place)	*hítardal* OI, *hítardal* ON
		hold	*halda* OI, *halda* ON, *haldast* OI, *haldast* ON, *haldi* OI, *haldi* ON
Helga (a name), holy	*helga* OI, *helga* ON		
Helgi (a name)	*helgi* OI, *helgi* ON		
Helluland (a place)	*helluland* OI, *helluland* ON	Holm (a place)	*hólmum* OI, *hólmum* ON
help	*duga* OI, *duga* ON	home	*bús* OI, *bús* ON, *heim* OI, *heim* ON, *heima* OI, *heima* ON, *heiman* OI, *heiman* ON
hence	*héðan* OI, *heðan* ON		
her	*hana* OI, *hana* ON, *hennar* OI, *hennar* ON, *henni* OI, *henni* ON		
		homeless	*vistlaus* OI, *vistlauss* ON
here	*hér* OI, *hér* ON, *hingað* OI, *hingat* ON	Hornstrandir (a place)	*hornströndum* OI, *hornströndum* ON

117

Word List (English to Norse)

English	Norse	English	Norse
Horse-Head (a name)	hesthöfða OI, hesthöfða ON	immediately	fljótast OI, fljótast ON
horse's	hestrinn ON, hesturinn OI	in	á OI, á ON, að OI, at ON, í OI, í ON, inn OI, inn ON, inni OI, inni ON, við OI, við ON
house	húsin ON		
house-besom	húsasnotru OI, húsasnotru ON, húsasnotruna OI, húsasnotruna ON	Ingolf (a name)	ingólfr ON, ingólfur OI
		Ingolf's (a name)	ingólfs OI, ingólfs ON
house-building	húsgerð OI, húsgerð ON	inhabit	byggjum OI, byggjum ON
houseman	húskarli OI, húskarli ON	injured	lestist OI, lestist ON
houses	hús OI, hús ON, húsa OI, húsa ON, húsanna OI, húsanna ON, húsin OI, húsin ON, húss OI, húss ON	in-need	þurftugir OI, þurftugir ON
		inside	innstr ON, innstur OI
		intend	ætlað OI, ætlat ON
		intended	ætlað OI, ætlaði OI, ætlaði ON, ætlaðr ON, ætlaður OI, ætlat ON, ætluðu OI, ætluðu ON
housewife	húsfreyja OI, húsfreyja ON, húsfreyju OI, húsfreyju ON	into	í OI, í ON
how	hvárt ON, hversu OI, hversu ON, hvort OI	invite	bjóða OI, bjóða ON
		invited	bauð OI
Hrafn (a name)	hrafn OI, hrafn ON	irritable	úrigt OI, úrigt ON
Hrafnsfjord (a place)	hrafnsfjörð OI, hrafnsfjörð ON	is	er OI, er ON, í OI, í ON
		island	ey OI, ey ON, eyjarinnar OI, eyjarinnar ON, eyju OI, eyju ON, eyland OI, eyland ON
hunsband's	bónda ON		
hunting	veiðum OI, veiðum ON		
husband	bónda OI, bónda ON, bóndi OI, bóndi ON		
husband's	bónda OI	islands	eyjótt OI, eyjótt ON, eyrar OI, eyrar ON
Hvarfsgnipu (a place)	hvarfsgnípu OI, hvarfsgnípu ON	is-named	heitir OI, heitir ON
		it	að OI, at ON, hann OI, hann ON, í OI, í ON, það OI, þat ON

I, i

English	Norse
I	eg OI, ég OI, ek ON
Iceland (a place)	ísland OI, ísland ON, íslands OI, íslands ON
Iceland (a place), Icelander	íslandi OI, íslandi ON
Icelander	íslenskum OI, íslenzkum ON
Icelanders	íslenskir OI, íslenzkir ON
if	ef OI, ef ON, hvárt ON, hvort OI
ill	illr ON, ills OI, ills ON, illur OI
ill-will	illsku OI, illsku ON

J, j

English	Norse
Jaeren (a place)	jaðri OI, jaðri ON
Jorund (a name)	jörundar OI, jörundar ON
journey	ferð OI, ferð ON, ferðar OI, ferðar ON, leið OI, leið ON

K, k

English	Norse
Karlsefni (a name)	karlsefni OI, karlsefni ON

Word List (English to Norse)

English	Norse	English	Norse
Karlsefni's (a name)	*karlsefnis* OI, *karlsefnis* ON	lake	*vatnið* OI, *vatninu* OI, *vatninu* ON, *vatnit* ON
keel	*kjölinn* OI, *kjölinn* ON	land	*jörð* OI, *jörð* ON, *land* OI, *land* ON, *landi* OI, *landi* ON, *landið* OI, *landinu* OI, *landinu* ON, *landit* ON, *lands* OI, *lands* ON, *landsins* OI, *landsins* ON, *lönd* OI, *lönd* ON
keep	*halda* OI, *halda* ON		
kept	*efndi* OI, *efndi* ON		
Ketil (a name)	*ketill* OI, *ketill* ON		
Ketilsfjord (a place)	*ketilsfjörð* OI, *ketilsfjörð* ON		
kill	*drepa* ON		
killed	*drepa* OI, *drepa* ON, *drepnir* OI, *drepnir* ON	land-benefits	*landkostr* ON, *landkostum* OI, *landkostum* ON, *landskostr* ON, *landskostur* OI
killing	*víga* OI, *víga* ON		
killing-of	*víg* OI, *víg* ON		
kin	*kyni* OI, *kyni* ON	land-exploring	*landaleitan* OI, *landaleitan* ON
kin-blessed	*kynsæll* OI, *kynsæll* ON		
kinds	*konar* OI, *konar* ON	lands	*landið* OI, *landit* ON, *lands* OI, *lands* ON, *löndum* OI, *löndum* ON
kinds-of	*konar* OI, *konar* ON		
kinsman	*frændi* OI, *frændi* ON		
kinsmen	*frændum* OI, *frændum* ON	land-sight	*landsýn* OI, *landsýn* ON
Kjalarnes (a place)	*kjalarnes* OI, *kjalarnes* ON	land-taking-man	*landnámamanns* OI, *landnámamanns* ON
Knarrarbringu (a name)	*knarrarbringu* OI, *knarrarbringu* ON	language	*mál* OI, *mál* ON
		larboard-side	*bakborða* OI, *bakborða* ON
knees	*knjám* OI, *knjám* ON		
knew	*kunni* OI, *kunni* ON, *skildu* OI, *skilðu* ON, *vissi* OI, *vissi* ON, *vissu* OI, *vissu* ON	large	*mikil* OI, *mikil* ON, *mikill* OI, *mikill* ON, *mikli* OI, *mikli* ON, *miklir* OI, *miklir* ON
		larger	*stærra* OI, *stærra* ON
know	*kann* OI, *kann* ON, *veit* OI, *veit* ON, *veita* OI, *veita* ON, *vísu* OI, *vísu* ON	last	*síðast* OI, *síðast* ON, *síðasta* OI, *síðasta* ON
		late	*seinn* OI, *seinn* ON
		launched	*skjóta* OI, *skjóta* ON, *skkutu* ON, *skutu* OI, *skutu* ON
known	*kennt* OI, *kennt* ON, *kunnu* OI, *kunnu* ON	law-taken	*lögtekin* OI, *lögtekin* ON
Krossanes (a place)	*krossanes* OI, *krossanes* ON	lay	*lá* OI, *lá* ON, *lægi* OI, *lægi* ON, *lagði* OI, *lagði* ON, *lagðist* OI, *lagðist* ON, *lágu* OI, *lágu* ON, *láta* OI, *láta* ON, *leggja* OI, *leggja* ON, *lögðu* OI, *lögðu* ON

L, l

English	Norse
laid	*búa* OI, *búa* ON, *lætr* ON, *lætur* OI, *lagði* ON, *lágu* OI, *lágu* ON, *látið* OI, *látit* ON, *legið* OI, *legit* ON, *leið* OI, *leið* ON, *lét* OI, *lét* ON, *létu* OI, *létu* ON, *lögðu* OI, *lögðu* ON
lead	*leiða* OI, *leiða* ON, *leiddu* OI, *leiddu* ON, *veita* OI, *veita* ON
leader	*höfðingi* OI, *höfðingi* ON, *réði* OI, *réði* ON

Word List (English to Norse)

English	*Norse*	English	*Norse*
left	*eftir* OI, *eftir* ON, *létu* OI, *létu* ON, *lokið* OI, *lokit* ON	loosened	*leystu* OI, *leystu* ON
		lost	*týndust* OI, *týndust* ON
Leif (a name)	*leif* OI, *leif* ON, *leifi* OI, *leifi* ON, *leifr* ON, *leifs* OI, *leifs* ON, *leifur* OI	loudly	*hátt* OI, *hátt* ON
		loved	*elskað* OI, *elskat* ON
		low	*lág* OI, *lág* ON
Leif's	*leifs* OI, *leifs* ON	lowered	*lægðu* OI, *lægðu* ON
Leif's-Camp (a place)	*leifsbúða* OI, *leifsbúða* ON	luck	*heill* OI, *heill* ON
		lucky	*heppni* OI, *heppni* ON
lent	*léði* OI, *léði* ON, *lutu* OI, *lutu* ON	Lysufjord (a place)	*lýsufirði* OI, *lýsufirði* ON
less	*minna* OI, *minna* ON, *minni* OI, *minni* ON	# M, m	
let	*láta* OI, *láta* ON, *látið* OI, *látit* ON, *leggja* OI, *leggja* ON, *lét* OI, *lét* ON, *létu* OI, *létu* ON	made	*gera* OI, *gera* ON, *gerði* OI, *gerði* ON, *gerðist* OI, *gerðist* ON, *gerðu* OI, *gerðu* ON, *gerður* OI, *gerðust* OI, *gerðust* ON, *gerir* OI, *gerir* ON, *gerr* ON, *gerst* OI, *gerst* ON, *gerzt* ON
life	*lífi* OI, *lífi* ON		
like	*líkar* OI, *líkar* ON, *líkast* OI, *líkast* ON		
little	*lítill* OI, *lítill* ON, *litla* OI, *litla* ON, *litlu* OI, *litlu* ON, *litlum* OI, *litlum* ON, *lítt* OI, *lítt* ON	make	*gera* OI, *gera* ON, *gerðu* OI, *gerðu* ON
little-man	*lítilmenni* OI, *lítilmenni* ON	man	*maðr* ON, *maður* OI, *manna* OI, *manna* ON, *manni* OI, *manni* ON, *manns* OI, *manns* ON
little-wide	*óvíða* OI, *óvíða* ON		
live	*lifa* OI, *lifa* ON		
lived	*bjó* OI, *bjó* ON, *bjuggu* OI, *bjuggu* ON, *lifði* OI, *lifði* ON	man's	*manna* OI
		man-worthiness	*mannvirðingar* OI, *mannvirðingar* ON
lives	*líf* OI, *líf* ON	many	*fjöldi* OI, *fjöldi* ON, *fjölmenni* OI, *fjölmenni* ON, *marga* OI, *marga* ON, *margir* OI, *margir* ON, *margt* ON, *mart* OI, *mörg* OI, *mörg* ON, *mörgum* OI, *mörgum* ON, *víða* OI, *víða* ON
livestock	*kvikfé* OI, *kvikfé* ON		
loan	*ljá* OI, *ljá* ON		
lodge	*vistar* OI, *vistar* ON		
lodging	*vistar* OI, *vistar* ON, *vistir* ON		
lodgings	*vistir* OI		
long	*langa* OI, *langa* ON, *langar* OI, *langar* ON, *langt* OI, *langt* ON, *lengi* OI, *lengi* ON, *lengst* OI, *lengst* ON		
		maple	*mösur* OI, *mösurr* ON
		mark	*mörk* OI, *mörk* ON
		Markland (a place)	*markland* OI, *markland* ON
long-as	*meðan* OI, *meðan* ON	married	*átti* OI, *átti* ON, *fekk* OI, *fekk* ON, *gefin* OI, *gefin* ON, *gift* OI, *gift* ON, *hafði* ON, *kvángaðr* ON, *kvángazt* ON, *kvongaður* OI, *kvongast* OI
longer	*lengr* ON, *lengur* OI		
looked	*leit* OI, *leit* ON, *sást* ON, *sáust* OI, *sjá* OI, *sjá* ON, *sjást* OI, *sjást* ON		
loose-eyed	*lauseygr* ON, *lauseygur* OI		

Word List (English to Norse)

English	*Norse*	English	*Norse*
master	*drottinn* OI, *dróttinn* ON	more	*fleira* OI, *fleira* ON, *fleiri* OI, *fleiri* ON, *meira* OI, *meira* ON
matters	*máldagi* OI, *máldagi* ON		
may	*má* OI, *má* ON, *mætti* ON, *mættu* OI, *mátti* OI, *mátti* ON, *máttu* OI, *máttu* ON	morning	*dagmála* ON, *dagmálastað* OI, *morgin* ON, *morgininn* ON, *morgun* OI, *morguninn* OI, *morguninn* ON
me	*mér* OI, *mér* ON, *mig* OI, *mik* ON		
meantime	*meðan* ON	most	*mesta* OI, *mesta* ON, *mestri* OI, *mestri* ON
meet	*fund* OI, *fund* ON, *fundar* OI, *fundar* ON, *fundi* OI, *fundi* ON, *mót* OI, *mót* ON, *móts* OI, *móts* ON	mother-of	*móður* OI, *móður* ON
		mountain	*féll* OI, *fell* ON
		mountainous	*fjöllótt* OI, *fjöllótt* ON
		mountains	*fjöll* OI, *fjöll* ON, *jöklanna* OI, *jöklanna* ON
men	*háseta* OI, *háseta* ON, *karla* OI, *karla* ON, *karlar* OI, *karlar* ON, *mann* OI, *mann* ON, *manna* OI, *manna* ON, *menn* OI, *menn* ON, *mönnum* OI, *mönnum* ON	mouth	*munn* OI, *munn* ON
		mouths	*munn* OI, *munn* ON
		much	*mikið* OI, *mikil* OI, *mikil* ON, *mikill* OI, *mikill* ON, *mikit* ON, *miklu* OI, *miklu* ON, *miklum* OI, *miklum* ON, *mjög* OI, *mjök* ON
men's	*manna* ON		
men's-heads	*mannshausi* OI, *mannshausi* ON	my	*mig* OI, *mínar* OI, *mínar* ON, *minnar* OI, *minnar* ON, *mitt* OI, *mitt* ON
men's-work	*mannaverk* OI, *mannaverk* ON		
merchant-ship	*kaupskipið* OI, *kaupskipit* ON		
met	*hittu* OI, *hittu* ON		
mid-afternoon	*eyktar* ON, *eyktarstað* OI		

N, n

English	*Norse*
middle	*miðjan* OI, *miðjan* ON, *miðri* OI, *miðri* ON
Midjokul (a place)	*miðjökul* OI, *miðjökul* ON
milk-products	*búnyt* OI, *búnyt* ON
mine	*mér* OI, *mér* ON, *mín* OI, *mín* ON, *mína* OI, *mína* ON, *minn* OI, *minn* ON, *míns* OI, *míns* ON, *mínu* OI, *mínu* ON, *mitt* OI, *mitt* ON
missing	*vant* OI, *vant* ON
moderate-man	*hófsmaðr* ON, *hófsmaðuR* OI
monks	*munka* OI, *munka* ON

English	*Norse*
name	*heiti* OI, *heiti* ON, *nafn* OI, *nafn* ON
named	*heita* OI, *heita* ON, *heiti* OI, *heiti* ON, *heitir* OI, *heitir* ON, *hét* OI, *hét* ON, *nafn* ON
namesake	*nafni* OI, *nafni* ON
near	*hjá* OI, *hjá* ON, *ná* OI, *ná* ON, *nær* OI, *nær* ON, *náim* ON, *náum* OI, *undir* OI, *undir* ON
nearest	*næstir* OI, *næstir* ON
near-the	*nær* OI, *nær* ON
necessity	*nauðsyn* OI, *nauðsyn* ON
need	*þurfa* OI, *þurfa* ON

Word List (English to Norse)

English	*Norse*	English	*Norse*
needed	þurfa OI, þurfa ON, þurfti OI, þurfti ON	of	á OI, á ON, að OI, af OI, af ON, at ON, hinn OI, inn ON, of OI, of ON, ór ON, úr OI
neither	hvárigir ON, hvárki ON, hvergi OI, hvergi ON, hvorigir OI, hvorki OI	off	af OI, af ON, ofan OI, ofan ON
new	nýnæmi OI, nýnæmi ON	offered	buðu OI, buðu ON
news	tíðenda ON, tíðinda OI, tíðindum OI, tíðindum ON	offspring	afkvæmi OI, afkvæmi ON
next	næst OI, næst ON, öðrum OI, öðrum ON	of-the	hinni OI, inni ON
night	nótt OI, nótt ON	of-them	þeira ON, þeirra OI
nights	nætr ON, nætur OI	on	á OI, á ON, í OI, í ON, ofan OI, ofan ON
no	engi OI, engi ON	one	ein OI, ein ON, eina OI, eina ON, einn OI, einn ON, einni OI, einni ON, einu OI, einu ON, einum OI, einum ON, eitt OI, eitt ON
no-curiosity	óforvitinn OI, óforvitinn ON		
none	engar ON, engi OI, engi ON, engum ON, öngar OI, öngum OI		
nor	né OI, né ON	one-such	einhverju OI, einhverju ON
Nordic	norænn OI, norrænn ON	on-the	á ON
norse	norrænu OI, norrænu ON	opposite	gegnt OI, gegnt ON
		or	eða OI, eða ON, eðr ON
north	norðan OI, norðan ON, norðr ON, norður OI, nyrðra OI, nyrðra ON	other	aðrir OI, aðrir ON, annan OI, annan ON, öðru OI, öðru ON, öðrum OI, öðrum ON
North-East-Wind	landnyrðingsveðr ON, landnyrðingsveður OI	others'	annars OI, annars ON
northwards	norðan OI, norðan ON	our	vár ON, vor OI
north-wind	norrænur OI, norrænur ON	ours	várn ON, várt ON, váru ON, vorn OI, vort OI, voru OI, vorum OI
Norway	noregi OI, noregs OI		
Norway (a place)	nóregi ON, nóregs ON	out	ór ON, úr OI, út OI, út ON, utan OI, útan ON, úti OI, úti ON
not	eigi OI, eigi ON, ekki OI, ekki ON, engi OI, engi ON		
not-be	eigi OI, eigi ON	outlawed	sekr ON, sekur OI
nothing	ekki OI, ekki ON, engi OI, engi ON, engu ON, öngu OI	out-of	ór ON, úr OI, út OI, út ON, utan OI, útan ON
		out-travel	utan OI, útan ON
now	nú OI, nú ON	over	efra OI, efra ON, yfir OI, yfir ON
nun's-vows	nunnuvígslu OI, nunnuvígslu ON	own	eigum OI, eigum ON
		Oxney (a place)	öxney OI, öxney ON

O, o

P, p

pale	fölleit OI, fölleit ON

Word List (English to Norse)

English	Norse	English	Norse
part-of	*hluti* OI, *hluti* ON	quickly	*fljótast* OI, *fljótast* ON, *skjótast* OI, *skjótast* ON
parts	*staði* OI, *staði* ON		
peaceful-men	*friðmenn* OI, *friðmenn* ON		
place	*stað* OI, *stað* ON		
place-names	*örnefni* OI, *örnefni* ON		

R, r

English	Norse
plan	*ráð* OI, *ráð* ON, *ráða* OI, *ráða* ON
plank	*fjöl* OI, *fjöl* ON
played	*léku* OI, *léku* ON
pledged	*heitið* OI, *heitit* ON
poor-wretch	*vesallegr* ON, *vesallegur* OI
possessions	*föng* OI, *föng* ON
preferably	*helst* OI, *helzt* ON
prepare	*búa* OI, *búa* ON, *búið* OI, *búið* ON
prepared	*bjó* OI, *bjó* ON, *bjóst* OI, *bjóst* ON, *bjuggu* OI, *bjuggu* ON, *bjuggust* OI, *bjuggust* ON, *brá* OI, *brá* ON, *búa* OI, *búa* ON, *búast* OI, *búast* ON, *búið* OI, *búit* ON, *búnir* OI, *búnir* ON, *býr* OI, *býr* ON
present	*fyrir* OI, *fyrir* ON
promising	*efnilegsti* OI, *efniligsti* ON
prophecy	*spá* OI, *spá* ON
propose	*beiddi* OI, *beiddi* ON
protection	*verja* OI, *verja* ON
provisions	*vist* OI, *vist* ON, *vistir* OI, *vistir* ON
prow	*framstafn* OI, *framstafn* ON
pulled	*dregil* OI, *dregil* ON
purchase	*kaupa* ON
purchases	*kaupför* OI, *kaupför* ON
pursuits	*sýslur* OI, *sýslur* ON
put	*láta* OI, *láta* ON

Q, q

English	Norse
quality	*gæða* OI, *gæða* ON, *gæði* OI, *gæði* ON, *gæðum* OI, *gæðum* ON

English	Norse
raise	*reisa* OI, *reisa* ON, *reisim* ON, *reisum* OI
raised	*reist* OI, *reist* ON
ran	*runnu* OI, *runnu* ON
rather	*heldr* ON, *heldur* OI
Raven-The-Dueller (a name)	*hólmgöngu-hrafns* OI, *hólmgöngu-hrafns* ON
ready	*albúinn* OI, *albúinn* ON, *búin* OI, *búin* ON, *búinn* OI, *búinn* ON, *búnir* OI, *búnir* ON
receded	*rénuðu* OI, *rénuðu* ON
receive	*þiggja* OI, *þiggja* ON
recluse	*einsetukona* OI, *einsetukona* ON
red	*rauði* ON
Red (a name)	*rauði* OI
referred	*veik* OI, *veik* ON
remained	*eftir* OI, *eftir* ON
remote	*fásinni* OI, *fásinni* ON
repaired	*bættu* OI, *bættu* ON
reproach	*ámæli* OI, *ámæli* ON
reproaching	*átölur* OI, *átölur* ON
resolved	*ráðið* OI, *ráðit* ON
respectable	*göfgasti* OI, *göfgasti* ON, *göfgustum* OI, *göfgustum* ON, *yfirlæti* OI, *yfirlæti* ON
resting-place	*hvíldarstaða* OI, *hvíldastaða* ON
return	*áðr* ON, *áður* OI, *aftr* ON, *aftur* OI
returned	*fór* ON
returning	*aftr* ON, *aftur* OI
Reykjanes (a place)	*reykjaness* OI, *reykjaness* ON
richer	*auðgara* OI, *auðgara* ON
riding	*reið* OI, *reið* ON
rises	*örglast* OI, *örglast* ON
rising	*félli* OI, *felli* ON

Word List (English to Norse)

English	*Norse*	English	*Norse*
river	*ána* OI, *ána* ON, *ánni* OI, *ánni* ON, *vatni* OI, *vatni* ON	sails	*segl* OI, *segl* ON
		salmon	*lax* OI, *lax* ON
		same	*sama* OI, *sama* ON, *senn* OI, *senn* ON
rock	*bjarg* OI, *bjarg* ON, *sker* OI, *sker* ON, *skerið* OI, *skerinu* OI, *skerinu* ON, *skerit* ON	sands	*sandar* OI, *sandar* ON, *sandinum* OI, *sandinum* ON
rode	*réðst* OI, *réðst* ON, *riðr* ON, *ríður* OI	sat	*sat* OI, *sat* ON, *sátu* OI, *sátu* ON, *setið* OI, *setit* ON, *settist* OI, *settist* ON, *settu* OI, *settu* ON, *settust* OI, *settust* ON, *sitr* ON, *situr* OI
room	*rúmi* OI, *rúmi* ON, *rúmið* OI, *rúmit* ON, *stofunni* OI, *stofunni* ON		
rorqual	*reyðr* ON, *reyður* OI	saw	*sá* OI, *sá* ON, *sáu* OI, *sjá* OI, *sjá* ON
rowed	*réru* OI, *reru* ON		
rule	*ráða* OI, *ráða* ON	Saxony (a place)	*saxlandi* OI, *saxlandi* ON
Runolf'S (a name)	*runólfs* OI, *runólfs* ON	say	*sagna* OI, *sagna* ON, *segir* OI, *segir* ON, *segja* OI, *segja* ON

S, s

English	*Norse*	English	*Norse*
		saying	*kveðst* OI, *kveðst* ON
sables	*safali* OI, *safali* ON	says	*segir* OI, *segir* ON
safe	*höldnu* OI, *höldnu* ON	sea	*haf* OI, *haf* ON, *hafa* OI, *hafa* ON, *hafs* OI, *hafs* ON, *sjávar* ON, *sjóinn* OI, *sjóinn* ON, *sjónum* OI, *sjónum* ON, *sjór* OI, *sjór* ON, *sjóvar* OI
saga	*sögu* OI, *sögu* ON		
said	*frásögn* OI, *frásögn* ON, *kvað* OI, *kvað* ON, *kvaðst* OI, *kvaðst* ON, *kváðu* OI, *kváðu* ON, *kváðust* OI, *kváðust* ON, *kveðr* ON, *kveðst* OI, *kveðst* ON, *kveður* OI, *mælt* OI, *mælt* ON, *mælti* OI, *mælti* ON, *mál* OI, *mál* ON, *sagði* OI, *sagði* ON, *sagðir* OI, *sagðir* ON, *sagt* OI, *sagt* ON, *segir* OI, *segir* ON, *segja* OI, *segja* ON, *sögðu* OI, *sögðu* ON		
		sea-poem	*hafgerðingadrápu* OI, *hafgerðingadrápu* ON
		search	*leita* OI, *leita* ON
		seat-posts	*setstokka* OI, *setstokka* ON
		second	*annan* OI, *annan* ON
		see	*sé* OI, *sé* ON, *sjá* OI, *sjá* ON, *sjáið* OI, *sjáið* ON
		seek	*leita* OI, *leita* ON
		seem	*þykja* OI, *þykkja* ON
		seemed	*sýndist* OI, *sýndist* ON, *þykir* OI, *þykkir* ON
		seems	*þykir* OI, *þykkir* ON
		seen	*séð* OI, *sét* ON
sail	*sigla* OI, *sigla* ON	sell	*selja* OI, *selja* ON
sailed	*sigla* OI, *sigla* ON, *sigldi* OI, *sigldi* ON, *sigldu* OI, *sigldu* ON, *siglir* OI, *siglir* ON, *siglt* OI, *siglt* ON	separate	*skilist* ON, *skiljist* OI, *skilnað* OI, *skilnað* ON
		separated	*fráskili* OI, *fráskili* ON, *skilja* OI, *skilja* ON
sailing	*sigla* OI, *sigla* ON, *siglingum* ON	set	*setja* OI, *setja* ON, *sett* OI, *sett* ON, *settu* OI, *settu* ON
sailors	*hásetar* OI, *hásetar* ON, *hásetum* OI, *hásetum* ON		

Word List (English to Norse)

English	*Norse*	English	*Norse*
settle	*byggja* OI, *byggja* ON	shortage	*skorti* OI, *skorti* ON, *skortir* OI, *skortir* ON
settled	*bjuggu* OI, *bjuggu* ON, *búi* OI, *búi* ON, *byggt* OI, *byggt* ON, *sætt* OI, *sætt* ON	shorten	*svipta* OI, *svipta* ON
		short-time-of-day	*skammdegi* OI, *skammdegi* ON
settlement	*bú* OI, *bú* ON, *búi* OI, *búi* ON, *búið* OI, *búit* ON, *bús* OI, *bús* ON, *byggð* OI, *byggð* ON, *óbyggð* OI, *óbyggð* ON	shot	*skaut* OI, *skaut* ON
		should	*mun* OI, *mun* ON, *mundu* OI, *muni* OI, *muni* ON, *munum* OI, *munum* ON, *myndi* ON, *skuluð* OI, *skuluð* ON, *skulum* OI, *skulum* ON, *skyldi* OI, *skyldi* ON, *skyldu* OI, *skyldu* ON
settles	*bjuggu* OI		
shadow	*skugga* OI, *skugga* ON		
shall	*mun* OI, *mun* ON, *muni* OI, *muni* ON, *munt* OI, *munt* ON, *muntu* OI, *muntu* ON, *munu* OI, *munu* ON, *munuð* OI, *munuð* ON, *skal* OI, *skal* ON, *skalt* OI, *skalt* ON, *skulum* OI, *skulum* ON		
		shout	*kall* OI, *kall* ON
		show	*sýni* OI, *sýni* ON
		sickness	*sótt* OI, *sótt* ON, *sóttin* OI, *sóttin* ON, *sóttina* OI, *sóttina* ON
		side	*megin* OI, *megin* ON
shall-be	*vera* OI, *vera* ON	Siglefjord (a place)	*siglufjörð* ON
shallows	*grunnsævi* OI, *grunnsævi* ON	silence	*þegði* ON, *þegðu* OI
		silent	*þagði* OI, *þagði* ON
shame	*skammar* OI, *skammar* ON	since	*sem* OI, *sem* ON, *síðan* OI, *síðan* ON, *því* OI, *því* ON
share	*deila* OI, *deila* ON		
she	*hana* OI, *hana* ON, *hon* ON, *hún* OI, *hún* ON	sister	*systur* OI, *systur* ON
		sit	*sæti* OI, *sæti* ON
shield	*skjaldarins* OI, *skjaldarins* ON	six	*sex* OI, *sex* ON
		Skagafjord (a place)	*skagafjörð* OI, *skagafjörð* ON
ship	*skip* OI, *skip* ON, *skipi* OI, *skipi* ON, *skipið* OI, *skipinu* OI, *skipinu* ON, *skipit* ON, *skips* OI, *skips* ON, *skipsins* OI, *skipsins* ON, *skipum* OI, *skipum* ON	skin-boats	*húðkeipa* OI, *húðkeipa* ON
		skin-cots	*húðföt* OI, *húðföt* ON
		skin-wares	*skinnavöru* OI, *skinnvöru* ON
		Skraeling	*skrælingi* OI, *skrælingr* ON
ships	*skipa* OI, *skipa* ON, *skipi* OI, *skipi* ON, *skips* OI, *skips* ON	skraelings	*skrælinga* ON, *skrælingar* ON, *skrælingja* OI, *skrælingjar* OI
ship's	*skipsins* OI, *skipsins* ON		
		slayed	*vegr* ON, *vegur* OI
ship's-berth	*skipborðsins* OI, *skipborðsins* ON	sleeping	*soföndum* ON, *sofundum* OI
ships-his	*skipsins* ON	slept	*sofna* OI, *sofna* ON, *sváfu* OI, *sváfu* ON
shoes	*skóklæðin* OI, *skóklæðin* ON, *skúa* OI, *skúa* ON		
		small	*smár* OI, *smár* ON
short	*skammt* OI, *skammt* ON	Snaefell (a place)	*snæfells* OI, *snæfells* ON

125

Word List (English to Norse)

English	Norse	English	Norse
Snaefellsjokli (a place)	*snæfellsjökli* OI, *snæfellsjökli* ON	Son-of-Thord (a name)	*þórðar* OI, *þórðar* ON, *þórðarsonar* OI, *þórðarsonar* ON
Snorri (a name)	*snorra* OI, *snorra* ON, *snorri* OI, *snorri* ON	Son-of-Thorgrim (a name)	*þorgrímsson* OI, *þorgrímsson* ON
snorting	*gjalla* OI, *gjalla* ON	Son-of-Ulf (a name)	*úlfssonar* OI, *úlfssonar* ON
so	*sá* OI, *sá* ON, *sé* ON, *séu* OI, *svá* ON, *svo* OI	Son-of-Vifil (a name)	*vífilsson* OI, *vífilsson* ON
sold	*keyptu* OI, *keyptu* ON, *seldi* OI, *seldi* ON	sons	*synir* OI, *synir* ON
solitary	*einþykkr* ON, *einþykkur* OI	soon	*brátt* OI, *brátt* ON
Solvadal (a place)	*sölvadal* OI, *sölvadal* ON	sought	*leitaði* OI, *leitaði* ON, *leitar* OI, *leitar* ON, *sækja* OI, *sækja* ON
Sölvi (a name)	*sölvi* OI, *sölvi* ON		
some	*einhverju* ON, *nokkuð* OI, *nokkurar* OI, *nökkurar* ON, *nokkurir* OI, *nökkurir* ON, *nökkut* ON, *sum* OI, *sum* ON, *sumir* OI, *sumir* ON	south	*suðr* ON, *suður* OI
		southern-man	*suðrmaðr* ON, *suðurmaður* OI
		south-islander	*suðreyskr* ON, *suðureyskur* OI
		South-West (a place)	*útsynnings* ON
something	*nokkur* OI, *nökkur* ON	south-west-wind	*útsynningsbyr* OI
sometime	*nokkuru* OI, *nökkuru* ON	speak	*máls* OI, *máls* ON
son	*son* OI, *son* ON, *sonar* OI, *sonar* ON, *sonr* ON, *sonur* OI	speech	*máli* OI, *máli* ON
		spoke	*mælti* OI, *mælti* ON
		sports	*hagleik* OI, *hagleik* ON, *leikar* OI, *leikar* ON
son-of	*son* OI, *sonr* ON, *sonur* OI	spring	*várar* ON, *vári* ON, *várit* ON, *vorar* OI, *vori* OI, *vorið* OI
Son-of-Bard (a name)	*bárðarson* OI, *bárðarson* ON		
Son-of-Erik (a name)	*eiríksson* OI, *eiríksson* ON, *eiríkssonar* OI, *eiríkssonar* ON	sprung	*vár* ON, *vor* OI
		stand	*standa* OI, *standa* ON, *standir* OI, *standir* ON
Son-of-Herjolf	*herjúlfsson* OI, *herjúlfssonar* OI	stave	*stef* OI, *stef* ON
Son-of-Herjolf (a name)	*herjólfsson* ON	stay	*búast* OI, *búast* ON, *vistar* OI, *vistar* ON
Son-of-Herjolf (a name), Son-of-Herjolf's (a name)	*herjólfssonar* ON	steep-looking	*brattleitr* ON, *brattleitur* OI
		steer	*stýra* OI, *stýra* ON, *stýrir* OI, *stýrir* ON
Son-of-Karlesfni (a name), Son-of-Karlsefni (a name)	*karlsefnissonar* OI, *karlsefnissonar* ON	steered	*stefndu* OI, *stefndu* ON, *stýrði* OI, *stýrði* ON, *stýrðu* OI, *stýrðu* ON
Son-of-Kodran (a name)	*koðránsson* OI, *koðránsson* ON	steering	*stjórn* OI, *stjórn* ON
Son-of-Oxna-Thori (a name)	*öxna-þórissonar* OI, *öxna-þórissonar* ON	stern	*skaut* OI, *skaut* ON, *stafn* OI, *stafn* ON
Son-of-Snorri (a name)	*snorrasonar* OI, *snorrasonar* ON	still	*enn* OI, *enn* ON, *kyrrt* OI, *kyrrt* ON
		stomachs	*mögum* OI, *mögum* ON
Son-of-Thorbrand (a name)	*þorbrandsson* OI, *þorbrandsson* ON	stone-slab	*hella* OI, *hella* ON

Word List (English to Norse)

English	*Norse*	English	*Norse*
stood	*stað* ON, *staðið* OI, *staðit* ON, *stóð* OI, *stóð* ON, *stóðst* OI, *stóðst* ON	**T, t**	
		take	*taka* OI, *taka* ON, *takast* OI, *takast* ON
stool	*stóli* OI, *stóli* ON, *stólinn* OI, *stólinn* ON, *stólinum* OI, *stólinum* ON	taken	*fært* OI, *fært* ON, *höfð* OI, *höfð* ON, *nema* OI, *nema* ON, *tekið* OI, *tekit* ON
stop	*hætti* OI, *hætti* ON	taking	*nema* OI, *nema* ON
stormy	*hvasst* OI, *hvasst* ON	talk	*tala* OI, *tala* ON, *umræða* OI, *umræða* ON
story	*saga* OI, *saga* ON, *sögn* OI, *sögn* ON		
straightaway	*þegar* OI, *þegar* ON	talked	*mælti* OI, *mælti* ON, *talaði* OI, *talaði* ON, *taldi* OI, *talði* ON
strait	*sund* OI, *sund* ON		
strange	*undarlegum* OI, *undarligum* ON	team	*lið* OI, *lið* ON, *liðið* OI, *liðit* ON
strangers	*ókunnugum* OI, *ókunnum* ON	ten	*tíu* OI, *tíu* ON
strength	*afli* OI, *afli* ON	tens	*tigi* OI, *tigu* ON
stretches	*þokar* OI, *þokar* ON	tent	*tjaldi* OI, *tjaldi* ON, *tjaldinu* OI, *tjaldinu* ON
strike	*höggva* OI, *höggva* ON		
striking	*skörulegastur* OI, *sköruligastr* ON	tester	*reyni* OI, *reyni* ON
strong	*rammlegan* OI, *rammligan* ON, *sköruleg* OI, *skörulig* ON, *sterk* OI, *sterk* ON, *sterkr* ON, *sterkur* OI	than	*en* OI, *en* ON, *það* OI, *þat* ON
		thanked	*þakkaði* OI, *þakkaði* ON
		that	*að* OI, *af* OI, *at* ON, *en* OI, *en* ON, *er* OI, *er* ON, *inn* OI, *inn* ON, *sá* OI, *sá* ON, *sem* OI, *sem* ON, *það* OI, *þann* OI, *þann* ON, *þat* ON, *þeim* OI, *þeim* ON, *þetta* OI, *þetta* ON, *því* OI, *því* ON
struck	*hjó* OI, *hjó* ON, *sló* OI, *sló* ON		
Styrr (a name)	*styrr* OI, *styrr* ON		
such	*slík* OI, *slík* ON, *slíkan* OI, *slíkan* ON, *svá* ON, *svo* OI		
summer	*sumar* OI, *sumar* ON, *sumarið* OI, *sumarit* ON, *sumars* OI, *sumars* ON, *sumri* OI, *sumri* ON	the	*á* OI, *á* ON, *að* OI, *at* ON, *hið* OI, *hin* OI, *hina* OI, *hina* ON, *hinn* OI, *hinni* OI, *hinu* OI, *hinum* OI, *in* ON, *ina* ON, *inn* OI, *inn* ON, *inni* ON, *inu* ON, *inum* ON, *it* ON, *sá* OI, *sá* ON, *sér* ON, *sinn* OI, *sinn* ON, *þann* OI, *þann* ON, *þeir* ON, *þeira* ON, *þeirra* OI
sun	*sól* OI, *sól* ON		
supply	*veita* OI, *veita* ON		
supported	*veitti* OI, *veitti* ON, *veittu* OI, *veittu* ON		
suppose	*ætla* OI, *ætla* ON		
supposed	*ætla* OI, *ætla* ON, *ætlaði* OI, *ætlaði* ON, *ætluðu* OI, *ætluðu* ON		
		the-bishop	*biskups* OI, *biskups* ON
		the-Black	*svarta* ON, *svartr* ON
Sviney (a place)	*svíney* OI, *svíney* ON	the-Black (a name)	*svarta* OI, *svarti* OI, *svarti* ON, *svartur* OI
swiftly	*tíðast* OI, *tíðast* ON	the-Black's	*svarta* ON

127

Word List (English to Norse)

English	*Norse*	English	*Norse*
the-Farmer	bónda OI, bónda ON, bóndi OI, bóndi ON	these	sitt OI, sitt ON, þau OI, þau ON, þeim OI, þeim ON, þenna OI, þenna ON, þess OI, þess ON, þessar OI, þessar ON, þessi OI, þessi ON, þessir OI, þessir ON, þessum OI, þessum ON
the-Foul	saurs OI, saurs ON		
the-inlet	mynni OI, mynni ON		
their	sinn OI, sinn ON, sú OI, sú ON, þar OI, þar ON, þeira ON, þeirar ON, þeirra OI, þeirrar OI		
theirs	sér OI, sér ON, sín OI, sín ON, sína OI, sína ON, sínar OI, sínar ON, sinn OI, sinn ON, sinni OI, sinni ON, síns OI, síns ON, sínu OI, sínu ON, sínum OI, sínum ON, sitt OI, sitt ON, þeira ON, þeirra OI	the-sea	sjónum OI, sjónum ON
		The-Sensible (a name)	glóra ON
		the-ship	skipinu OI, skipinu ON
		the-sun	sól OI, sól ON
		the-way	háttað OI, háttat ON
		they	sér OI, sér ON, sinn ON, sinni OI, þá OI, þá ON, það OI, þær OI, þær ON, þann OI, þann ON, þar OI, þat ON, þau OI, þau ON, þeim OI, þeim ON, þeir OI, þeir ON
the-island	eyjar OI, eyjar ON		
the-land	landið OI, landit ON		
them	sér OI, sér ON, sín OI, sín ON, þá OI, þá ON, þau OI, þau ON, þeim OI, þeim ON, þeir OI, þeir ON, þeira ON, þeirra OI		
		things	hluti OI, hluti ON
		think	hygg OI, hygg ON
		thinks	þótti OI, þótti ON
the-matter	málum OI, málum ON	third	þriðja OI, þriðja ON
themselves	sig OI, sik ON	thirty	þriði OI, þriði ON
then	á OI, á ON, en OI, en ON, er OI, er ON, inn OI, inn ON, síðan OI, síðan ON, þá OI, þá ON, þann OI, þann ON, þegar OI, þegar ON	this	sá OI, sá ON, það OI, þann OI, þann ON, þat ON, þess OI, þess ON, þessa OI, þessa ON, þessi OI, þessi ON, þessu OI, þessu ON, þetta OI, þetta ON, þette ON
there	þá OI, þá ON, þaðan OI, þaðan ON, þangað OI, þangat ON, þar OI, þar ON, þeir OI, þeir ON, þeira ON, þeirar ON, þeirra OI, þeirrar OI	Thjodhild (a name)	þjóðhildar OI, þjóðhildar ON
		Thorbjarnardottur (a name)	þorbjarnardóttur OI, þorbjarnardóttur ON
		thorbjorg	þorbjargar ON
		Thorbjorg (a name)	þorbjargar OI
the-Red	rauða OI, rauða ON, rauði OI, rauði ON	Thorbjorn (a name)	þorbjörn OI, þorbjörn ON
therefore	því OI, því ON	Thorbrand (a name)	þorbrands OI, þorbrands ON
		Thorfin (a name)	þorfinnur OI
		Thorfin (a name), Thorfin (a name)	þorfinnr ON
		Thorgeir (a name)	þorgeir OI, þorgeirr ON

128

Word List (English to Norse)

English	Norse	English	Norse
Thorgerd (a name)	þorgerðr ON, þorgerður OI	time	hríð OI, hríð ON, skipti OI, skipti ON, stund ON, tíma OI, tíma ON
Thorgest (a name)	þorgesti OI, þorgesti ON	times	tíma OI, tíma ON
Thorgest's-Sons (a name)	þorgestlingum OI, þorgestlingum ON	to	á OI, á ON, að OI, at OI, at ON, í OI, i ON, í ON, þeim ON, til OI, til ON, við OI, við ON
Thori (a name)	þóri OI, þóri ON, þóris OI, þóris ON		
Thorir (a name)	þórir OI, þórir ON	together	saman OI, saman ON, samfarir OI, samfarir ON, samflota OI, samflota ON, samt OI, samt ON
Thorlak (a name)	þorláks OI, þorláks ON		
Thorsnes-Assembly (a name)	þórsnessþingi OI, þórsnessþingi ON		
Thorstein (a name)	þorstein OI, þorstein ON, þorsteini OI, þorsteini ON, þorsteinn OI, þorsteinn ON, þorsteins OI	to-him	honum OI, honum ON
		told	sagði OI, sagði ON, taldi OI, taldi ON, taldist OI, talðist ON, telgja OI, telgja ON, töluðu OI, töluðu ON
Thorstein's	þorsteins OI, þorsteins ON		
Thorun (a name)	þórunnar OI, þórunnar ON	to-me	mér OI, mér ON
Thorvald (a name)	þorvald OI, þorvald ON, þorvaldi OI, þorvaldi ON, þorvaldr ON, þorvaldur OI	took	færði OI, færði ON, námu OI, námu ON, taka ON, tekst OI, tekst ON, tók OI, tók ON, tóku OI, tóku ON, tókust OI, tókust ON
Thorvald (a name), Thorvard (a name)	þorvarðr ON		
Thorvald's (a name)	þorvalds OI, þorvalds ON	tortured	píndi OI, píndi ON
		to-them	þeim OI, þeim ON
Thorvard (a name)	þorvarður OI	towards	á OI, á ON, móti OI, móti ON, til OI, til ON
those	þau OI, þau ON, þeir OI, þeir ON	to-you	þér OI, þér ON
though	þó OI, þó ON	tradition	sið OI, sið ON
thought	hugðum OI, hugðum ON, hyggja OI, hyggja ON, þótti OI, þótti ON, þóttist OI, þóttist ON, þóttu OI, þóttu ON, þóttust OI, þóttust ON	travel	færi ON, færu OI, fara OI, fara ON, farar OI, farar ON, fari OI, fari ON, farið OI, farit ON, ferð OI, ferð ON, förum OI, förum ON
thoughts	hug OI, hug ON		
three	þrem OI, þremr ON, þrjá OI, þrjá ON, þrjár OI, þrjár ON, þrjú OI, þrjú ON	travelled	færðu OI, færðu ON, fara OI, fara ON, fór OI, fór ON, fórst OI, fórst ON, fóru OI, fóru ON
threw	köstuðu ON, varp OI, varp ON	travelling	förum OI, fórum ON
		travelling-men	förunautum OI, förunautum ON
thriving	þrifum OI, þrifum ON	tree	tré OI, tré ON
thus	þetta OI, þetta ON	trees	mörkina OI, mörkina ON, viðinn OI, viðinn ON
tide	fjöru OI, fjöru ON		
tidings	tíðendi ON, tíðindi OI	true	
		true	

Word List (English to Norse)

English	Norse	English	Norse
turn	*horfa* OI, *horfa* ON	vessel	*farkost* OI, *farkost* ON
turned	*settu* OI, *settu* ON, *snúa* OI, *snúa* ON	Vestribyggd (a place)	*vestribyggðar* OI, *vestribyggðar* ON
twelve	*tólf* OI, *tólf* ON	vines	*vínvið* OI, *vínvið* ON, *vínviði* OI, *vínviði* ON
twenty	*tög* ON, *tögr* ON, *tug* OI, *tugur* OI	Vinland (a place)	*vínland* OI, *vínland* ON, *vínlandi* OI, *vínlandi* ON, *vínlands* OI, *vínlands* ON
two	*tvá* ON, *tvau* ON, *tveir* OI, *tveir* ON, *tvennar* OI, *tvennar* ON, *tvo* OI, *tvö* OI	Vinland-voyage	*vínlandsferð* OI, *vínlandsferð* ON, *vínlandsför* OI, *vínlandsför* ON
Tyrkir (a name)	*tyrkir* OI, *tyrkir* ON	visit	*fund* OI, *fund* ON, *vitja* OI, *vitja* ON

U, u

		Vog (a place)	*vágs* ON
ulf	*úlfs* ON	Vogs (a place)	*vogs* OI
Ulf (a name)	*úlfs* OI	voyage	*ferð* OI, *ferð* ON, *ferðar* OI, *ferðar* ON, *förinni* OI, *förinni* ON, *reiðfara* OI, *reiðfara* ON
unbroken-sea	*ósæbratt* OI, *ósæbratt* ON		
under	*undan* ON, *undir* OI, *undir* ON		
uninjured	*óskatt* OI, *óskatt* ON	voyages	*farar* OI, *farar* ON, *ferðum* OI, *ferðum* ON
uninviting	*ógagnvænlegt* OI, *ógagnvænligt* ON		
unload	*bera* OI, *bera* ON		

W, w

until	*til* OI, *til* ON		
unwise	*óvitrlig* ON	wait	*bíða* OI, *bíða* ON
unwisely	*óviturleg* OI	waited	*beið* OI, *beið* ON
up	*upp* OI, *upp* ON, *uppi* OI, *uppi* ON	wake	*vaki* OI, *vaki* ON
		wares	*varnað* OI, *varnað* ON, *varning* OI, *varning* ON
upholstery	*breiðabólstað* OI, *breiðabólstað* ON	warlike	*ófriði* OI, *ófriði* ON
up-to	*undir* OI, *undir* ON	was	*enn* OI, *enn* ON, *er* OI, *er* ON, *gerði* OI, *gerði* ON, *gert* OI, *gert* ON, *væri* OI, *væri* ON, *var* OI, *var* ON, *varð* OI, *varð* ON, *varstu* OI, *varstu* ON, *váru* ON, *vera* OI, *vera* ON, *voru* OI
urged	*fýstu* OI, *fýstu* ON		
us	*oss* OI, *oss* ON		

V, v

valiant	*vaskasti* OI, *vaskasti* ON		
Vatnahverfi (a place)	*vatnahverfi* OI, *vatnahverfi* ON	was-named	*hét* OI, *hét* ON, *héti* OI, *héti* ON
Vatnshorn (a place)	*vatnshorni* OI, *vatnshorni* ON	water	*vatn* OI, *vatn* ON
		water-taken	*vatnað* OI, *vatnat* ON
vehemence	*þjósti* OI, *þjósti* ON	way	*hætti* OI, *hætti* ON, *leið* OI, *leið* ON, *veg* OI, *veg* ON
very	*ákafliga* ON, *mikið* OI, *mikill* OI, *mikill* ON, *mikit* ON, *mjög* OI, *mjök* ON	ways	*vega* OI, *vega* ON

Word List (English to Norse)

English	Norse	English	Norse
we	*okkr* ON, *okkur* OI, *oss* OI, *oss* ON, *várum* ON, *vér* OI, *vér* ON	while	*en* OI, *en* ON, *meðan* OI, *meðan* ON, *sem* ON, *stund* OI, *stund* ON
wealth	*fjár* OI, *fjár* ON	white	*hvítir* OI, *hvítir* ON
wealthy	*stórauðigr* ON, *stórauðigur* OI	who	*er* OI, *er* ON, *hver* OI, *hverr* ON, *sem* OI, *sem* ON
weapon	*vápn* ON, *vopn* OI	whole	*heilu* OI, *heilu* ON
weapons	*vápn* ON, *vápnin* ON, *vopn* OI, *vopnin* OI	why	*hví* OI, *hví* ON
we-are	*erum* OI, *erum* ON	widely	*víða* OI, *víða* ON
weather	*veðr* ON, *veðri* OI, *veðri* ON, *veður* OI	wife	*kona* OI, *kona* ON, *konu* OI, *konu* ON
wedding	*brúðhlaup* OI, *brúðlaup* ON	will	*mun* OI, *mun* ON, *vár* ON, *vil* OI, *vil* ON, *vilda* ON, *vildi* OI, *vildi* ON, *vilið* ON, *vilja* OI, *vilja* ON, *viljið* OI, *vill* ON, *vilt* OI, *vor* OI
week	*vika* OI, *vika* ON		
welcomed	*fagnað* OI, *fagnat* ON		
well	*vel* OI, *vel* ON		
well-built	*vexti* OI, *vexti* ON		
well-tempered	*skapgott* OI, *skapgott* ON	willed	*vildi* OI, *vildi* ON, *vildu* OI, *vildu* ON, *vilja* OI, *vilja* ON, *viljað* OI, *viljat* ON, *vill* OI, *vill* ON
went	*ganga* OI, *ganga* ON, *gekk* OI, *gekk* ON, *gengr* ON, *gengu* OI, *gengu* ON, *gengur* OI, *réðst* OI, *réðst* ON	will-you	*villtu* ON, *viltu* OI, *viltu* ON
		wind	*byr* ON, *veðrið* OI, *veðrit* ON, *vinda* OI, *vinda* ON
were	*er* OI, *er* ON, *eru* OI, *eru* ON, *væri* OI, *væri* ON, *var* OI, *var* ON, *varð* OI, *varð* ON, *váru* ON, *vera* OI, *vera* ON, *voru* OI	winds	*veðr* ON, *veður* OI
		winter	*vetr* ON, *vetra* OI, *vetra* ON, *vetrar* OI, *vetrar* ON, *vetri* OI, *vetri* ON, *vetrinn* ON, *vetrum* OI, *vetrum* ON, *vetrvist* ON, *vetur* OI, *veturinn* OI, *veturvist* OI
west	*vestr* ON, *vestur* OI		
western	*vestan* OI, *vestan* ON, *vestri* OI, *vestri* ON		
westward	*vestarlega* OI, *vestarliga* ON		
westwards	*vestrætt* ON, *vesturátt* OI	wintered	*vetr* ON, *vetur* OI
		winters	*vetrum* OI, *vetrum* ON
wet	*vát* ON, *vot* OI	wise	*fróðir* OI, *fróðir* ON, *vitr* ON, *vitur* OI
whale	*hvalinn* OI, *hvalinn* ON		
what	*hvað* OI, *hvat* ON	wish	*annt* OI, *annt* ON
when	*er* OI, *er* ON, *þá* OI, *þá* ON, *þegar* OI, *þegar* ON	wished	*vilda* ON, *vill* OI, *vill* ON
		with	*með* OI, *með* ON, *við* OI, *við* ON, *vit* ON
where	*er* OI, *er* ON, *hvar* OI, *hvar* ON, *hvert* OI, *hvert* ON	within	*innan* OI, *innan* ON
		without-mountains	*ófjöllótt* OI, *ófjöllótt* ON
whether	*hvárt* ON, *hvort* OI	without-quality	*gæðalaust* OI, *gæðalaust* ON
which	*er* OI, *er* ON, *hvert* OI, *hvert* ON, *sem* OI, *sem* ON	without-supplies	*óbirgir* OI, *óbirgir* ON

Word List (English to Norse)

English	Norse	English	Norse
woman	*kona* OI, *kona* ON, *konan* OI, *konan* ON, *konu* OI, *konu* ON	young	*ung* OI, *ung* ON, *unga* OI, *unga* ON
women	*konum* OI, *konum* ON, *konur* OI, *konur* ON	your	*þitt* OI, *þitt* ON, *ykkur* OI
wood	*tré* OI, *tré* ON, *við* OI, *við* ON, *viði* OI, *viði* ON, *viðu* OI, *viðu* ON	yours	*þik* ON, *þínir* OI, *þínir* ON, *þinnar* OI, *þinnar* ON, *þíns* OI, *þíns* ON, *þitt* OI, *þitt* ON, *yðUr* OI, *yðUr* ON
woods	*skóginn* OI, *skóginn* ON, *viði* OI, *viði* ON	you-two	*þið* OI, *þit* ON
word	*orð* OI, *orð* ON, *orðið* OI, *orðit* ON		
words	*orði* OI, *orði* ON		
work	*verk* OI, *verk* ON		
worse	*verra* OI, *verra* ON		
worth	*verðr* ON, *verður* OI		
worthiness	*mannvirðingar* OI, *mannvirðingar* ON, *virðingar* OI, *virðingar* ON, *virðingu* OI, *virðingu* ON		
worthy	*vert* OI, *vert* ON		
would	*mun* OI, *mun* ON, *mundi* OI, *mundi* ON, *mundu* OI, *mundu* ON, *muni* OI, *væri* OI, *væri* ON, *vilja* OI, *vilja* ON		
would-be	*mun* OI, *mun* ON		
wound	*sár* OI, *sár* ON		
wounded	*sárir* OI, *sárir* ON		
woundingly	*sárlega* OI, *sárliga* ON		
wounds	*sárir* OI, *sárir* ON		
wretched	*vesæll* OI, *vesall* ON		
wrote	*orti* OI, *orti* ON		

Y, y

English	Norse
yet	*enn* OI, *enn* ON, *þó* OI, *þó* ON
Yngvild (a name)	*yngveldar* OI, *yngvildar* ON
you	*þér* OI, *þér* ON, *þið* OI, *þig* OI, *þik* ON, *þinn* OI, *þinn* ON, *þit* ON, *þú* OI, *þú* ON, *yðr* ON, *yðUr* OI, *ykkar* OI, *ykkr* ON, *ykkrar* ON, *ykkur* OI, *ykkur* ON